IFIP Advances in Information and Communication Technology 743

IFIP Advances in Information and Communication Technology

The IFIP AICT series publishes state-of-the-art results in the sciences and technologies of information and communication. The scope of the series includes: foundations of computer science; software theory and practice; education; computer applications in technology; communication systems; systems modeling and optimization; information systems; ICT and society; computer systems technology; security and protection in information processing systems; artificial intelligence; and human-computer interaction.

Edited volumes and proceedings of refereed international conferences in computer science and interdisciplinary fields are featured. These results often precede journal publication and represent the most current research.

The principal aim of the IFIP AICT series is to encourage education and the dissemination and exchange of information about all aspects of computing.

More information about this series at https://link.springer.com/bookseries/6102

Dominique Verdejo · Eunika Mercier-Laurent
Editors

Artificial Intelligence for Global Security

First IFIP WG 12.13 International Conference, AI4GS 2024
Paris, France, November 19, 2024
Proceedings

Springer

Editors
Dominique Verdejo
Université Reims Champagne-Ardenne
Reims, France

Eunika Mercier-Laurent
Université Reims Champagne-Ardenne
Reims, France

ISSN 1868-4238 ISSN 1868-422X (electronic)
IFIP Advances in Information and Communication Technology
ISBN 978-3-031-96521-0 ISBN 978-3-031-96522-7 (eBook)
https://doi.org/10.1007/978-3-031-96522-7

This Springer imprint is published by the registered company Springer Nature Switzerland AG
The registered company address is: Gewerbestrasse 11, 6330 Cham, Switzerland

Foreword

Artificial Intelligence for Global Security – Proceedings of the AI4GS 2024 Conference

As we stand at the threshold of 2025, with globalization reshaping the contours of threats to our societies, artificial intelligence (AI) emerges as an indispensable strategic tool for law enforcement and defense institutions. This volume, compiling the proceedings of the conference "AI for Global Security," organized under the auspices of COMCYBER and INRIA, held in Paris on November, 19th 2024, underscores the urgency and relevance of exploring AI's potential in addressing the evolving landscape of organized crime and terrorism. These phenomena, now transnational and technologically sophisticated, demand a coordinated and innovative response, where scientific research and operational applications converge to ensure sovereignty and peace.

General Patrick Perrot, AI Coordinator for the Gendarmerie's Cyber Command (COMCYBER), emphasizes the critical need to integrate AI into the core of internal security strategies. In his view, "we cannot overlook the fact that the current level of artificial intelligence already surpasses human capabilities in many domains: it computes better, remembers better, detects better." For the Gendarmerie, grappling with globalized criminality—ranging from illicit trafficking networks to terrorist attacks orchestrated via digital platforms—AI provides unparalleled analytical and predictive capacities. It enables the exploitation of vast data volumes to uncover complex criminal patterns, thereby freeing up resources for law enforcement to enhance their field presence. Yet, as Patrick Perrot cautions, this tool must not supplant human judgment: it requires a robust ethical and legal framework to ensure human oversight and respect for individual freedoms. At the European level, this perspective aligns with a shared ambition to co-develop common standards, essential for tackling security challenges that transcend national borders.

Meanwhile, Frédérique Segond, Director of Security and Defense Activities at INRIA, highlights the pivotal role of AI research in securing technological sovereignty amidst a rapidly changing world. Since the establishment of Inria's Security-Defense Mission in 2020, the institute has committed to developing solutions tailored to the needs of public stakeholders, particularly in cybersecurity and intelligence. "Digital security and mastery of AI are foundational to a society of trust," she asserts, stressing that research must anticipate the challenges posed by emerging disruptive technologies, such as quantum computing or autonomous systems. In a global race for innovation, where major powers leverage AI for strategic purposes—whether for mass surveillance or targeted military operations—sovereignty hinges on a concerted effort to produce independent knowledge and tools. Partnerships between academic institutions like INRIA and operational entities like the Gendarmerie are thus vital to translating scientific advances into tangible capabilities.

We find ourselves at a pivotal juncture in history, characterized by hybrid conflicts where technology redefines power dynamics. AI, with its capacity to bolster the resilience of law enforcement and counter asymmetric threats, becomes a linchpin for maintaining order and peace. This volume illustrates this dynamic through the contributions of experts gathered at the conference. It invites reflection on the delicate balance between innovation, ethics, and sovereignty in a context where global security depends as much on technological mastery as on international cooperation. May this publication inspire new synergies to address the challenges of tomorrow.

Dominique Verdejo

Preface

Considering the growing interest in various aspects of security in a globalized world in digital transformation, with growing concerns about cybersecurity, while transverse technologies like AI tend to infiltrate every domain of human activity, it appeared clear to the Organizing Committee that it was time to gather interested researchers in a single workshop.

This conference was the first in the world and the first of a series devoted to multiple facets of security. The main themes that appeared were Defense, Cybersecurity, Homeland Security, and Financial Security.

A welcome speech was given Anthony Wong, IFIP President, followed by an introductory presentation given by Eunika Mercier-Laurent about the big picture of AI for Global Security.

General Patrick Perrot, AI coordinator for French COMCYBER-MI, gave a keynote about AI for Homeland Security, and Serena Villata, Research Director of CNRS, detailed the current research context in AI.

The conference was composed of three panels on AI in defense, cybersecurity, and regulation and presentations of research papers covering various aspects of security in the key areas.

From 45 submitted papers, the program committee made a first selection based on abstracts only. This selection included new contributions in any research area concerning the use of all AI fields for all system components of Global Security. Selected articles were then single- or double-blindly reviewed with submissions receiving on average two reviews each, and 21 papers were selected. All papers were thoroughly tested for plagiarism with the Ithenticate tool and none of them raised suspicion. From these 21 papers, 12 were proposed for a full presentation while 9 were proposed for a poster presentation. Eventually, 14 extended and revised papers were successfully reviewed and are published in the present volume.

A specific focus was placed on Cybersecurity during this session held at the French Campus Cyber, which led to the presentation of 6 papers in that category. As the conference was patronized by the French COMCYBER-MI, 5 papers are dedicated to various applications in homeland security. Finally, one paper is about biometry and AI, another is about fraud detection in Financial Security and the last one is about AI in military applications.

For the sake of convenience, we have grouped the articles by theme, beginning with Defense and Homeland Security, then focusing on Cybersecurity, and eventually ending with Regulation and Financial Security.

Defense

The first article "How can LLM improve efficiency of C4ISR" presents the intricate landscape of modern military operations as heavily relying on effective Command, Control,

Communications, Computers, Intelligence, Surveillance, and Reconnaissance (C4ISR) systems. The article explores the exciting prospect of leveraging Large Language Models (LLMs) to significantly enhance the efficiency and precision of these critical systems. Acknowledging the existing hurdles within current C4ISR architectures, the authors posit that LLMs, with their advanced capabilities in large-scale data analysis, linguistic translation, and versatile text generation, offer a compelling path forward. Through a detailed examination of current scholarly work, the paper investigates the technological facets and potential gains of embedding LLMs within C4ISR, emphasizing advancements in areas such as the fusion of diverse data sources, the detection and analysis of threats, and the augmentation of decision-making processes. Crucially, it also scrutinizes the inherent constraints and challenges associated with LLM deployment in this sensitive field, including vital considerations of data security, model interpretability, the reduction of biases, and ethical implications. Ultimately, the article charts a course for future inquiry, highlighting promising research directions in multi-agent systems, autonomous functionalities, context-aware processing, and active learning methodologies for anomaly detection within the evolving C4ISR paradigm.

Homeland Security

The paper "ODIP: A state-of-the-art Child Sexual Abuse Material detection model" introduces ODIP (Outil de Détection d'Images Pédopornographiques), a state-of-the-art tool developed by the French Ministry of the Interior Cyberspace Command for the automatic detection of Child Sexual Abuse Material (CSAM). This system aims to enhance the efficiency of investigations by rapidly analyzing digital storage devices. ODIP employs a two-stage process: first, it transforms images into digital vectors using a Vision Transformer (MetaCLIP), allowing for analysis without direct exposure to the content. Second, a binary classifier, consisting of two dense layers, is trained on these vectors to discriminate between CSAM and non-CSAM images. The development of ODIP emphasizes computational performance and the protection of investigators. The model achieved a high Area under the ROC Curve (AUC) of 0.968 on its test dataset and a recall rate of over 95% at a specific decision threshold, indicating a strong ability to identify CSAM. The authors highlight the potential of ODIP to significantly aid digital forensic investigations, while also noting the importance of future work focused on expanding the training dataset to improve the model's generalizability.

The following paper "A responsible crime evolution analysis for homeland security" addresses the critical need for effective and explainable criminality forecasting to enhance public safety and optimize law enforcement resource allocation. It introduces an adaptive time series analysis method that integrates tendency (short-term trends) and seasonality (long-term patterns) by analyzing a five-year dataset of interventions by the French Gendarmerie, covering approximately 80% of France's territory. The model employs an adaptive weighting scheme that gives higher importance to more recent data while considering historical patterns. A key feature of this approach is its explain ability, allowing each prediction to be traced back to specific incidents and their weights, which is crucial for legal accountability and informed decision-making. The evaluation of the method highlights a balance between precision and recall, demonstrating its solid predictive capabilities and its potential to support proactive policing strategies.

The paper titled "Swarms of thermal and optical drones for searching for missing persons" presents the development of advanced technology for the automated deployment of drone swarms equipped with thermal cameras aimed at locating missing persons or fugitives. It addresses the limitations of traditional search methods and highlights how integrating drones provides real-time thermal imaging without interfering with existing protocols. The research details the selection of the DJI Mavic 3T Enterprise Thermal drone and the use of UGCS Commander software for coordinated flight planning, collision avoidance, and energy management. Experimental results demonstrate the increased efficiency of swarm flights in grid formations at different altitudes compared to single drone operations, emphasizing the benefits of multi-battery charging and adjustable thermal settings. The paper also outlines ongoing research focused on optimizing image quality, characterizing post-mortem thermal signatures, and using machine learning to differentiate between human and animal thermal signatures. Ultimately, this initiative aims to equip law enforcement with cutting-edge tools for improved operational efficiency in search and rescue through automated drone management and real-time thermal and optical data analysis.

The next article, "The security of the territory: everyone's business. Towards an intelligent security network," explores the integration of Artificial Intelligence (AI) within French Municipal Police forces as a means to improve urban security. Focusing on the substantial amount of local security data managed by these forces, the authors, Isabelle Cimino and Jérôme Marcenac from the Municipal Police of Nice Côte d'Azur, investigate the potential of AI technologies, such as intelligent video surveillance and predictive analysis, to optimize resources and enhance crime resolution. The study, conducted in Nice, also examines the development of an analytical framework for sharing local security data in critical domains such as radicalization and narcotics. While highlighting the benefits, the article addresses the crucial challenges related to privacy and ethics in the implementation of AI, underscoring the necessity of adhering to regulatory guidelines. The authors conclude by anticipating the future role of local security data analysts within Municipal Police forces in response to the ongoing digitalization of their operations.

The paper "Human-Centric AI for enhancing security in smart city anomaly detection", addresses the growing security challenges in smart cities by proposing a novel approach using Human-Centric Artificial Intelligence (HCAI) and deep learning for anomaly detection in CCTV surveillance. The study introduces a Hybrid Spatial Weighted Attention Layer Pooling Convolutional Neural Network (NeuroNet) model designed to improve the accuracy and reliability of surveillance systems. To ensure transparency and trust, the model incorporates HCAI-based Local Interpretable Model-agnostic Explanations (LIME) for predictions and visualizations, providing insights into its decision-making process. The proposed model demonstrates high performance metrics, achieving an accuracy of 0.9825, precision of 0.9826, recall of 0.9825, and an F1-score of 0.9824 on a smart city CCTV violence detection dataset. The research emphasizes aligning AI systems with human values and ethical principles to create more intelligent and secure digital urban environments.

Cybersecurity

The following article, "Design & development of health monitoring system with IoT cryptography scheme for wind turbine," introduces a hardware-based system for monitoring and controlling a small-scale wind turbine prototype. The system utilizes various sensors to collect critical performance data such as speed, temperature, and vibration, which is then processed by an Arduino Nano and transmitted to the cloud via an ESP8266 module and the Ubidots STEM cloud for real-time monitoring and preventive maintenance. A central focus of the work is on securing temperature sensor data before transmission by implementing and comparing three distinct AES encryption techniques (AES-128, AES-192, and AES-256) to ensure data confidentiality and integrity. The system is designed to automatically detect abnormalities and trigger a shutdown to prevent damage. The research aims to enhance the security and efficiency of small-scale wind energy systems through the combination of real-time data collection, preventive maintenance, and robust encryption.

Addressing the critical need for more dynamic and adaptive security measures in modern database systems, the paper titled "Enhancing RDBMS security through Metaheuristics, Reinforcement Learning, and Triple Loop Learning" presents a novel integrated framework. It highlights the increasing inadequacy of traditional static security mechanisms like RBAC and IDS in the face of evolving cyber threats. To address these challenges, the paper proposes leveraging Metaheuristics for optimizing security configurations, Reinforcement Learning for real-time adaptation to emerging threats, and Triple-Loop Learning for the continuous evolution of security policies. Through multiple case studies, the framework demonstrates significant improvements in security performance, including reduced unauthorized access and enhanced intrusion detection accuracy, suggesting a scalable and proactive approach to securing RDBMS environments.

The next paper, entitled "Explainable contextual anomaly detection: a focus on QCAD," addresses the integration of explain ability techniques in anomaly detection systems, which is crucial for improving transparency and trust in various application domains. This paper presents a detailed review of methods designed to enhance the explain ability of anomaly detection models based on machine learning and artificial intelligence. In particular, the study focuses on a recent explainable contextual anomaly detection method using quantile regression forests: QCAD. The authors highlight the importance of taking context into account for a more effective detection of anomalies. The paper evaluates the impact of context size on QCAD's performance using the real-world "Bodyfat" dataset and exploits QCAD's explain ability layer to analyze its mitigated results on this dataset. The experimental results suggest that QCAD's performance is influenced by the context size and the method of anomaly injection, underscoring the necessity of considering the specificities of each dataset. Finally, the paper proposes adding a preprocessing step to QCAD to dynamically define the different contexts, opening perspectives for future work.

The article "Prevention of DDoS using AI" presents a novel AI-based system for the prevention of Distributed Denial of Service (DDoS) attacks, a critical threat to modern network infrastructures. The proposed approach integrates end-to-end encryption utilizing AES for secure communication, with the exchange of encryption keys facilitated by RSA asymmetric encryption between the Internet Service Provider (ISP) and the server. A key aspect of this system is the implementation of real-time request validation at the ISP level through a Gateway Server, which authenticates user requests before they reach the target server. Furthermore, the article highlights the essential role of Artificial Intelligence (AI) in monitoring network traffic, dynamically managing an allow list of legitimate IPs, and identifying patterns in both benign and malicious traffic to proactively prevent potential attacks. The system's capabilities include generating statistical visualizations and clustering of rejected IP addresses, providing actionable intelligence to network administrators. The performance of machine learning algorithms such as Random Forest and Support Vector Machines (SVM) in classifying network traffic for DDoS detection is also evaluated. This research contributes a robust and scalable solution for enhancing network resilience against the evolving landscape of DDoS threats through the synergistic application of AI and encryption techniques.

Addressing the pressing challenges in contemporary information security, the next paper of this Cybersecurity section, titled "Challenges in information security management system," delves into the limitations of current security paradigms, specifically focusing on aspects like sovereignty, storage and access control, security, privacy, and safeguarding. To overcome these limitations, the authors propose and investigate the potential of a self-sovereign AI information management system, particularly concerning identity. The paper further introduces a model for a self-sovereign AI system leveraging blockchain technology, emphasizing its capacity to ensure principles of sovereignty, security, reliability, and genericity. Through an analysis of various features and an evaluation methodology yielding a "High adherence" level, the research highlights the effectiveness of the proposed model in meeting the dynamic requirements for identity and addressing current challenges in information security management.

The next paper, entitled "LLM-based data annotation and augmentation for NERand relationship extraction models enhancement," deals with the realm of Cyber Threat Intelligence (CTI), the effective analysis and decision-making processes that hinge on a robust understanding of various concepts and their interrelationships, such as threat actors, tools, and malware. This paper presents an innovative approach to automating the annotation of a corpus using large language models (LLMs), addressing the challenges posed by manual annotation, which is often costly and time-consuming due to the semantic ambiguities and the scarcity of certain concepts and relationships in the data. The proposed method involves a two-step process: initially, LLMs are employed to extract relevant concepts and relationships from existing texts, followed by a data augmentation phase where new synthetic documents are generated to fill in the gaps of underrepresented concepts and relationships. This dual approach not only enhances the quality of the annotated corpus but also significantly reduces the need for expert intervention, making the process more efficient and cost-effective. The results indicate that the error rate in concept extraction is less than 5%, showcasing the effectiveness of this method in producing high-quality annotations suitable for training supervised machine learning models. By leveraging LLMs, this research contributes to the advancement of automated STIX file generation, ultimately facilitating better interoperability among cybersecurity tools and enhancing the overall capability of threat intelligence systems.

Regulation

The paper, titled "The definition of biometric data in the context of French legislative experimentation and the implementation of EU regulation on artificial intelligence," examines the evolving definition of biometric data in European and French law, particularly in light of the upcoming EU AI Act. The author traces the definitional shifts from the 1995 Directive and the GDPR to the AI Act, highlighting the inclusion of categorization and emotion recognition alongside identification and authentication in the AI Act's definition. The paper discusses the potential interplay and coherence issues between the AI Act, the GDPR, the Law Enforcement Directive, and the French law experimenting with augmented cameras for the Paris 2024 Olympic Games. It also explores the debate surrounding whether the French experimental algorithms, despite claims to the contrary, process biometric data by analyzing behaviours. Ultimately, the paper proposes to discuss the norm hierarchy and the implications for technical design and fundamental rights concerning personal data and artificial intelligence.

Financial Security

The following article, "Explainability in fraud detection: Trustworthy AI and pattern detection," explores the integration of explainable artificial intelligence (XAI) tools with machine learning models, specifically focusing on tree-based algorithms like Random Forest and XGBoost. The research addresses the challenges posed by highly imbalanced datasets, where fraudulent transactions often represent a mere 5-6% of the total data, complicating effective model training and evaluation. By employing techniques such as SMOTE for oversampling and utilizing various XAI methods including LIME, SHAP, and PyXAI, the study aims to provide robust explanations for model predictions, thereby fostering trust among domain experts. The findings reveal that rule-based explanations are crucial for understanding the conditions under which transactions are deemed legitimate, while feature importance methods assist in identifying key variables influencing fraud detection. This work not only contributes to the development of more reliable AI systems but also emphasizes the importance of transparency in automated decision-making processes, ultimately aiming to empower experts in combating financial fraud effectively.

We express our deep gratitude to the members of the Program Committee for reviewing the submitted papers and helping put together an interesting program. We also thank all authors and our invited speakers, Patrick Perrot and Serena Villata, and our panelists for their inspiring presentations.

Panel About AI for Cybersecurity

This panel was chaired by Joël Courtois of P4S, with panel members Pierre Parrend from the University of Strasbourg, Simon Marstol of Sopra Steria, Général Didier Tisseire of DIRISI, and Hélène Chinal of Capgemini.

Panel About IA and Regulation

This panel was chaired by Dominique Verdejo of AI4GS, with panel members Luc Chausson of LNE, Sabine Marcellin, lawyer and author of "Droit de l'Intelligence artificielle", and Nathalie Beslay from NAAIA.

Panel About AI for Defense

This panel was chaired by Frédérique Segond, Inria, with panel members Nizar Touleimat of CEA, Pierre Memheld from the University of Strasbourg, and David Olivier of Sopra Steria.

Finally, our thanks go out to all the supporting institutions and organizations that helped make this conference possible: French Association for Artificial Intelligence (AFIA), Inria (National Institute for Research in Digital Science and Technology), and Sopra Steria.

We hope that you enjoy reading these papers as much as we had pleasure in collecting and reviewing them.

March 2025

Dominique Verdejo
Eunika Mercier-Laurent

Organization

Program Chairs and Volume Editors

Dominique Verdejo	University of Reims Champagne Ardenne, France
Eunika Mercier-Laurent	University of Reims Champagne Ardenne, France
Frédérique Segond	Inria, France
Patrick Perrot	Gendarmerie Nationale and COMCYBER-MI, France

Program Committee

Joël Courtois	P4S, France
Antoine Guilmoto	Independent Consultant, France
Ammar Mohammed	MSA University and Cairo University, Egypt
Didier Mascarelli	KADLOG, France
Brett Van Niekerk	Durban University, South Africa
Albrecht Schmidt	Ludwig Maximilian University of Munich, Germany
Sanjeet Kumar Nayat	Indian Institute of Information Technology, Design and Manufacturing, Kancheepuram, India
Perumal Thinagaran	Universiti Putra Malaysia, Malaysia
Renumol V. G.	Cochin University, India
Patrick Hebrard	RHEA Group, France
Reda Yaich	IRT SystemX, France
Kave Salamatian	Université de Savoie, France
Guillaume Acca	Cyber Defense Command, France
Paul Askell Dowland	Edith Cowan University, Australia
William Puech	LIRMM, Université de Montpellier, CNRS, France
Ysens de France	Aivancity, France
Simeon Simoff	Western Sydney University, Australia
Solange Ghernaouti	University of Lausanne, Switzerland

Contents

How Can LLM Improve Efficiency of C4ISR? 1
Dominique Verdejo and Eunika Mercier Laurent

ODIP : A State-of-the-Art Child Sexual Abuse Material Detection Model 18
Jérémy Billuart, Romain Gemignani, and Patrick Perrot

A Responsible Crime Evolution Analysis for Homeland Security 28
Daniel Camara and Patrick Perrot

Swarms of Thermal and Optical Drones for Searching for Missing Persons 42
Thibaut Heckmann and Gautier Filardo

La Sécurité Du Territoire: L'affaire De Tous. Vers Un Maillage Sécuritaire Intelligent 62
Cimino Isabelle and Marcenac Jérôme

Human-Centric AI for Enhancing Security in Smart City Anomaly Detection 75
Sanjay Misra, Kousik Barik, Petter Kvalvik, and Sabarathinam Chockalingam

Design and Development of Health Monitoring System with IoT Cryptography Scheme for Wind Turbine 91
Manimegalai Somasundaram and Chamundeswari Arumugam

Enhancing RDBMS Security Through Metaheuristics, Reinforcement Learning, and Triple Loop Learning 100
William Kandolo

Explainable Contextual Anomaly Detection: A Focus on QCAD 114
Gauderic Gumbs, Maurras Togbe, Yousra Chabchoub, and Patrick Perrot

Prevention of DDoS Using AI 127
N. S. Gowri Ganesh, Karthi Govindharaju, K. Mohanish, K. J. Dinesh Karthick, and J. Mohammed Faizal

Challenges in Information Security Management System 143
Mariya Evtimova-Gardair and Frederique Segond

LLM Based Data Annotation and Augmentation for NER and Relationship Extraction Models Enhancement 153
Skander Soltani and Elias Limouni

The Definition of Biometric Data in the Context of French Legislative Experimentation and the Implementation of the AI Act 161
Amélie Turci

Explainability in Fraud Detection: Trustworthy AI and Pattern Detection 178
Hugues Ali-Mehenni, Steve Bellart, and Ahmad Chamma

Author Index 191

How Can LLM Improve Efficiency of C4ISR?

Dominique Verdejo(✉) and Eunika Mercier Laurent

CReSTIC Centre de Recherche en Sciences et Technologies de l'Information et de la Communication - UR 3804, University of Reims Champagne Ardenne, Reims, France
dominique.verdejo@etudiant.univ-reims.fr,
eunika.mercier-laurent@univ-reims.fr

Abstract. The effective Command, Control, Communications, Computers, Intelligence, Surveillance, and Reconnaissance (C4ISR) systems are crucial for modern military operations providing clear situational awareness and vital elements for decision-making. Various AI techniques have been already applied to enhance data integration and some other C4ISR components.

This article proposes to explore the potential of Large Language Models (LLMs) to enhance the current C4ISR capacities such as analyzing vast amounts of data, translating languages, and generating diverse creative text formats that make them useful for heterogeneous data and information fusion, threats and fakes detection and analysis and decision support. After the introduction, the literature review discusses the technical considerations and potential benefits from the integration of LLMs into C4ISR systems. This discussion includes the functionalities such as multisource and multimodal data integration, detection, analysis and prediction of threats and misinformation, decision support through analysis of complex scenarios, identifying potential courses of action, and providing real-time recommendations to commanders working in evolving situations.

The main challenges related to the use of today's LLMs to enhance C4ISR framework such as data security, model interpretability, and bias mitigation will be studied during this research. The specific challenges will be derived from the main case study. This article includes also some characteristics that may serve to elaborate the best-suited framework. This article ends by perspective for future work.

Keywords: Global security · cognitive artificial intelligence · LLMs · C4ISR · military decision support systems · data fusion · intelligence analysis · cybersecurity · misinformation

1 Introduction

1.1 AI in Military C4ISR Systems

C4ISR (Command, Control, Communications, Computers, Intelligence, Surveillance, and Reconnaissance) is an integrated framework used by armed forces, intelligence agencies, and defense organizations to coordinate missions, manage battlefield operations

Published by Springer Nature Switzerland AG 2025
D. Verdejo and E. Mercier-Laurent (Eds.): AI4GS 2024, IFIP AICT 743, pp. 1–17, 2025.
https://doi.org/10.1007/978-3-031-96522-7_1

and ensure strategic advantage. It integrates multiple capabilities to enhance situational awareness, decision-making, and operational effectiveness. Among the applications of C4ISR are also detection of cyber treats, various fakes including propaganda, maintaining of boarder security and management of emergency and crisis situations. C4ISR networks collect massive amounts of data through multiple sensors, drones, intelligence offices, and other sources worldwide. This data is stored, processed and shared with authorized users to make more informed strategic decisions and for missions' execution.

Various AI techniques have been employed to support the key components of C4ISR, with some of these techniques recently being renamed. Notably, Reinforcement Learning and Cognitive AI (also known as Knowledge-based AI or Symbolic AI) have been successfully used to enhance multi-agent system-based simulations, enabling them to make tactical decisions in dynamic environments (Möbius et al., 2023). Cognitive Artificial Intelligence within the C4ISR framework emulates human-like reasoning and decision-making by processing complex information and providing actionable insights (Sumari et al., 2017). Additionally, cognitive systems are applied in Electronic Warfare (EW) to enhance situational awareness and decision-making by interpreting large datasets to identify patterns and anticipate adversary courses of action (COA) (Barbu, 2024). Machine Learning algorithms are extensively used in military intelligence to analyze vast amounts of data from various sources, including SIGINT (Signal Intelligence) and OSINT (Open-Source Intelligence). These algorithms help identify patterns, predict threats, and support decision-making (Szabadföldi & Négyesi, 2023) (Marlin, 2018). ML-based systems can process large datasets to minimize information overload and cognitive biases in intelligence analysis, enabling analysts to focus on synthesizing knowledge and building situational understanding.

Deep Learning (DL) techniques, such as Convolutional Neural Networks (CNNs) have been used for image recognition, classification, and processing in military applications. The related models are optimized to run on tactical mobile edge devices with limited computing resources (Park et al., 2024).

Natural Language Processing (NLP) helps improve communication between humans and AI systems in military applications. This includes the issuance of doctrines and objectives in natural language, enabling AI agents to understand and execute complex commands (Möbius et al., 2023). The chat bots and conversational AI systems, such as Copilot and Gemini, have been tested for decision support in military command and control processes, demonstrating their potential for providing accurate and complete information (Vráb & Zezula, 2024).

1.2 Challenges and Research Proposal

There are still some key challenges to address for better efficiency and accuracy of existing systems, such as:

- Intelligent integration of various data sources with consistency verification and "garbage collector" for data,
- Prediction and early detection of cybersecurity threats that can compromise sensitive information and operational integrity,
- Smart multimodal data/information mining to derive meaningful insights,

- Adequate human-AI interaction for effective Decision Support Systems.

Such challenges require innovative solutions to improve the whole life cycle of data collection, management and processing, user-AI interaction, even synergy and streamline communication across various platforms. The aspects such as speed, accuracy, scalability and cost have also be considered.

To address the above challenges we propose to explore the potential of Large Language Models (LLMs). They are able to analyze a huge amount of data, identify patterns, and generate relevant insights, thereby streamlining operations and improving situational awareness. Their integration capabilities have been studied in various contexts, both from a generic software component perspective (Weber, 2024) and as a specific category of tools for military applications, where rapid decision-making is essential in dynamic environments (Kapiamba et al., 2024).

LLMs, such as GPT-4, have demonstrated their capabilities in natural language "understanding", generation, translation, and "reasoning". Integrating LLMs into C4ISR systems may enhance their efficiency and accuracy by improving data processing, information dissemination to the right actors, decision support, and human-machine interaction.

This research work aims to study the LLMs capacities to address the C4ISR needs, providing more intuitive systems, enabling predictive analytics, automating routine tasks, and allowing involved actors to focus on higher-level analysis and decision-making, thereby increasing overall operational efficiency.

The proposed research method consists in analysis of the main case study - US DoD C4ISR framework in aim identifying and discovering the needs for improvement. Then we will explore if and how the LLMs can address the detected needs and for what results. The relevant cases from specific military context will be selected for implementation and evaluation of potential benefits and perspectives of deployment.

This research begins by the study of initial state of the art in applying LLMs to C4ISR systems.

2 State of the Art

This initial state of the art is composed of several parts exploring the challenges from the users' point of view and from technological perspectives.

2.1 Historical Perspective on C4ISR Systems Within US DoD

The C4ISR Architecture Framework was originally developed in the late 1990s to provide a structured approach for describing, analyzing, and integrating C4ISR architectures within the U.S. Department of Defense (DoD). Acting as a set of rules or guidelines, the framework aims to help various military groups create cohesive plans or "architectures" that ensure interoperability and coherence across different systems. These groups include geographic and functional unified Commands, Military Services, and Defense Agencies, each playing specific roles such as managing particular regions or handling specialized functions.

This framework ensures that the plans cover three main perspectives, promoting integration across various dimensions (vertical, horizontal, temporal, and functional) to ensure interoperability and coherence:

- Operational View: This perspective focuses on how missions are executed, detailing the steps and procedures involved in operational activities.
- Systems View: This view concentrates on the tools and equipment used, such as computers, communication systems, and other technological assets.
- Technical View: This aspect deals with the technical details, including how different systems connect, communicate, and share data information and expertise.

The Architecture Framework underwent several iterations before being superseded by the Department of Defense Architecture Framework (DoDAF) in 2003. The most recent major version, DoDAF 2.0, was released in 2010 and introduced significant changes, including a more data-centric approach and the concept of "fit-for-purpose" architectures. This version emphasizes the importance of tailoring architectures to specific operational needs and strategic goals, ensuring that C4ISR systems are well-designed, interoperable, and aligned with the DoD's objectives.

Since 2003, DoDAF has undergone several updates, providing a standardized methodology for describing, analyzing, and developing complex military systems, with C4ISR being a prime example. It ensures that these systems are not only technologically advanced but also strategically aligned to meet the evolving demands of modern warfare.

In 2023, the Atlantic Council, a prominent American Think Tank based in Washington, D.C., published a comprehensive report (Davis, 2023) on the future trajectory of NATO's C4ISR capabilities. The report highlights significant shortcomings in existing C4ISR systems, deeming them inadequate for addressing projected threats. It emphasizes the need for prompt measures to enhance interoperability and integration across various military domains, asserting that multi-domain operations require substantial modifications to NATO's command frameworks to ensure preparedness for collective defense scenarios.

The report highlights the importance of enhancing intelligence capabilities and augmenting surveillance efforts through innovative policies and technologies to effectively address the challenges set by peer adversaries. It also stressed the need for standardized protocols and data architectures to facilitate data sharing and management, which is vital for crisis prevention and the resolution of enduring security dilemmas. Furthermore, the incorporation of artificial intelligence and advanced data management tools was identified as essential for augmenting the efficacy of NATO's C4ISR operations.

In conclusion it mentions five critical steps transatlantic decision-makers can take to modernize NATO C4ISR and help the Alliance maintain its military edge against potential adversaries in an increasingly contested geopolitical environment:

1. Share more data and intelligence,
2. Transform digitally,
3. Implement new concepts, policies, and plans to clarify C4ISR requirements,
4. Modernize, augment, and acquire capabilities to meet new C4ISR requirements - promoting innovation and adoption of emergent and disruptive technologies such as Artificial Intelligence, autonomy, space-based capabilities, and quantum computing

5. Continue to invest in C4ISR interoperability, readiness, resilience, innovation, and adaptation collective awareness, decision-making, and action.

In this research, we focus on the advantages the LLMs can bring to the C4IRS framework.

2.2 Overview of Large Language Models Development

The development of Large Language Models (LLMs) has evolved significantly from early statistical models to sophisticated architectures capable of understanding and generating human-like text. As research continues to advance, LLMs are poised to play an increasingly critical role in various applications, enhancing operational efficiency and decision-making capabilities across diverse fields.

The evolution of LLMs can be traced through several key milestones:

Transformers and Attention Mechanism: The introduction of the Transformer architecture in 2017 marked a pivotal moment in LLM development. Presented in the paper "Attention is All You Need" (Vaswani et al., 2017), Transformers utilized self-attention mechanisms to process input data more efficiently and effectively. This innovation allowed models to weigh the significance of different words in a sentence based on context rather than position, leading to significant improvements in tasks such as translation, summarization, and conversational agents.

The GPT Series: OpenAI's Generative Pre-trained Transformer (GPT) series exemplifies the advancements in LLMs. Starting with GPT in 2018, followed by GPT-2 in 2019 and GPT-3 in 2020, these models showcased increasing scale and capability. GPT-3, with 175 billion parameters, demonstrated remarkable proficiency in generating coherent and contextually relevant text across diverse prompts, establishing a new benchmark in natural language processing (NLP). The release of GPT-4 further pushed the boundaries, introducing enhanced reasoning abilities and a more nuanced understanding of context, thereby broadening its applications in various fields such as education, content creation, and customer service.

Fine-Tuning and Transfer Learning: The ability to fine-tune pre-trained models on specific tasks further enhanced LLM capabilities. This approach allowed organizations to adapt general language understanding to specialized domains, improving performance in applications ranging from chatbots to content generation. This adaptability not only maximized efficiency but also ensured that the models could meet the unique needs of different industries, paving the way for more personalized and effective interactions with users.

Continued Research and Innovation: The field has continued to innovate with the development of even larger models, such as GPT-4, which further refine language understanding and generation. Research has also focused on addressing challenges such as bias mitigation, model interpretability, and ethical considerations surrounding LLM deployment in sensitive environments.

Retrieval-Augmented Generation (RAG): Pushing the boundaries, RAG is an innovative approach that combines the strengths of information retrieval and text generation.

This technique enhances the capabilities of language models by enabling them to access external knowledge bases or document collections during the generation process. By retrieving relevant information from these sources, RAG models can produce more accurate, contextually rich, and informative responses. This hybrid method addresses some limitations of traditional language models, which may struggle with factual accuracy or up-to-date information, thus making RAG particularly valuable in applications such as question answering, summarization, and conversational agents.

Applications in Various Domains: LLMs have found applications across multiple sectors, including healthcare, finance, and military operations. In military contexts, their ability to process and analyze vast datasets, detect threats, and support decision-making processes has highlighted their transformative potential, particularly within frameworks like Command, Control, Communications, Computers, Intelligence, Surveillance, and Reconnaissance (C4ISR). This capability not only enhances situational awareness but also facilitates rapid response strategies, ensuring that military personnel are equipped with timely and relevant information in high-stakes environments.

2.3 Some Examples of LLMs Applications in C4ISR

Large Language Models (LLMs), such as OpenAI's GPT series represents interesting capacities in natural language processing exploring vast datasets and generating contextually relevant insights. The information fusion allows the integration of heterogeneous, multimodal data including sensors and drones feeds, text reports, and social media, thereby providing an overall view of the operational environment. Furthermore, LLMs are adept at threat detection and analysis, utilizing historical data and real-time "intelligence" to identify anomalies and predict adversary actions from past situations, crucial for proactive defense strategies.

In the context of maritime security, C4ISR systems play a strategic role in enhancing the capabilities of naval forces. They support the integration of intelligence and surveillance data to improve maritime domain awareness and address complex security threats, such as those posed by hybrid warfare (Dolonseda, 2022).

In addition to enhancing data processing and situational awareness, LLMs also serve as decision support tools. By analyzing complex scenarios and providing real-time recommendations, these models helps commanders to make informed choices in rapidly evolving situations. According to Davis (Davis, 2023) LLMs play a vital role in combating misinformation and disinformation, ensuring that accurate intelligence reaches decision-makers, which is paramount in maintaining operational integrity. As an example, LLMs can analyze vast amounts of data from various sources to identify patterns of misinformation, such as detecting false narratives posted on social media platforms. This capability allows timely intervention before misinformation spreads widely.

In specific situations, LLMs may be used for mission planning and execution. As military organizations continue to navigate the challenges of modern warfare, the integration of LLMs into C4ISR architecture promises to revolutionize capabilities, ensuring that personnel are equipped with the tools necessary to respond swiftly and effectively to emerging threats.

Recent studies reveal that LLMs can be instrumental in designing multi-agent architectures that enhance situational awareness and operational planning (Liu et al., 2024.a). Frameworks such as DyLAN allow for real-time agent collaboration, optimizing task execution based on situational demands (Liu et al., 2023). Project AIOS provides an operating system designed to optimize resource allocation and context management among multiple LLM agents, crucial for maintaining operational efficiency in C4ISR environments (Mei et al., 2024), indicating the emergence of a real LLM ecosystem.

According to Wang (Wang et al., 2023) LLMs stand out as a progress compared to previous software generations as they exhibit continuous learning capacities, for instance with Active Learning and the Learning through Communication (LTC) paradigm. This enables LLM agents to adapt to new tasks through iterative learning, enhancing their effectiveness in dynamic military scenarios. Moreover, LLMs step out of the software ontology by their unique capability of fine-tuning the models to adapt their vocabulary and responses to the Army domain specificities. This process is crucial due to the unique requirements and specific vocabulary of military contexts, which are not typically addressed by general-purpose LLMs. The development of specialized models like TRACLM and evaluation frameworks such as MilBench exemplifies efforts to enhance LLM performance in military applications (Ruiz & Sell, 2024).

Hereafter, we emphasize major advancements in LLM technology that are shaping the future of military operations, including enhanced data analysis, predictive modeling, and real-time communication systems that improve situational awareness on the battlefield.

2.3.1 Information Fusion

Integrating disparate data sources presents numerous challenges, including data inconsistency and compatibility issues. LLMs have demonstrated in the biomedical field that they can extract, interpret, and standardize metadata from various sources, significantly outperforming traditional methods and achieving a 50% recovery rate of manually curated metadata (Higashi et al., 2024). In financial applications, LLMs are fine-tuned using data fusion techniques, combining datasets from different tasks to improve model performance across diverse financial tasks (Cao et al., 2024).

In C4ISR, LLMs can play a crucial role in facilitating multi-source data integration by efficiently processing and synthesizing information from various formats. They can analyze sensor feeds, text reports, and social media data, providing a comprehensive view of the situation at hand. Effective sensor fusion techniques enhance situational awareness by intelligently combining observations, allowing operators to focus on the most relevant information (Reily et al., 2021). This integration significantly enhances situational awareness, allowing organizations to respond more effectively to emerging events and trends.

2.3.2 Threat Detection and Analysis

Real-time threat assessment is crucial in security, as it enables organizations to respond swiftly to potential risks. Training LLMs on both historical and real-time data enhances their ability to recognize patterns and detect anomalies effectively. Various techniques for anomaly detection and prediction play a vital role in identifying threats before they happen. LLMs leverage their advanced language "understanding" capabilities to analyze and detect threats by integrating natural language processing (NLP) and machine learning techniques into security frameworks. These models enhance threat detection, anomaly analysis, and automated incident response by processing vast amounts of security data, identifying patterns, and generating contextually appropriate responses (Molleti et al., 2024).

LLMs integrated into existing security systems, such as Security Information and Event Management (SIEM) systems can improve threat detection and response automation. They achieve predictive threat intelligence by recognizing linguistic and non-linguistic patterns in IT security logs, identifying potential threats before they manifest (Bokkena, 2024). They outperform traditional models in detection speed and accuracy, particularly in identifying zero-day exploits, thus supporting proactive security management.

2.3.3 Decision Support

The complexity of modern battlefield scenarios necessitates advanced tools for effective analysis and decision-making. LLMs play a crucial role in scenario analysis and course-of-action development, providing real-time recommendations that can significantly influence the decision-making process. By leveraging LLMs, military strategists can navigate the intricate dynamics of contemporary conflicts, ensuring that their responses are both informed and timely, ultimately enhancing operational effectiveness on the battlefield.

According to Cabalerro (Caballero & Jenkins, 2024) LLMs accelerates the transition from data to actionable decisions, enabling decision-makers to quickly analyze information in applications like war gaming and automatic summarization. They facilitate intelligence officers' tasks, including data collection, fusion, analysis, report generation, and information sharing (Snidaro, 2023). Multimodal LLMs can help C4ISR systems interpret and extract meaningful information from vast amounts of data. Image-to-text analytics can play a crucial role by converting visual data into textual information, which can be more easily processed and analyzed, allowing for better decision-making and situational awareness in military operations (Patra et al., 2017).

2.3.4 Misinformation and Disinformation Detection

The threat of false information in military operations poses significant challenges to national security, as misinformation can lead to misguided strategies and compromised missions. Leveraging advanced LLM capabilities can enhance the detection of such misinformation, enabling military personnel to discern credible intelligence from deceptive narratives. By ensuring the integrity of intelligence reports, armed forces can maintain operational effectiveness and make informed decisions, ultimately safeguarding their objectives against the pervasive influence of false information.

LLMs can help with discourse analysis, detecting disinformation by analyzing discourse derailment, which involves identifying when a conversation is intentionally shifted away from its original topic (Kryoniuk et al., 2024). By cross-referencing new information against the vast corpus of data they are trained on, LLMs can identify inconsistencies and potential misinformation by comparing new inputs with their stored knowledge (Pendyala & Hall, 2024). LLMs surpass traditional methods in accuracy and efficiency for detecting fake news and profiles, utilizing text classification, fact-checking, and contextual analysis to identify false information (Papageorgiou et al., 2024).

To detect propaganda for instance, LLMs utilize text classification techniques to analyze language patterns commonly found in propaganda, such as emotionally charged language or misleading claims. This allows them to identify and flag potentially manipulative content effectively.

2.3.5 Automated Planning and Resource Allocation

Tactical planning and resource management often face significant challenges, particularly in aligning operational objectives with available resources.

Techniques like REPL-Plan allow LLMs to interactively execute and evaluate code, enabling them to handle errors dynamically and adapt to changing scenarios, which is essential for real-time decision-making in C4ISR (Liu et al., 2024). In simulation environments, LLMs, when integrated with Generative Agent-Based Models, can simulate human behavior and interactions, providing insights into complex systems. This capability is beneficial for modeling and predicting outcomes in C4ISR environments, where human-like decision-making is often required (Lu et al., 2024). However, applying LLMs for planning and resource allocation generate important environmental impact (https://hai.stanford.edu/news/regulation-needed-ai-technology-environmental-impact).

Constraint Programming has been largely used with less environmental impact over the last decades for efficient resource allocation, mission planning and scheduling operations.

2.3.6 Risk Assessment and Operational Planning

In naval operations, LLMs can assist in generating operational plans by assessing and quantifying risks, thus supporting strategic planning and execution within the C4ISR framework (Kapiamba et al., 2024). While LLMs offer substantial benefits, their integration into C4ISR systems should be carefully considered. Challenges such as data privacy concerns, potential hallucinations, and vulnerability to adversarial attacks necessitate rigorous safeguards to ensure accuracy and reliability (Caballero & Jenkins, 2024). Additionally, the evolving nature of LLMs requires ongoing research to address biases and improve energy efficiency, which are critical for their sustainable deployment in military applications (Varghese & Ramasamy, 2024).

3 Limitations of LLMs and Challenges to Address for C4ISR

While Large Language Models (LLMs) offer substantial benefits, their integration into Command, Control, Communications, Computers, Intelligence, Surveillance, and Reconnaissance (C4ISR) systems presents several challenges and limitations that must be addressed to ensure their effective and responsible deployment.

3.1 Privacy and Security Risks

The integration of LLMs in national security applications necessitates robust countermeasures to mitigate risks associated with adversarial attacks and disinformation. LLMs can inadvertently leak sensitive information or be manipulated to spread misinformation, posing significant threats to operational integrity. Implementing rigorous safeguards, such as encryption, access controls, and regular security audits, is crucial to protect the accuracy and reliability of information shared among C4ISR users (Yang, 2024; Caballero & Jenkins, 2024).

3.2 Hallucinations and Data Reliability

LLMs are known to occasionally produce "hallucinations," generating outputs that sound confident but are factually incorrect. This issue is particularly concerning in military contexts, where decisions based on inaccurate information can have severe consequences. To mitigate this risk, it is essential to develop mechanisms for verifying the outputs of LLMs against reliable data sources and implementing cross-checking protocols to ensure the validity of the information (Caballero & Jenkins, 2024).

3.3 Adversarial Attacks and Robustness

LLMs are vulnerable to adversarial attacks, where malicious inputs are designed to deceive the model and produce erroneous outputs. Enhancing the robustness of LLMs against such attacks is critical for their deployment in C4ISR systems. Research efforts should focus on developing defensive strategies, such as adversarial training and anomaly detection, to safeguard LLMs from potential threats (Caballero & Jenkins, 2024).

3.4 Interpretability and Transparency

The interpretability of LLMs is a critical concern in military applications, where understanding the rationale behind model outputs is essential for trust and accountability. Approaches like the Concept Bottleneck Large Language Model (CB-LLM) aim to enhance transparency by providing clear explanations for model decisions. Ensuring that LLMs can offer interpretable insights is crucial for their acceptance and effective integration into C4ISR systems (Sun et al., 2024).

3.5 Ethical Implications and Bias Mitigation

The deployment of LLMs within the Department of Defense (DoD) must consider ethical implications, including biases in training data that can lead to unfair or discriminatory outcomes. Collaboration between industry, academia, and government is essential to address these issues and ensure the responsible and equitable deployment of LLMs. Developing frameworks for ethical guidelines and continuous monitoring of model biases can help mitigate these concerns (Blowers et al., 2024).

Ethical aspects should be addressed applying, for instance AI act principles (*EU AI Act: First Regulation on Artificial Intelligence*, n.d.)

3.6 Role and Autonomy in Decision-Making

LLMs are best suited for supporting roles rather than leading strategic decisions due to their lack of autonomous agency. Their use in training and wargaming can provide valuable insights and personalized learning experiences, improving operational readiness without compromising security or decision-making integrity. The ontological characterization of LLMs as non-autonomous agents raises questions about their role in decision-making processes, necessitating careful integration and oversight to ensure they complement human expertise effectively (Barandiaran & Almendros, 2024). They are currently limited primarily to decision making in simulation environments but modern battlefield makes increasing use of drones and autonomous vehicles that will soon require LLMs capabilities.

3.7 Data Privacy and Compliance

Data privacy is a critical concern in the deployment of LLMs, particularly in sensitive military and intelligence operations. Ensuring compliance with data protection regulations and implementing robust data governance frameworks is essential to safeguard personal and operational data. Addressing data privacy challenges requires a multi-faceted approach, including anonymization techniques, secure data storage, and strict access controls (Jalil, 2023; Albtosh, 2024). Notwithstanding ethical aspects, Europe has deeply analyzed and regulated AI usage and the principles for a trustworthy AI should be taken into account in military LLM deployment (https://Digital-Strategy.Ec.Europa.Eu/En/Library/Ethics-Guidelines-Trustworthy-Ai, n.d.).

3.8 Misinformation and Disinformation Detection

LLMs face challenges in detecting and mitigating misinformation and disinformation, which can undermine the integrity of intelligence reports and decision-making processes. Developing advanced techniques for discourse analysis, fact-checking, and contextual verification can enhance the ability of LLMs to identify and counter false information, ensuring the reliability of intelligence in C4ISR systems (Pendyala & Hall, 2024).

3.9 Energy Efficiency and Sustainability

The computational demands of LLMs raise concerns about energy efficiency and environmental sustainability. Optimizing model architectures and training processes to reduce energy consumption is crucial for the long-term viability of LLMs in military applications. Research efforts should focus on developing energy-efficient algorithms and leveraging renewable energy sources to support sustainable deployment (Varghese & Ramasamy, 2024).

The big challenge is still huge environmental impact of generative AI and powering and cooling data centers and for models generation (Mercier-Laurent, 2024), Stanford HAI study (https://hai.stanford.edu/news/regulation-needed-ai-technology-environmental-impact). These aspects will be studied in our further research.

3.10 Continuous Learning and Adaptation

LLMs must adapt to evolving threats and operational environments through continuous learning and updates. Implementing active learning frameworks and real-time data integration can enhance the adaptability of LLMs, ensuring they remain effective in dynamic military scenarios. Collaboration with domain experts and regular model evaluations can help identify areas for improvement and drive ongoing innovation (Wang et al., 2023).

Addressing these challenges and limitations is essential to harness the full potential of LLMs in C4ISR systems. By implementing robust safeguards, enhancing interpretability, mitigating biases, and ensuring ethical deployment, military organizations can leverage LLMs to enhance operational efficiency and decision-making while maintaining the integrity and security of their operations.

Neuro-symbolic AI (NesyAI) is an interesting option that could significantly enhance the real-time capabilities of Large Language Models (LLMs) by integrating structured symbolic reasoning with neural network flexibility. This combination addresses critical challenges such as factual accuracy, logical reasoning, and adaptability in dynamic environments. The merging of symbolic and connectionist paradigms enables LLMs to navigate complex environments effectively, enhancing decision-making and adaptability (Tilwani et al., 2024).

4 Perspectives on Evaluation of Benefits/Effects from Integration of LLMs to C4ISR Systems

In this research we also plan to prototype the assessment of benefits and effects related to the integration of Large Language Models (LLMs) into Command, Control, Communications, Computers, Intelligence, Surveillance, and Reconnaissance (C4ISR). The initial assessment can be inspired by World Economic Forum "simulator" (WEF 2025).

Among others, the main aspects to consider will be the following:

4.1 Accuracy and Performance

Accuracy determines the reliability of LLMs in processing and interpreting data within C4ISR systems. High accuracy ensures that the information provided by LLMs is dependable for decision-making processes (Găitan, 2024). Performance metrics, such as the Unified Performance Ranking Metric, offer a holistic evaluation by integrating qualitative and quantitative assessments, enabling a comprehensive comparison of LLM capabilities (León, 2024).

The Situational Awareness Dataset (SAD) benchmark demonstrates that LLMs can recognize and predict their own behavior, which is crucial for autonomous planning and action. This ability enhances the model's capacity to support C4ISR operations by providing reliable and context-aware responses (Laine et al., 2024).

4.2 Offensive and Defensive Cyber Capabilities

Benchmarks like the Catastrophic Cyber Capabilities Benchmark (3CB) evaluate the offensive cyber capabilities of LLMs, such as reconnaissance and exploitation. This is particularly relevant for cyber military applications, where understanding and countering offensive capabilities is crucial (Anurin et al., 2024).

4.3 Reasoning Capabilities

The ability of LLMs to perform complex reasoning tasks is crucial in C4ISR contexts, where multi-step reasoning and logical operations are often required. The Chain-of-Thought Hub provides benchmarks to evaluate these reasoning capabilities, highlighting the importance of model scale and development in enhancing reasoning performance (Fu et al., 2023).

4.4 Value Alignment

Aligning LLMs with human values is essential to ensure that their outputs are ethically and socially acceptable. The A2EHV system evaluates value rationality, assessing how well LLMs align with diverse human values, which is critical in sensitive C4ISR applications (Zhang et al., 2023). Ensuring value alignment helps mitigate risks associated with biased or unethical outputs, promoting trust and accountability in LLM-driven decisions.

4.5 Continuous Evaluation and Adaptation

Given the dynamic nature of LLMs and the evolving requirements of C4ISR systems, continuous updates and refinements in evaluation methodologies are necessary. Establishing frameworks for ongoing assessment ensures that LLMs remain effective and relevant in the face of technological advancements and changing operational landscapes.

More details on metrics will be provided all along this research to help military organizations explore the full potential of LLMs to enhance operational efficiency, decision-making, and situational awareness, while ensuring ethical and responsible deployment.

5 Future Research

The integration of Large Language Models (LLMs) into C4ISR architectures opens large perspectives for future research.

5.1 Multi-agent Systems and Autonomous Operations

Autonomous LLM-powered multi-agent systems are being explored to tackle complex and interconnected tasks within C4ISR architectures. These systems decompose user-prompted goals into manageable tasks, orchestrating their execution through a collective of specialized agents. This approach enhances the cognitive synergy among agents, allowing for more effective goal-driven task management and multi-agent collaboration, which are essential for C4ISR operations (Händler, 2023). By leveraging the strengths of individual agents, these systems can handle intricate tasks more efficiently, providing a robust framework for autonomous operations in dynamic environments.

5.2 Context Handling and Information Processing

LLMs are equipped to handle larger context lengths, which is crucial for processing the vast amounts of data in C4ISR systems. Techniques like Extensible Embedding allow LLMs to access a broader scope of context efficiently, supporting long-context language modeling and understanding tasks. This capability is vital for maintaining situational awareness and making informed decisions in C4ISR environments (Shao et al., 2024).

The ability of LLMs to reason over structured environments, such as knowledge graphs and tables, further enhances their utility in C4ISR architectures. Frameworks like "Readi" enable LLMs to generate and edit reasoning paths, improving the accuracy and efficiency of information processing and decision-making (Cheng et al., 2024). This structured reasoning capability allows LLMs to provide more reliable and contextually relevant insights, supporting complex analytical tasks in military contexts.

5.3 Active Learning in Anomaly Detection

Active learning involves selecting the most informative data points for labeling, which helps in building a more accurate classifier with fewer labeled instances. This approach is particularly useful in intrusion detection, where the volume of data is large, and labeling is resource-intensive (Gu & Zydek, 2014; Dang, 2020).

The integration of active learning with machine learning models, such as deep learning, can enhance the detection of anomalies by incorporating expert feedback to refine the model's understanding of what constitutes an anomaly (Pimentel et al., 2020). This iterative process not only improves detection accuracy but also reduces the reliance on extensive labeled datasets, making it more feasible for real-world applications.

6 Conclusion and Perspectives

Command, Control, Communications, Computers, Intelligence, Surveillance, and Reconnaissance (C4ISR) is the military's "nervous system," crucial for operations and various actions in complex environments and facing the growing global threats. The geopolitical tensions growing in many places of the planet require continuous improvement of C4ISR architecture to maintain a competitive edge against state-based adversaries and emerging challenges.

The integration of Large Language Models (LLMs) into C4ISR systems represents a transformative leap in military and defence operations. This article presents the initial literature review of existing works covering various aspects, potential advantages and challenges related to heterogeneous data collection, management and processing, situational awareness, and decision-making in dynamic military environments.

This review represents the large spectrum of interconnected topics with promising research and growing challenges due to dynamic environment and requirements of C4ISR.

In addition to efficiency and performance, the ethical and environmental challenges should be considered. Addressing hallucinations, security and vulnerability to adversarial attacks, among others requires considering not only data but also the whole life cycle from collection, managing and exploring. In this aim we wish to explore the hybrid approaches combining the exploration of multi-agent systems and dynamic context handling.

While C4ISR systems are primarily focused on military applications, their principles and technologies can also be adapted for civilian uses, such as effective management of growing natural and human provoked disasters, border security and citizens security.

References

Weber, I.T.: Large language models as software components: a taxonomy for LLM-integrated aplications (2024). https://doi.org/10.48550/arxiv.2406.10300

Kapiamba, S., Fouad, H., Moskowitz, I.S.: Responsible integration of large language models (LLMs) in navy operational plan generation (2024). https://doi.org/10.1609/aaaiss.v3i1.31179

DODAF Version 2.02: DODAF (2003). https://dodcio.defense.gov/Library/DoD-Architecture-Framework/

Vaswani, A., et al.: Attention is all you need. In: Neural Information Processing Systems (2017)

Dolonseda, N.A.: Strategic role of the defense industry in answering the needs of KRI capability C4ISR to achieve maritime security in Indonesian national jurisdictions (2022). https://doi.org/10.55208/jebe.v16i2.251

Davis, G.B.: "Skip". In: Council, A. (ed.) The Future of NATO C4ISR (2023). https://www.atlanticcouncil.org/in-depth-research-reports/report/the-future-of-nato-c4isr-assessment-and-recommendations-after-madrid/

Liu, Z., et al.: AgentLite: a lightweight library for building and advancing task-oriented LLM agent system. arXiv.Org (2024). https://doi.org/10.48550/arxiv.2402.15538

Liu, Z., Zhang, Y., Li, P., Liu, Y., Yang, D.: Dynamic LLM-agent network: an LLM-agent collaboration framework with agent team optimization. arXiv.Org (2023). https://doi.org/10.48550/arxiv.2310.02170

Mei, K., Li, Z., Xu, S., Ye, R., Ge, Y., Zhang, Y.: AIOS: LLM agent operating system. arXiv.Org (2024). https://doi.org/10.48550/arxiv.2403.16971

Wang, K., Lu, Y., Santacroce, M., Gong, Y., Zhang, C., Shen, Y.: Adapting LLM agents through communication. arXiv.Org (2023). https://doi.org/10.48550/arxiv.2310.01444

Ruiz, D.G., Sell, J.: Fine-tuning and evaluating open-source large language models for the army domain (2024). https://doi.org/10.48550/arxiv.2410.20297

Higashi, K., Nakagawa, Z., Yamada, T., Mori, H.: Automated harmonization and large-scale integration of heterogeneous biomedical sample metadata using large language models (2024).https://doi.org/10.1101/2024.10.26.620145

Cao, Y., Yao, Z., Zhi, C., Deng, Z.: CatMemo at the FinLLM challenge task: fine-tuning large language models using data fusion in financial applications (2024). https://doi.org/10.48550/arxiv.2407.01953

Reily, B., Reardon, C., Zhang, H.: Multi-modal sensor fusion and selection for enhanced situational awareness (2021).https://doi.org/10.1117/12.2587985

Molleti, R., Goje, V., Luthra, P., Raghavan, P.: Automated threat detection and response using LLM agents. World J. Adv. Res. Rev. (2024). https://doi.org/10.30574/wjarr.2024.24.2.3329

Bokkena, B.: Enhancing IT security with LLM-powered predictive threat intelligence (2024) https://doi.org/10.1109/icosec61587.2024.10722712

Caballero, W.N., Jenkins, P.R.: On large language models in national security applications (2024). https://doi.org/10.48550/arxiv.2407.03453

Snidaro, L.: ChatGPT Act as an Intelligence Officer (2023). https://doi.org/10.1109/techdefense59795.2023.10380914

Patra, T.K., Rani, R., Dayal, P.: Analytics for image, text and audio analysis for military surveillance, command & control systems (2017). https://doi.org/10.1109/ICECCT.2017.8118039

Kryoniuk, K., Hopkin-King, C., Roberts, S.G.: Detecting disinformation with measures of discourse derailment using LLMs (2024). https://doi.org/10.31234/osf.io/cspdw

Pendyala, V.S., Hall, C.E.: Explaining misinformation detection using large language models. Electronics (2024). https://doi.org/10.3390/electronics13091673

Pendyala, V.S., Hall, E.: Explaining misinformation detection using large language models (2024b). https://doi.org/10.20944/preprints202404.1513.v1

Papageorgiou, E., Chronis, C., Varlamis, I., Himeur, Y.: A survey on the use of large language models (LLMs) in fake news. Future Internet (2024). https://doi.org/10.3390/fi16080298

McDaniel, E., Ruvinsky, A.: Building holistic situation awareness through large language models. EPiC Ser. Comput. (2024). https://doi.org/10.29007/bb8h

Liu, A.Z., et al.: Interactive and expressive code-augmented planning with large language models (2024). https://doi.org/10.48550/arxiv.2411.13826

Lu, Y., Aleta, A., Du, C., Shi, L., Moreno, Y.: LLMs and generative agent-based models for complex systems research. Phys. Life Rev. (2024). https://doi.org/10.1016/j.plrev.2024.10.013

Varghese, N., Ramasamy, G.: Unveiling the potential of large language models. Adv. Comput. Intell. Robot. Book Ser. (2024). https://doi.org/10.4018/979-8-3693-5288-5.ch015

Yang, J.: Large language models privacy and security. Appl. Comput. Eng. (2024). https://doi.org/10.54254/2755-2721/76/20240584

Sun, C.-E., Oikarinen, T., Weng, T.-W.: Crafting large language models for enhanced interpretability (2024). https://doi.org/10.48550/arxiv.2407.04307

Blowers, M., Salinas, S.S., Bailey, S.A.: Risk considerations for the department of defense's fielding of large language models (2024). https://doi.org/10.1117/12.3014424

Jalil, S.: The transformative influence of large language models on software development. arXiv.Org (2023). https://doi.org/10.48550/arxiv.2311.16429

Albtosh, L.: Challenges and limitations of using LLMs in software security. Adv. Inform. Secur. Priv. Ethics Book Ser. (2024). https://doi.org/10.4018/979-8-3693-9311-6.ch012

Barandiaran, X.E., Almendros, L.S.: Transforming agency. on the mode of existence of large language models. arXiv.Org (2024). https://doi.org/10.48550/arxiv.2407.10735

Găitan, N.C.: Performance and accuracy research of the large language models. Int. J. Adv. Comput. Sci. Appl. (2024). https://doi.org/10.14569/ijacsa.2024.0150807

León, M.: Benchmarking large language models with a unified performance ranking metric. Int. J. Found. Comput. Sci. Technol. (IJFCST) (2024). https://doi.org/10.5121/ijfcst.2024.14302

Laine, R., et al.: Me, Myself, and AI: the situational awareness dataset (SAD) for LLMs (2024). https://doi.org/10.48550/arxiv.2407.04694

Anurin, A., Ng, J., Schaffer, K., Wang, Z., Schreiber, J.M., Kran, E.: Catastrophic cyber capabilities benchmark (3CB): robustly evaluating LLM agent cyber offense capabilities (2024). https://doi.org/10.48550/arxiv.2410.09114

Fu, Y., Ou, L., Peng, H.-C., Khot, T.: Chain-of-Thought Hub: a continuous effort to measure large language models' reasoning performance. arXiv.Org (2023). https://doi.org/10.48550/arXiv.2305.17306

Zhang, Z., Liu, N., Qi, S., Zhang, C., Yang, Y., Cui, S.: Heterogeneous value evaluation for large language models. arXiv.Org (2023). https://doi.org/10.48550/arXiv.2305.17147

Heterogeneous Value Evaluation for Large Language Models (2023). https://doi.org/10.48550/arxiv.2305.17147

Händler, T.: Balancing autonomy and alignment: a multi-dimensional taxonomy for autonomous LLM-powered multi-agent architectures. arXiv.Org (2023). https://doi.org/10.48550/arxiv.2310.03659

Shao, N., Xiao, S., Liu, Z., Zhang, P.: Extensible embedding: a flexible multipler for LLM's context length (2024). https://doi.org/10.48550/arxiv.2402.11577

Cheng, S., et al.: Call me when necessary: LLMs can efficiently and faithfully reason over structured environments. arXiv.Org (2024). https://doi.org/10.48550/arxiv.2403.08593

Gu, Y., Zydek, D.: Active learning for intrusion detection (2014). https://doi.org/10.1109/NWRCS.2014.26

Dang, Q.-V.: Active learning for intrusion detection systems (2020). https://doi.org/10.1109/RIVF48685.2020.9140751

Pimentel, T., Monteiro, M., Veloso, A., Ziviani, N.: Deep active learning for anomaly detection. In: International Joint Conference on Neural Network (2020). https://doi.org/10.1109/IJCNN48605.2020.9206769

Möbius, M., Kallfass, D., Flock, M., Doll, T., Kunde, D.: Incorporation of military doctrines and objectives into an AI agent via natural language and reward in reinforcement learning (2023). https://doi.org/10.1109/wsc60868.2023.10408462

Sumari, A.D.W., Ahmad, A.S., Artificial, C.: The application of cognitive artificial intelligence within C4ISR framework for national resilience. In: Asian Conference on Defence Technology (2017). https://doi.org/10.1109/ACDTJ.2017.8259600

Barbu, A.: The cognitive electronic warfare in the age of artificial intelligence (2024). https://doi.org/10.53477/2784-2487-24-02

Szabadföldi, I., Négyesi, I.: The comprehensive approach of military strategic operations planning and its support by artificial intelligence. Honvédségi Szemle (2023). https://doi.org/10.35926/hdr.2023.1-2.1

Marlin, E.M.: Using artificial intelligence to minimize information overload and cognitive biases in military intelligence (2018)

Park, S.C., Kim, Y.-J., Oh, S., Jeong, C.: Robust bare-bone CNN applying for tactical mobile edge devices. IEEE Access (2024). https://doi.org/10.1109/access.2024.3445911

Vráb, V., Zezula, J.: The role of artificial intelligence in military (2024). https://doi.org/10.3849/cndcgs.2024.58

EU AI Act: First Regulation on Artificial Intelligence (n.d.). https://www.europarl.europa.eu/topics/en/article/20230601STO93804/eu-ai-act-first-regulation-on-artificial-intelligence#ai-act-different-rules-for-different-risk-levels-6

EU Ethics guidelines for trustworthy AI. (n.d.). https://digital-strategy.ec.europa.eu/en/library/ethics-guidelines-trustworthy-ai

World Economic Forum: Strategic Intelligence | World Economic Forum. Stategic Intelligence. https://intelligence.weforum.org

Tilwani, D., Venkataramanan, R., Sheth, A.: Neurosymbolic AI approach to Attribution in Large Language Models (2024). https://doi.org/10.48550/arxiv.2410.03726

Regulation Needed for AI, Technology Environmental Impact. 27 juillet 2022. https://hai.stanford.edu/news/regulation-needed-ai-technology-environmental-impact

WEF 2025. https://intelligence.weforum.org/topics/a1Gb0000000pTDREA2. Accessed 6 Mar 2025

ODIP : A State-of-the-Art Child Sexual Abuse Material Detection Model

Jérémy Billuart(✉), Romain Gemignani(✉), and Patrick Perrot(✉)

Ministry of interior's cyberspace command, Paris, France
billuartjeremy@gmail.com, romain.gemignani@gmail.com,
patrick.perrot@gendarmerie.interieur.gouv.fr

Abstract. Child abuse is a criminal offense that needs investigation tools to be more efficient as well as to protect investigators. This is the double objective covered by the ODIP application. This tool has been developed by the French Ministry of Interior Cyberspace Command to provide a child abuse images automatic detection tool to analyze a hard disk or any other physical storage device with great precision and efficiency. The architecture is divided into two major components: a Vision Transformer (ViT) and a Classifier. The ViT model enables us to extract a digital vector from an image, capturing its semantic content. The Classifier is trained to distinguish between vectors representing CSAM and those representing non-CSAM. To train the classifier, we created a corpus of positive and negative images, and all the positive data has been preprocessed by specialist investigator. Thus, when analyzing a hard disk, the program is able to classify each new image as either child abuse or not. This result is still validated by the investigator's or analyst's expertise.

Keywords: CSAM detection · Vision Transformer · Deep learning

1 Introduction

The widespread dissemination of Child Sexual Abuse Material (CSAM) on digital platforms has become a critical issue for law enforcement agencies. The challenge is not only the vast amount of material but also the rapid evolution of techniques used by perpetrators to evade detection. Technological advancements are crucial for detecting, preventing, and mitigating the impact of this illegal content.

1.1 Related Work

The detection of CSAM is a critical challenge in the fight against the online distribution of illegal content. The detection problem can be split into two primary categories: the identification of known CSAM through hashing techniques and the detection of new CSAM using advanced methods such machine learning.

Published by Springer Nature Switzerland AG 2025
D. Verdejo and E. Mercier-Laurent (Eds.): AI4GS 2024, IFIP AICT 743, pp. 18–27, 2025.
https://doi.org/10.1007/978-3-031-96522-7_2

Detection of Known CSAM. The detection of known CSAM primarily relies on hashing techniques, which enable platforms to identify and block the distribution of illegal content. Major tech companies like Microsoft, Apple, and Google have made important efforts to tackle the issue of CSAM, offering various solutions to curb its dissemination on their platforms. These tools are useful for protecting users while assisting law enforcement agencies in taking appropriate action against offenders.

One of the most commonly utilized solutions is PhotoDNA, developed by Microsoft. PhotoDNA generates a fuzzy hash, a hashing technique designed to produce an approximate digital fingerprint of an image. Unlike traditional cryptographic hashes, which are highly sensitive to even the slightest alteration of data, fuzzy hashes allow for the identification of images even if they have undergone minor modifications, such as cropping or changes in color. This hashed signature is then compared against a database of known CSAM hashes, enabling platforms to detect and block identical or near-identical images without the need to expose the actual content. PhotoDNA has been proven highly effective in detecting known CSAM, with a remarkably low false-positive rate, making it one of the leading tools in the fight against illegal content online.

In addition to Microsoft's efforts, Apple has also developed its own CSAM detection system, leveraging a technique known as a neural hash. Neural hashes use machine learning models to generate a digital fingerprint of an image based on its semantic features, capturing complex visual patterns that go beyond simple pixel comparisons. Apple's system was designed to be deployed within its iCloud service to detect known CSAM while maintaining user privacy. The approach compares neural hashes of user-uploaded images with a database of CSAM image hashes.

However, these techniques are inherently limited to detecting content that has already been identified and hashed. Newly generated CSAM remains outside the scope of these systems until it is manually classified and added to the hash databases. This limitation highlights the need for complementary approaches, such as proactive detection methods based on artificial intelligence, to address the emergence of previously unknown illegal content.

Detection of New CSAM. Detecting new CSAM is a much more complex challenge, requiring more sophisticated techniques that go beyond hash-based matching.

Early efforts to detect CSAM in images primarily relied on nudity detection techniques, often based on skin color classification. Tools like NuDetective [1] exemplify this approach, using algorithms that identify large regions of skin in images to flag potentially explicit content. These systems were effective at detecting nudity but lacked the granularity to distinguish between adult pornography and CSAM. Moreover, they narrowly defined pedopornography as mere nudity, overlooking the wider spectrum of abusive content that CSAM can represent.

In response to this limitation, researchers sought to enhance nudity detection by integrating age estimation models. For example, Sae-Bae et al. (2014) introduced a system in their study [5], that combined skin-based nudity detection with algorithms capable of estimating the age of individuals. However, these methods relied heavily on facial recognition for age prediction, making them ineffective when the subject's face was not visible in the image. The reliance on facial features remains a significant drawback, as many CSAM images obscure or omit facial details.

Building on this, the methodology outlined by Macedo et al. (2018) explored the combination of Yahoo's open-source deep learning solution for detecting Not Safe For Work (NSFW) images with age estimation algorithms [3]. While this approach improved classification accuracy, it still faced the same limitation-age estimation models predominantly require facial information, which is not always present in CSAM.

With the rise of deep learning, particularly Convolutional Neural Networks (CNNs), more sophisticated techniques were applied to CSAM detection. A notable example is the work made by Vitorino et al. [7] titled Leveraging Deep Neural Networks to Fight Child Pornography in the Age of Social Media, which employed fine-tuning and transfer learning techniques on pre-trained models like GoogLeNet [6]. In this approach, CNNs were used as feature extractors, allowing the system to automatically learn and classify CSAM images based on visual patterns. This marked a significant advancement, as the model could generalize better to unseen images without relying solely on skin or facial detection.

Despite these advancements, one of the biggest challenges in CSAM detection is the lack of comprehensive datasets for training machine learning models. Due to legal and ethical constraints, researchers are limited in their access to real CSAM images, which results in models being trained on small or unbalanced datasets. This severely hampers the ability of such systems to generalize across the diverse range of CSAM content, which varies in ethnicity, background, and image quality.

Finally, to avoid directly analyzing visual content, some researchers have explored detection methods based on metadata. These approaches analyze file characteristics—such as file paths, directory structures, and naming conventions—rather than the content itself. For example Pereira et al. proposed a deep learning model [4] that analyzed file metadata to detect CSAM, achieving high accuracy rates without requiring access to the image data itself. This method is particularly effective for large-scale scanning operations where it is impractical or legally risky to process image content directly. However, the main drawback of this method is that criminals always try to conceal evidence. In our case, they often obfuscate file names and folder paths. As a result, the file path or name of CSAM may become useless and irrelevant, as it no longer contains the necessary information to ensure proper detection.

In conclusion, while significant progress has been made in CSAM detection, each method has its own limitations. Skin-based nudity detection lacks specificity, age estimation models often require facial visibility, and CNN-based classifiers face challenges related to the scarcity of training data. Metadata-based approaches offer a promising alternative, but they cannot entirely replace visual content analysis. Future research will need to address these gaps, particularly in developing models that can handle diverse, unseen CSAM content and scale effectively in real-world applications.

1.2 Context

The investigators of the French National Gendarmerie work on several thousand cases of Child Sexual Abuse each year. These investigations are partially based on CSAM research on various mass storage devices (usb keys, sd cards, hard disks ...) or mobile phones. As the rapidity of detection of CSAM is a key element of Child Abuse offense characterization during police custody, investigators have to accurately discriminate CSAM from other nudity and sexual images and videos present on these supports. Usually, this process involves some investigators who are exposed to psychologically harmful content. To help them, several tools can be used to reduce the amount of data to analyze. First, known CSAM can be detected by comparing each image with a database of previously identified CSAM. They also have the possibility to use a nudity detection. However, in some cases it can lead to a large number of false positives.

In this context the French Ministry of Interior Cyberspace Command has developped a CSAM automatic detection system based on state of the art AI model discriminating CSAM from other sexual material by image semantic capture in an embedding vectors space. This system called ODIP (Outil de Détection d'Images Pédopornographiques) tackles the False Positive images problem keeping high level of computationnal performances. As image processing stage is clearly separated from the classification stage it preserve investigators exposition by design.

1.3 Legal Framework

CSAM data are very sensitive and subject to a strict legal framework, which is why we have collaborated with the CNAIP (French National Center for the Analysis of Child Sexual Abuse Material Images). Together, we were able to obtain the authorization of a magistrate to use the images from an ongoing investigation for exploratory purposes. We also want to stress that, as research scientists, we never had possession of any such material. All the data was processed by the CNAIP, which provided us only with feature vectors containing solely the semantic information of the images.

2 Dataset

The tool we developed is a binary classifier that evaluates each image and, based on a predefined threshold, determines whether the image should be classified as exhibiting CSAM. To train and test our model, we created a dataset consisting of positive images containing CSAM and negative images.

Table 1. Training dataset details

Negative: 44 097 images			Positive
Hard	Weak		
various : 30 269 images	**children** : 7 100 images	**porno** : 6 728 images	33 294 images

Table 2. Validation dataset details

Negative: 11 025 images			Positive
Hard	Weak		
various : 7 568 images	**children** : 1 775 images	**porno** : 1 682 images	8 323 images

Table 3. Test dataset details

Negative	Positive
103 images	103 images

The dataset used for classifier training is made of almost % 40 of positive data. Negative data was made mixing hard negatives and weak negatives images (70 and 30% respectively). Weak negatives contains pornographic and children images. This dataset was split into train (Table 1) and validation (Table 2) datasets (80 and 20% respectively). Another small dataset composed of manually chosen images was used for test. The test dataset (Table 3) was made in order for performance evaluation of the classifier on various representative targets.

3 Architecture

The architecture of our model (see Fig. 1) is divided into two main components: a Vision Transformer [2] used as a feature extractor, followed by a classifier responsible for predicting the category based on the extracted representations.

3.1 Vision Language Model Backbone

In the field of multimodal AI research, Vision-Language Models (VLM) have made great progress in recent years, particularly in the embedding representation of both images and text into a shared vector space using alignment methods such as contrastive learning. ODIP rely on a such model: MetaCLIP [8] This particular model, train on over 400 millions of image text pairs, exhibits excellent performance in inference step even on CPU.5 In our case, we utilize MetaCLIP as a feature extractor for our images. The extensive dataset used to train MetaCLIP, combined with its robust architecture, makes it an excellent candidate for extracting meaningful features. The latent space where image embeddings are projected contains a wealth of semantic information about the image, capturing both fine-grained and high-level details.

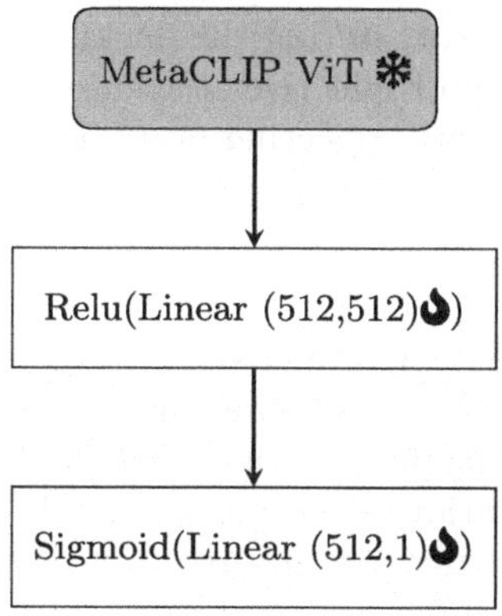

Fig. 1. Model architecture, ❄ represents frozen parameters, 🔥 represents trainable parameters.

3.2 Capability Validation of the Model in Zero-Shot Learning Tasks

To validate the model's capability in distinguishing positive images from negative images based on semantic representation, we first conducted a basic zero-shot binary classification using both vision and language encoders of the model and measuring the cosine distance of various images dataset to well chosen text descriptions. This prelimary works successfuly demonstrate the ability of MetaCLIP to capture image semantic in this specific usecase. However, the cosine distance between true and false positives is not significant enough for simple zero-shot classification, and this is the reason why we trained a classifier on top of MetaCLIP, to enable our model to discriminate CSAM properly.

3.3 Vision Transformer Based Classifier

The ODIP classifier is a binary model that operates on vector representations of images computed by the VisionTransformer module of pretrained MetaCLIP model. It consists of two dense layers. The first dense layer maps the 512-dimensional input vector to another 512-dimensional output, followed by a ReLU activation function. The second layer reduces the output to a single scalar value, which is then passed through a sigmoid activation function to produce a classification score between 0 and 1.

The training loss is a simple Binary Cross Entropy function L defined by:

$$L = \frac{-1}{N} \sum_{i=1}^{N} (y_i \log(p_i) + (1 - y_i) \log(1 - p_i)) \qquad (1)$$

BCE works by comparing the predicted probability for each image with the actual label (CSAM or non-CSAM). It penalizes incorrect predictions more heavily as they diverge from the true label, thereby guiding the model to adjust its weights to minimize these errors during the backpropagation. Through this process, the classifier becomes more effective at accurately identifying CSAM images (*sensitivity*) while also correctly rejecting non-CSAM content (*specificity*).

4 Results

Our primary evaluation metric was the Receiver Operating Characteristic (ROC) curve, a well-established tool for assessing the performance of binary classifiers. The ROC curve plots the true positive rate (*sensitivity*) against the false positive rate (1-*specificity*) across various decision thresholds. This allows us to visualize the trade-off between detecting true positives and avoiding false positives.

The area under the ROC curve (AUC) provides a quantifiable measure of the model's ability to discriminate between positive (CSAM) and negative (non-CSAM) images. An AUC of 0.5 represents a random classifier, indicating no discriminative power, while an AUC of 1.0 signifies perfect classification performance.

As shown in Fig. 2, our model achieves an AUC of 0.968 on the test dataset.

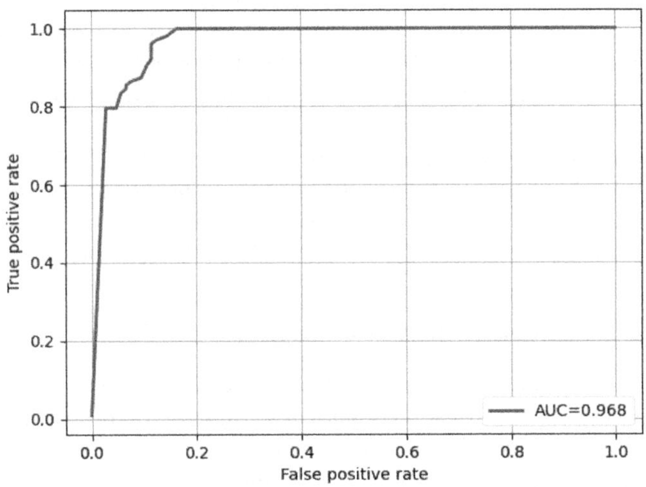

Fig. 2. ROC Curve of our Model Evaluated on the Test Dataset (see Table 3).

After testing, our model, has been optimized with a decision threshold set at 0.3 to minimize the false negative rate while maintaining a reasonable false positive rate. The performance of the model at this threshold yielded a recall rate of over 95%, significantly improving its ability to correctly identify CSAM content. This adjustment ensures that the risk of missing harmful content is minimized.

At this threshold, the confusion matrix (see Fig. 3) shows 99 true positives and only 4 false negatives, indicating the model's strong capability to detect

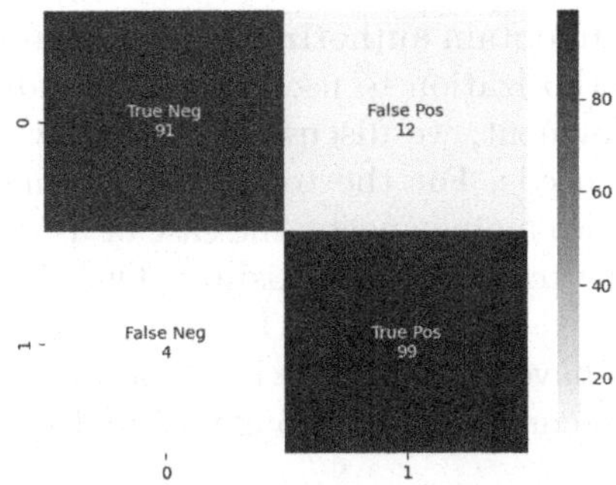

Fig. 3. Confusion Matrix of our Model with a Threshold of 0.3.

CSAM instances. Meanwhile, the false positive rate remains reasonable, with 12 false positives compared to 91 true negatives. These results highlight the model's balance between maximizing detection and controlling false alarms, crucial for real-world applications where identifying as many CSAM instances as possible is essential, even if it means a slight increase in false positives.

However, in some cases it can be difficult to determine whether an image falls under child sexual abuse material. When conducting an investigation, context allows investigators to judge if an image is indeed a CSAM. This is why even though the decision threshold is set to 0.3, it can be adjusted to fit the needs of the investigators and the trade-off between false positive and false negative permitted within their analysis. Furthermore, it is important to emphasize the fact that ODIP has no intention of doing autonomous analysis, it is supposed to serve as an assistant for the investigators. The topic is too sensitive to allow the AI to make the final decisions. Investigators need to be the final decision maker as well as being involved during the whole process.

5 Discussion

The ODIP tool shows great potential for automating CSAM detection, providing an efficient and portable solution that runs on standard CPUs. However, the tool's effectiveness is currently constrained by the size and diversity of the training dataset. To improve the model's generalizability and ensure reliable performance across various scenarios, it is crucial to expand the dataset to include a broader range of CSAM and non-CSAM images. Although the current architecture is effective, future work could explore more advanced techniques, such as fine-tuning MetaCLIP or integrating additional modalities like video or metadata, to further enhance the tool's capabilities. Additionally, as the dataset grows, addressing legal considerations will become increasingly important.

The final objective of our work is to make ODIP available to cyber investigators dedicated to content analysis. This objective raises two challenges: the first is to obtain legal authorizations, and the second is to deploy the tool. At present, ODIP is only authorized for exploratory purposes, and we are working on the legal framework to obtain authorization to re-train our model on a larger database and obtain authorization to use ODIP in a judicial investigation.

Regarding the deployment, we discuss with the investigors to get a better understanding of their needs. For the tool to be the most helpful toward the investigators, their are two main aspects: the ease of use and the level of integration of the tool with the tools already existant. One deployment option would be to éadd ODIP to an existing toolbox. To use the tool and analyze a storage space, investigators will have to justify the need for automatic analysis by ODIP. This protocol aims to secure the use of our tool and provide full transparency on its use.

6 Conclusion

ODIP offers a robust solution for the rapid identification of CSAM while shielding investigators from exposure to harmful content. With ongoing development, including dataset expansion, ODIP has the potential to become an indispensable asset for digital forensic investigators, contributing to a more efficient and humane approach to handling CSAM cases. The tool, utilizing state-of-the-art techniques and strategic technological choices, is well-positioned to support law enforcement in digital investigations.

Acknowledgments. We would like to thank the investigators at CNAIP for their time and dedication. Their hard work and support were essential to the success of this project. We greatly appreciate their contributions.

References

1. de Castro Polastro, M., da Silva Eleuterio, P.M.: Nudetective: a forensic tool to help combat child pornography through automatic nudity detection. In: 2010 Workshops on Database and Expert Systems Applications, pp. 349–353 (2010). https://doi.org/10.1109/DEXA.2010.74
2. Dosovitskiy, A., et al.: An image is worth 1t6x16 words: Transformers for image recognition at scale. CoRR abs/2010.11929 (2020). https://arxiv.org/abs/2010.11929
3. Macedo, J., Costa, F., A. dos Santos, J.: A benchmark methodology for child pornography detection. In: 2018 31st SIBGRAPI Conference on Graphics, Patterns and Images (SIBGRAPI), pp. 455–462 (2018). https://doi.org/10.1109/SIBGRAPI.2018.00065
4. Pereira, M., Dodhia, R., Brown, R.: Metadata-based detection of child sexual abuse material. CoRR **abs/2010.02387** (2020), https://arxiv.org/abs/2010.02387
5. Sae-Bae, N., Sun, X., Sencar, H.T., Memon, N.D.: Towards automatic detection of child pornography. In: 2014 IEEE International Conference on Image Processing (ICIP).,pp. 5332–5336 (2014). https://doi.org/10.1109/ICIP.2014.7026079
6. Szegedy, C., et al.: Going deeper with convolutions. CoRR abs/1409.4842 (2014). arXiv:1409.4842

7. Vitorino, P., Avila, S., Perez, M., Rocha, A.: Leveraging deep neural networks to fight child pornography in the age of social media. J. Vis. Commun. Image Represent. **50**, 303–313 (2018)
8. Xu, H., et al.: Demystifying clip data (2024). https://arxiv.org/abs/2309.16671

A Responsible Crime Evolution Analysis for Homeland Security

Daniel Camara[1(✉)] and Patrick Perrot[2]

[1] Gendarmerie Nationale, 4 Rue Claude Bernard, 92130 Issy Les Moulineaux, France
daniel.camara@gendarmerie.interieur.gouv.fr
[2] Commandement du Ministère de L'intérieur Dans Le Cyberespace, 4 Rue Claude Bernard, 92130 Issy Les Moulineaux, France
patrick.perrot@gendarmerie.interieur.gouv.fr

Abstract. Effective criminality forecasting enhances public safety by optimizing the knowledge of crime evolution, increasing the transparency of police actions at the condition to be at a the right decision making level. This kind of tools is dedicated for tactical and strategic issue in order to optimize the operational level. It is not built as an execution tool but needs to be used at the decision making level. This paper presents an adaptive time series analysis method that improves both the accuracy and interpretability of crime predictions. Utilizing a five-year dataset of interventions by the French Gendarmerie—covering approximately 80% of France's territory—the model analyzes historical incidents to forecast future occurrences. It integrates two components: **tendency**, capturing short-term trends from recent incidents with higher weights assigned to more recent data, and **seasonality**, accounting for long-term patterns using data from the same periods over the past four years with decreasing weights for older data. Developed and validated using real-world data, the method produces accurate and explainable forecasts. This explainability satisfies legal requirements for accountability and aids law enforcement in decision-making processes. The approach effectively captures evolving crime patterns, offering valuable insights for proactive policing while balancing Precision and interpretability.

Keywords: Criminality Forecast · Time Series Analysis · Explainability

1 Introduction

Criminality forecasting is vital for enhancing public safety and optimizing law enforcement resource allocation. This kind of tools is dedicated for tactical and strategic issue in order to optimize the operational level. It is not built as an execution tool but needs to be used at the decision making level. Accurate predictions of crime patterns enable authorities to implement proactive measures, deploy personnel effectively, and devise strategic interventions. Traditional forecasting methods often rely on static analyses of historical data, which may not account for the dynamic nature of urban environments where factors influencing criminal activities evolve rapidly.

Published by Springer Nature Switzerland AG 2025
D. Verdejo and E. Mercier-Laurent (Eds.): AI4GS 2024, IFIP AICT 743, pp. 28–41, 2025.
https://doi.org/10.1007/978-3-031-96522-7_3

Advancements in time series analysis have introduced models that capture temporal dependencies and trends in crime data. However, many of these models function as opaque "black boxes," offering limited transparency into their predictive mechanisms. This lack of explainability poses challenges in legal contexts where authorities must justify decisions based on model outputs. In such settings, the ability to provide clear, evidence-based explanations is as crucial as the accuracy of the predictions.

This paper proposes an adaptive time series analysis method designed to enhance both the accuracy and explainability of criminality forecasting. The method integrates two key components: tendency and seasonality. The tendency component captures short-term trends by analyzing recent data—such as the past week, the same day over the past four weeks, and similar parts of the week—with weights that decrease over time. The seasonality component accounts for long-term patterns by incorporating data from the same week and month over the past four years, also weighted to reflect temporal proximity.

The weighting scheme is grounded in the understanding that urban landscapes and social behaviors influencing crime are subject to continuous change. Factors like economic shifts, legislative changes, population movements, and climatic variations can alter crime dynamics. By assigning greater influence to more recent data, the model adapts to current conditions while acknowledging historical patterns that may still exert residual effects.

Explainability is a central feature of the proposed method. Each prediction is accompanied by transparent reasoning that details the contribution of various factors, enabling law enforcement agencies to provide clear justifications in judicial proceedings and policy decisions. This approach aligns with the growing emphasis on accountable and interpretable AI systems, particularly in sensitive domains like criminal justice.

The remainder of this paper is structured as follows: Sect. 2 reviews existing literature on criminality forecasting and the importance of explainable models in legal contexts. Section 3 outlines the methodology, detailing the data collection processes and the adaptive weighting mechanisms employed. Section 4 presents the results of applying the method to real-world crime data, evaluating its performance. Finally, Sect. 5 concludes the paper by discussing the method, summarizing key contributions, and suggesting directions for future research.

2 Related Works

The forecasting of criminal activity has been extensively studied, with various methodologies developed to understand and predict crime patterns. Central to this endeavor is recognizing that crime is influenced by social, environmental, and spatial factors that can be systematically analyzed and modeled.

Studies have shown that social factors significantly influence criminality, suggesting these variables can be leveraged for crime prediction. Ruiz and Sawant emphasize the impact of social determinants on crime rates, highlighting the importance of understanding these factors in prediction models [1]. The role of location is also well-documented; Eck and Weisburd discuss the significance of spatial factors, noting that not all places are equally conducive to crime [2].

Crime Pattern Theory provides a framework explaining why crimes occur in certain areas by examining the overlap between the activity spaces of offenders and potential victims. An individual's activity space includes personal nodes—home, work, school, recreational areas—and the connecting paths, forming their awareness space. Crime is more likely when an offender's awareness space intersects with that of a victim in locations offering opportunities for crime. High-traffic areas like shopping malls often experience higher crime rates due to the convergence of potential victims and offenders [2]. By analyzing these movement patterns, Crime Pattern Theory aids law enforcement in understanding and predicting where crimes are likely to happen.

The ability to study and model crime patterns, including spatial components, has led to significant advancements in spatiotemporal crime prediction methods. Environmental criminology theories have been scientifically tested, resulting in progress across various research fields. In the past decade, studies by Caplan et al. [3], Perry et al. [4], Wang and Brown [5], and Yu et al. [6] have developed methods for crime prediction and evaluation.

Data mining techniques are crucial in criminality forecasting, extracting meaningful patterns from extensive crime data. Gendre et al. classify primary methods into association rule mining, classification, and clustering [7]. Association rule mining uncovers hidden relationships in unlabeled data, revealing correlations between crime types, locations, and times—often using algorithms like Apriori. Classification assigns data instances to predefined categories based on attributes, aiding in predicting crime likelihood under specific conditions using methods like decision trees, nearest neighbor algorithms, and neural networks. Clustering groups similar data without predefined labels to identify patterns or hotspots, utilizing techniques such as k-means clustering and hierarchical clustering. These methods enable law enforcement to analyze crime data effectively, enhance resource allocation, and develop proactive policing strategies by identifying relationships and predicting crime occurrences.

Advancements in Geographic Information Systems (GIS) have significantly enhanced predictive policing by improving crime mapping and analysis capabilities. The U.S. Department of Homeland Security's SAVER program detailed how GIS tools are instrumental in plotting and visualizing crime locations, aiding in detecting spatial and temporal crime patterns [8]. GIS enables law enforcement agencies to overlay crime data with non-crime data—such as population density, income levels, and land use—to better understand environmental and societal factors contributing to crime, thereby formulating more effective response strategies.

Most prediction techniques in criminality forecasting rely on retrospective forecasting, predicting future events through historical data analysis. Historical crime data are used alone or with crime attractors and generators—demographic, environmental, or socioeconomic factors—in various prediction models. Kounadi et al. present a systematic review of spatial crime forecasting methods, explaining and comparing diverse methodologies [9]. For instance, models may incorporate data on unemployment rates, school dropout rates, and urban decay indicators alongside past crime incidents to forecast future trends.

Existing literature underscores the feasibility of criminality forecasting by leveraging social, environmental, and spatial factors. Through data mining techniques and GIS tools, researchers can model crime patterns and develop strategies to predict and prevent criminal activities. Continued advancements in analytical methods and technology promise further improvements in the precision and utility of crime forecasting models, contributing to more effective law enforcement and enhanced public safety.

3 Methodology

3.1 Data Collection

The data utilized in this study comprise all interventions conducted by the French Gendarmerie in response to emergency calls within their jurisdiction, which encompasses approximately 80% of France's territory, including overseas departments. The dataset spans five years and includes every call and subsequent intervention recorded in the Gendarmerie's competency zone.

Each record in the dataset contains (i) *Date and Time of Intervention*: Precise timestamps of when interventions occurred. (ii) *Geographic Location*: Latitude and longitude coordinates pinpointing the location of each intervention, divided into approximately 1 km $\times$ 1 km grid squares covering the entire French territory. (iii) *Reason for Intervention*: Coded classifications of the incidents prompting interventions, standardized across French Police and Gendarmerie services.

While the interventions range widely—from addressing hazards like dead animals on roads to responding to serious crimes such as burglaries and assaults—the study focuses primarily on incidents related to criminal activities. For simplicity, all interventions are referred to as "crimes" throughout this paper, acknowledging that some interventions involve non-criminal matters like public safety hazards or assistance to vulnerable individuals.

Access and Permissions

The data were obtained directly from the Gendarmerie's operational records. The study has been presented to the French data protection authority and is in the process of declaration for conformity, ensuring compliance with relevant data protection regulations.

Timeframe and Geographical Coverage

The dataset covers a continuous five-year period, allowing for robust analysis of both short-term trends and long-term seasonal patterns in criminal activity. The geographical coverage includes the entire French territory managed by the Gendarmerie, divided into a lattice of approximately 1 km $\times$ 1 km squares. This granularity enables detailed spatial analysis of crime patterns at the local level.

For each target day in the forecasting model, the following temporal data segments are collected:

- **Last Seven Days**: Incidents from the seven days immediately preceding the target day.
- **Same Day of the Week Over the Last Four Weeks**: Incidents occurring on the same weekday in each of the four weeks prior.

- **Same Part of the Week Over the Last Four Weeks**: Incidents from the same portion of the week (weekdays or weekends) over the past four weeks.
- **Last Four Weeks**: All incidents from the past four weeks.
- **Last Four Months**: Incidents from the past four months.
- **Same Week Over the Last Four Years**: Incidents from the same ISO week number in each of the past four years.
- **Same Month Over the Last Four Years**: Incidents from the same calendar month in each of the past four years.

This sliding window approach ensures that the model captures both recent trends (tendency) and recurring patterns (seasonality) relevant to each day and location.

Types of Crimes Analyzed

The dataset includes a wide array of crime types, with particular emphasis on burglaries and auto thefts due to their prevalence and impact on public safety. Crimes are categorized according to standardized codes defined by French law enforcement agencies. Operators assign these codes during the call and may update them during or after interventions if initial information is misleading.

Data Preprocessing

Data cleaning was minimal due to the dataset's inherent quality from the Gendarmerie's automated call system. The primary task involved removing anomalies such as erroneous geocoding—approximately 1% of records with incorrect geographic coordinates outside French territory or within the Police Zone—and incomplete records missing critical information like date, time, crime type, or location. A temporal aggregation was assigned to each incident to appropriate time frames—daily, weekly, monthly, and annually—to facilitate the calculation of the tendency and seasonality components in the forecasting model. The spatial aggregation task involves mapping incidents onto 1 km × 1 km grid squares covering the French territory, enabling localized analysis and forecasting of criminal activity.

Normalization

To standardize the danger levels across different grid squares, a normalized dangerosity score was calculated for each cell, ranging from 0 to 1. The raw dangerosity is determined based on each cell's weighted sum of incidents. The normalization process scales these values relative to the maximum and minimum raw dangerosity scores observed, enabling comparative analysis across the entire territory.

Ethical Considerations

The study exclusively uses anonymized data without personal identifiers such as names or phone numbers. The only potentially sensitive information is the geographic location of interventions; however, without additional context, this data does not compromise individual privacy. The use of this data complies with ethical standards and data protection regulations in France.

3.2 Adaptive Time Series Analysis

Overview of the Approach

The adaptive time series analysis method integrates both tendency and seasonality components to forecast criminal activity in each 1 km × 1 km grid square across France. The model operates by collecting and weighting historical incident data relevant to each target day and location, emphasizing more recent events to capture current trends while accounting for seasonal patterns observed over previous years (Fig. 1).

The model's framework involves:

- **Tendency Component**: Captures short-term trends by analyzing recent data segments, such as incidents from the last seven days, the same day over the past four weeks, and the same part of the week over the past four weeks. This component adapts quickly to sudden changes in criminal activity, reflecting environmental or societal shifts affecting specific areas.
- **Seasonality Component**: Accounts for long-term patterns by incorporating data from the same week and month over the past four years. This component captures recurring seasonal effects, such as increased crime rates during certain holidays or tourist seasons, providing a stable view of expected behavior based on historical patterns.

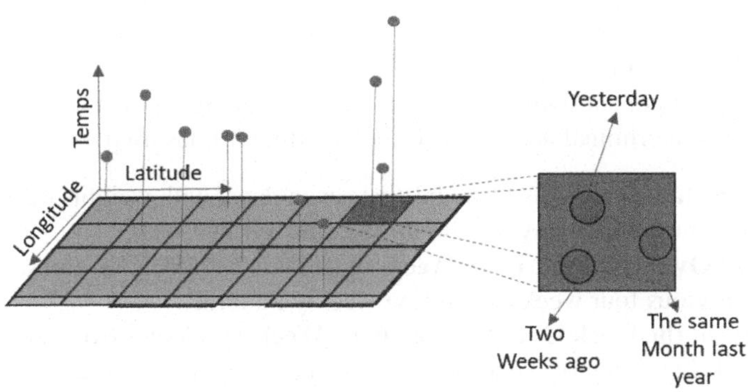

Fig. 1. The division of the area into latices of ~1 square km, and the attribution of the past events over the lattice. Here, we consider two dimensions: a geographic one, denoted by the lattice, and a temporal one, denoted by the height of the events, which are depicted as red dots. The weight of each class of event gives the ponderation of the temporal distance. Color figure online

Mathematical Formulation

The dangerosity score for each grid cell sss on a target date *d* is calculated as the sum of weighted incidents across all relevant time frames:

$$\text{cell\_dangerosity}_s(d) = \sum_t \left(\sum_i \left(\text{weight}_{t,i} \times \text{incidents}_{s,t,i}(d) \right) \right)$$

where:

- t represents each type of temporal segment (e.g., daily, weekly, monthly).
- i index the specific periods within each temporal segment (e.g., days in the last week, months in the last four months).
- s represents the s-th 1 square kilometre cell on the grid
- d represents a given data
- $weight_{t,i}$ is the weight assigned to the i-th period of temporal segment t, that is linked to the function of the period (week, day, last year month…).
- $incidents_{s,t,i}(d)$ is the number of incidents in grid cell s during the i-th period relevant to date d.

Weighting Mechanism

Weights are assigned to incidents based on their temporal proximity to the target date, with more recent events receiving higher weights. The initial weights were set to follow a regular decay pattern, starting with a maximum weight of 2 for the most recent data points and decreasing by approximately 10% with each subsequent period. For specific segments like the last days of the week, weights decrease by 5%.

A genetic algorithm optimized the weighting scheme, allowing weights to vary within a 10% range of their initial values. The algorithm iteratively adjusted the weights to maximize the model's performance, focusing on increasing true positives and reducing false negatives.

Tendency Component

The tendency component focuses on recent data to capture short-term fluctuations and sudden changes in criminal activity. The specific time frames used are:

- **Last Seven Days**: Incidents from the past seven days, with weights decreasing from 1.85 for the most recent day to 1.00 for the days further back.
- **Same Day Over the Last Four Weeks**: Incidents occurring on the same weekday over the previous four weeks, capturing weekly patterns.
- **Same Part of the Week Over the Last Four Weeks**: Incidents from the same portion of the week (weekday or weekend) over the past four weeks, recognizing different crime patterns between weekdays and weekends.
- **Last Four Weeks**: Aggregated weekly incidents over the past four weeks, with decreasing weights to reflect recency.
- **Last Four Months**: Incidents from each of the last four months, capturing medium-term trends.

These time frames align with how law enforcement agents might recall and assess recent criminal activity, emphasizing recent incidents that may influence current conditions. The weighting scheme ensures that the model remains sensitive to new developments, such as environmental factors or criminal behavior changes.

Seasonality Component

The seasonality component incorporates long-term historical data to account for recurring patterns in criminal activity associated with specific times of the year. The time frames used are:

- **Same Week Over the Last Four Years**: Incidents from the same ISO week number in each of the past four years, weighted to prioritize more recent years.
- **Same Month Over the Last Four Years**: Incidents from the same calendar month over the past four years, capturing broader seasonal trends.

Seasonal effects, such as increased tourism during summer months or heightened activity during holiday seasons, significantly influence crime patterns. By including data from the same periods in previous years, the model accounts for these predictable fluctuations while allowing for the diminishing relevance of older data due to environmental or societal changes.

Integration of Components

After weighting, incidents from both the tendency and seasonality components are combined to calculate the raw dangerosity score for each grid cell. This integrated approach ensures that the model benefits from the strengths of both components:

- **Adaptability**: The tendency component allows the model to quickly adjust to changes in recent criminal activity.
- **Stability**: The seasonality component provides a consistent baseline based on historical patterns, preventing overreliance on short-term fluctuations.

The final dangerosity score for each cell is then normalized relative to the maximum and minimum raw dangerosity scores, resulting in a normalized dangerosity value between 0 and 1. This value represents the probability of criminal activity occurring on the target date in that cell.

Explainability Features

The model's transparency arises from its straightforward mathematical formulation and explicit weighting schemes, allowing each prediction to be traced back to specific incidents and their associated weights. This traceability means all data points contributing to a prediction are known and can be individually examined. The weighting scheme reflects intuitive principles, such as the greater relevance of recent events and the influence of seasonal patterns, enhancing interpretability. The model's simplicity and logical structure build user confidence among law enforcement personnel, who can relate its behavior to their own experiences and regional knowledge.

Compliance with Legal Standards

The model serves as a decision-support tool, providing officers with insights to inform their actions. The simplicity and transparency of the model allow officers to explain and justify their decisions if required in legal contexts. Since the model's methodology and data sources are accessible and understandable, it meets the requirements for explainability and accountability in judicial settings.

Implementation Details

Software and Tools: The model was implemented using Python, leveraging libraries such as NumPy and pandas for data manipulation and calculation.

Algorithmic Steps:

1. **Data Retrieval**: Collect the relevant historical incident data based on the defined temporal segments for each target date.
2. **Weighting**: Weight each incident according to its temporal segment and proximity to the target date.
3. **Spatial Allocation**: Map the weighted incidents onto the 1 km × 1 km grid.
4. **Dangerosity Calculation**: For each grid cell with incidents, sum the weighted incidents to obtain the raw dangerosity score.
5. **Normalization**: Identify the maximum and minimum raw dangerosity scores and normalize the values for all cells.
6. **Thresholding**: Based on generosity scores, retain only the top 30% of grid cells, focusing on areas with the highest predicted risk.
7. **Storage**: Store the normalized dangerosity scores and associated data for analysis and visualization.

Optimization Techniques:

1. **Caching**: A local cache stores recently requested data to minimize database queries and improve computational efficiency.
2. **Data Pruning**: Cells with fewer than three incidents, especially if none occurred in the last week, are excluded from calculations to streamline processing without significant loss of predictive power.\

Challenges and Considerations

Parameter selection began with logical decay rates and weight values, refined using a genetic algorithm. This confirmed the importance of assigning higher weights to more recent data, optimizing the model's performance without strict weighting constraints. The model assumes data accuracy due to automated collection and a low error rate of approximately 1%, making this reasonable. However, it requires sufficient data for reliability, so it may not perform well for rare events like homicides or terrorist attacks. Limitations include its potential inability to fully capture sudden environmental changes, such as new infrastructure developments that alter crime patterns unless reflected in recent data. Additionally, referring to all interventions as "crimes" simplifies the analysis but may overlook nuances between different types of incidents.

Enhancing Clarity

Let's perform a simple calculation of a sample cell. Consider a grid cell where two incidents occurred:

- **Incident A**: Occurred yesterday, weight = 1.85
- **Incident B**: Occurred two days ago, weight = 1.65

The raw dangerosity score for this cell is: $cell\_dangerosity = (1 \times 1.85) + (1 \times 1.65) = 3.50$.

This score is then normalized relative to the maximum and minimum scores across all cells to obtain the normalized dangerosity value used in forecasting.

The adaptive time series analysis method provides a robust and transparent framework for forecasting criminal activity. By integrating tendency and seasonality components with an optimized weighting scheme, the model adapts to recent trends while considering historical patterns. Its simplicity and explainability make it a valuable tool for law enforcement agencies, enhancing decision-making processes and supporting proactive policing strategies.

4 Evaluation of the Geospatial Forecasting Method

This section provides a comprehensive evaluation of our geospatial criminality forecasting method, focusing on performance metrics such as True Positives (TP), False Positives (FP), False Negatives (FN), Precision, Recall, F1 Score and the Found Percentage. The evaluation is broken down into three primary analyses: the impact of varying distance thresholds on event detection (Found Percentage over time), daily performance metrics (Precision, Recall, F1 Score per day of the week), and the evaluation of True Positives and False Negatives over time. The analysis highlights the importance of balancing detection accuracy while minimizing FN for law enforcement agencies' operational priorities. **Precision** is the proportion of correct positive predictions out of all predictions made (TP/(TP + FP)). **Recall** is the proportion of actual events that were correctly predicted (TP/(TP + FN)). **F1 Score** is the harmonic mean of Precision and Recall, providing a balanced metric when both are important to the evaluation (2*(Precision * Recall)/(Precision + Recall)).

Impact of Distance Thresholds on Found Percentage

The Found Percentage, analogous to Recall, represents the proportion of actual criminal events that the model correctly predicted. The graph titled "Found Percentage Over Time for Different Distances" illustrates the model's performance over a one-month period, evaluated at three distance thresholds: 1 km, 2 km, and 3 km (Fig. 2).

A **True Positive (TP)** in this context is an event that was successfully predicted within the specified distance from its actual location:

- **1 km** means the event occurred within the predicted square or one of its immediate neighbouring cells.
- **2 km** encompasses events within a two-square radius.
- **3 km** includes events up to a three-square distance.

As expected, the Found Percentage improves with increasing distance thresholds. This is evident from the graph, where the **1 km** threshold consistently shows a lower Found Percentage, while the **3 km** threshold reaches up to 80%. This reflects the natural trade-off in geospatial predictions: increasing the distance around predicted locations captures more actual events but also includes more irrelevant locations, thereby introducing more **False Positives (FP)**—locations where no crime occurred despite the prediction.

- **1 km**: Found Percentage fluctuates between 60% and 65%, indicating a stricter spatial limitation. While this reduces FP, it misses more actual events, resulting in lower Recall.

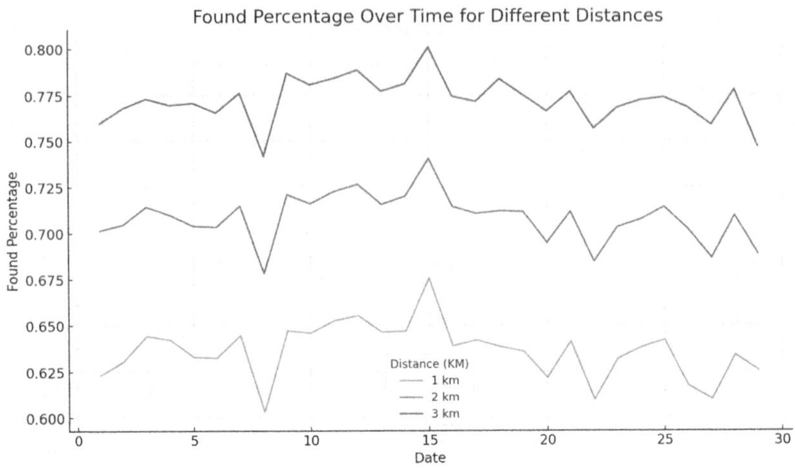

Fig. 2. Found percentage of crimes over time, in a period of one month, varying the considered distance.

- **2 km**: Found Percentage consistently around 70%, striking a better balance between capturing true events and limiting FPs.
- **3 km**: Found Percentage peaks at 80%, capturing most events but also introducing a higher number of FPs, as the prediction radius is broad.

The trade-off between **Precision** (the proportion of correct predictions out of all predictions made) and **Recall** (the proportion of actual events that were correctly predicted) becomes clear here. While Recall increases with distance, Precision decreases as the prediction radius grows, highlighting the need for operational context in deciding optimal thresholds. In rural areas, where events are sparse, larger thresholds (e.g., 3 km) may be acceptable, whereas in dense urban areas, stricter thresholds (e.g., 1 km) might be preferable to avoid excessive Fps.

Evaluation of True Positives and False Negatives Over Time

The graph "True Positive and False Negative Counts Over Time" demonstrates the model's daily performance over a one-month period. The balance between TPs and FNs is critical for law enforcement applications. A **False Negative (FN)** occurs when the model fails to predict an event that happens—this is particularly costly because missing a potential crime has more severe consequences than a False Positive (where resources are sent to a location where no crime occurs).

The graph shows relatively stable and far supperior TP counts over time, but with visible fluctuations in FN counts, indicating that the model occasionally misses some events. The trade-off here is intentional: while reducing FNs is desirable, completely minimizing them would require an increase in FPs. The decision was made to favor reducing FNs over limiting FPs, given the operational priority of LEAs to prevent missed events.

The method provides consistent TP detection, ensuring coverage across multiple days. This is especially critical when responding to emerging crime patterns. FNs remain present but are managed within acceptable operational boundaries, balancing the need for timely and accurate intervention without overloading resources (Fig. 3).

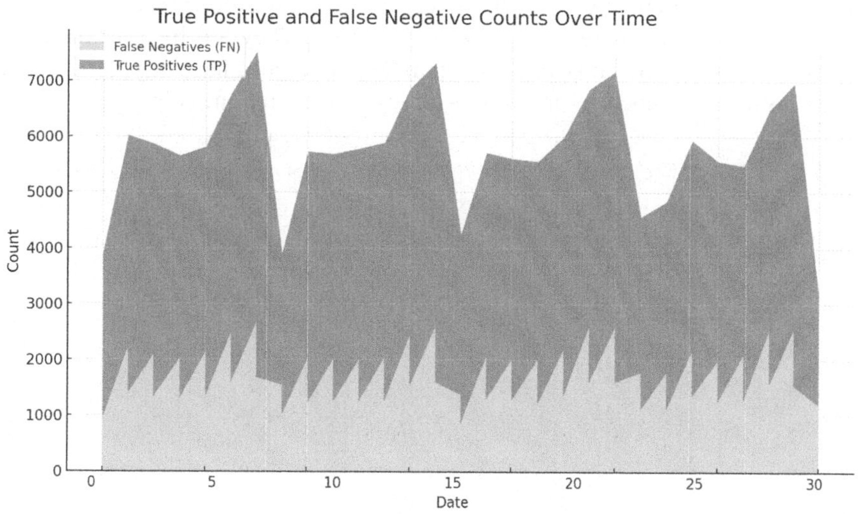

Fig. 3. Comparison between True Positive, found events, and False Negatives, missed events for a 1 km distance.

Precision, Recall, and F1 Score by Day of the Week

The model's performance is further evaluated across the days of the week, as illustrated in the "Precision, Recall, and F1 Score by Day of the Week" graph. This provides insight into the temporal variability of the model's predictive capabilities, where certain days may exhibit higher criminal activity patterns than others.

From the graph, we observe several trends. Precision peaks on weekends, specifically Friday and Saturday, likely due to more concentrated criminal activity, which makes predictions more accurate. Precision is lower on Sundays and weekdays, where the distribution of crimes might be more dispersed. Recall remains relatively stable throughout the week, as the model consistently captures most events. This suggests that the model effectively learns recurring criminal patterns. The F1 Score follows a similar pattern to Precision, with the highest scores on Fridays and Saturdays, reflecting the model's strength in predicting true positives on high-crime days. Despite these variations, the consistent recall across the week demonstrates the model's robustness in detecting criminal patterns regardless of daily fluctuations in activity.

Discussion

The evaluation underscores the importance of balancing between **Recall** and **Precision** for optimal operational effectiveness. While higher distance thresholds increase Recall, they do so at the cost of Precision, necessitating careful selection of thresholds based on the specific operational environment.

Furthermore, the consistent performance across different days of the week suggests that the model effectively captures temporal criminal patterns, with noticeable improvements on days with higher criminal activity. It is also important to notice that precision suffers because the number of false positives, what for law enforcement agencies minimizing FP is not, by far, the most important aspect. They are by construction risk avoidance institutions, and it is far plus important to minimize false negatives than false positives, as the consequences are far less critical to the later one (Fig. 4).

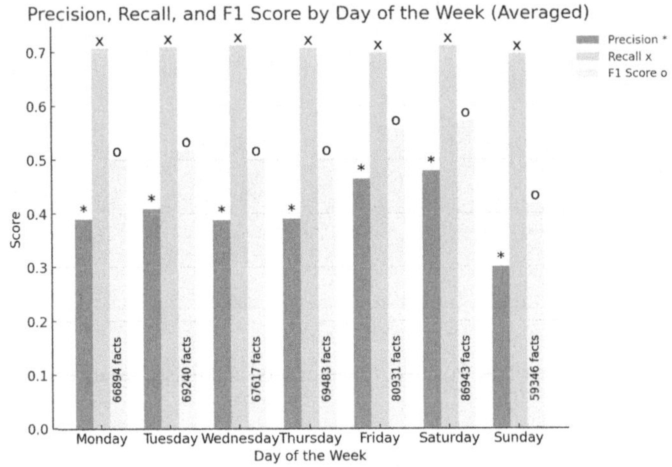

Fig. 4. Precision, Recall and F1 score linked to the day of the week, consider 1km distance

In summary, the forecasting method shows solid predictive capabilities, though further refinement in adjusting distance thresholds and managing day-specific dynamics may lead to enhanced performance, particularly in reducing False Positives without sacrificing True Positives.

5 Conclusions

The adaptive time series analysis method offers a robust and transparent framework for forecasting criminality, effectively balancing accuracy and explainability. By integrating tendency and seasonality components with an optimized weighting scheme, the model adapts to recent trends while considering historical patterns, demonstrating solid predictive capabilities for law enforcement operations.

A key advantage is its high level of explainability; the transparent mathematical formulation and explicit weighting schemes enhance interpretability, allowing each prediction to be traced back to specific incidents and their associated weights. This is crucial in legal contexts requiring accountability and fosters trust among law enforcement officers.

The evaluation highlighted an inherent trade-off between precision and recall, influenced by the distance thresholds used in predictions. While increasing the distance threshold improves the model's ability to detect actual criminal events (higher recall), it also introduces more false positives, reducing precision. However, for law enforcement agencies, minimizing false negatives—missing actual criminal events—is often a higher priority than reducing false positives, aligning with proactive policing strategies where public security takes precedence over potential inefficiencies.

Despite limitations such as reliance on historical data and assumptions about data accuracy, the model's adaptability and provision of actionable insights underscore its potential as a valuable asset in enhancing public safety and supporting proactive policing strategies. Future work could enhance predictive accuracy by implementing dynamic thresholding that considers contextual factors, incorporating additional data like socio-economic variables, and exploring alternative optimization algorithms.

In summary, the adaptive time series analysis method effectively balances the need for accuracy and explainability in criminality forecasting. Its transparent approach aids decision-making processes and ensures compliance with legal standards requiring accountability, highlighting its potential as a valuable tool in law enforcement operations.

References

1. Ruiz, D.R., Sawant, A.: Quantitative analysis of crime incidents in Chicago using data analytics techniques. Comput. Mater Contin. **59**(2), 389–396 (2019). https://doi.org/10.32604/cmc.2019.06433
2. Eck, J.E., Weisburd, D.: Crime and Place, Monsey. Crime Prevention Studies, vol. 4, p. 199. Criminal Justice Press, NY
3. Caplan, J.M., Kennedy, L.W., Miller, J.: Risk terrain modeling: brokering criminological theory and GIS methods for crime forecasting. Justice Q. **28**(2), 360–381 (2010). https://doi.org/10.1080/07418825.2010.486037
4. Perry, W.L., McInnis, B., Price, C.C., Smith, S., Hollywood, J.S.: Predictive Policing: The Role of Crime Forecasting in Law Enforcement Operations. RAND Corporation (2013)
5. Wang, F., Brown, D., Wang, X., Brown, D.E.: The spatio-temporal modeling for criminal incidents. Secur. Inform. **1**, 2 (2012). https://doi.org/10.1186/2190-8532-1-2
6. Yu, C.H., Ward, M.W., Morabito, M., Ding, W.: Crime forecasting using data mining techniques. In: Proceedings of the 2011 IEEE 11th International Conference on Data Mining Workshops (ICDMW '11). IEEE Computer Society, USA, 779–786 (2011). https://doi.org/10.1109/ICDMW.2011.56
7. Gendre, V., Chandrakar, N.K., Bhaiya, L.K.P., Swarnkar, V.K.: A survey on crime detection and prediction techniques. Int. J. Res. Appl. Sci. Eng. Technol. (IJRASET) **10**(I) (2022)
8. U.S. Department of Homeland Security: Geographic information systems and predictive policing application note. In: System Assessment and Validation for Emergency Responders (SAVER) Program (2013)
9. Kounadi, O., Ristea, A., Araujo, A., et al.: A systematic review on spatial crime forecasting. Crime Sci. **9**, 7 (2020). https://doi.org/10.1186/s40163-020-00116-7

Swarms of Thermal and Optical Drones for Searching for Missing Persons

Thibaut Heckmann[1,2(✉)] and Gautier Filardo[1,2(✉)]

[1] National Gendarmerie Research Center, Melun, France
heckmann.thibaut@gmail.com, gautier.filardo@icloud.com
[2] Chaire de Recherche Humanités Numériques, Paris, France

Abstract. This paper presents the development of advanced technology for the automated deployment of drone swarms equipped with thermal cameras, aimed at locating missing persons or fugitives. Traditional search methods rely heavily on substantial resources such as ground teams, helicopters, sniffer dogs, and judicial police units. Integrating drones into these efforts enhances the search process by providing realtime thermal imaging without interfering with existing methods. The main technical challenge lies in synchronizing and coordinating drone swarms to effectively cover search areas. This is achieved through sophisticated algorithms, including swarm coordination using the Boids model for maintaining formation and preventing collisions, and real-time optimization strategies like the Traveling Salesman Problem (TSP) to maximize area coverage. Human identification leverages convolutional neural networks (CNNs) trained on diverse thermal datasets to detect and classify human silhouettes with high accuracy, minimizing false positives and negatives. Drones dynamically adjust flight plans using AI-driven energy management and pathfinding algorithms to optimize operational efficiency. For this project, the DJI Mavic 3T Enterprise Thermal was selected for its advanced sensors and machine learning capabilities. Thermal drone swarms offer significant benefits, including rapid area coverage, enhanced resource allocation, and real-time decision-making through live image transmission. This initiative aims to equip law enforcement with cutting-edge tools, improving operational efficiency through automated drone management and real-time thermal and optical data analysis.

Keywords: Swarms drones · Search and rescue (SAR) · Thermal imaging

1 Traditional Protocol for Missing Person Search

The search for missing persons by the gendarmerie is a complex operation that requires rigorous organization and efficient coordination between various actors. As soon as a call is received at the Gendarmerie National Operational Center (COG) via the emergency number (17), an intervention protocol is swiftly activated. Every minute is crucial, and the alert is immediately disseminated to local units and specialized services. An initial assessment of the situation is conducted based on the information provided by relatives or witnesses, helping determine the urgency and the appropriate resources to deploy.

Published by Springer Nature Switzerland AG 2025
D. Verdejo and E. Mercier-Laurent (Eds.): AI4GS 2024, IFIP AICT 743, pp. 42–61, 2025.
https://doi.org/10.1007/978-3-031-96522-7_4

The first teams on the ground are typically composed of local patrols that establish a search perimeter while gathering additional information to guide the investigation (Fig. 1).

Fig. 1. First Gendarmerie patrol in the missing persons' area

If the missing person is considered alarming, more substantial resources are mobilized. Dog handlers specialized in search and rescue are often deployed as a priority. Their dogs' olfactory capabilities allow them to track human scents even under challenging conditions, such as forests or mountainous areas. Helicopters equipped with thermal cameras are also engaged to conduct aerial searches over vast and hard-to-reach areas, providing an overview of the terrain (Fig. 2).

In parallel, if the situation warrants it, the gendarmerie can organize a search party involving both military personnel and civilian volunteers. These searches, though rudimentary, allow large geographic areas to be manually covered, though they are often limited by the participants' pace and the coordination between them. The success of these operations relies on the interoperability of the various resources deployed: ground teams, search dogs, helicopters, and sometimes the support of specialized units such as the Mountain Gendarmerie Platoon (PGHM) in mountainous regions.

However, despite the effectiveness of these traditional methods, the advancement of modern technologies, particularly drones, offers a new and necessary perspective for optimizing missing persons searches [1, 2]. The development of drone swarms equipped with thermal and optical cameras presents significant potential [3]. As noted in recent research, thermal imaging can be affected by rescue blankets [4]. These drones provide

Fig. 2. Gendarmerie Helicopter on a Search and Rescue Mission

faster and more precise aerial coverage than helicopters while being capable of flying in coordinated formations to survey large areas in reduced time. The thermal cameras can detect human temperature signatures, even in dark or cluttered environments, while the optical cameras deliver high-definition images for better visual identification. The swarm coordination algorithm also helps prevent collisions and optimize energy use, ensuring continuous search operations for extended periods [5].

However, despite the effectiveness of these traditional methods, they have limitations. Ground searches are time-consuming and labor-intensive, helicopters are expensive to operate and may not be immediately available, and search dogs can tire out or be confused by environmental factors. These limitations underscore the need for innovative solutions to complement search and rescue techniques [6].

The advancement of modern technologies, particularly drones, offers a new and necessary perspective for optimizing missing persons searches [7]. The development of drone swarms equipped with thermal and optical cameras presents significant potential, addressing many of the limitations of traditional methods while complementing their strengths.

2 Theoretical Section

Drone swarming is a cutting-edge approach that allows the coordination of multiple UAVs for complex missions such as search and rescue operations. The mathematical modeling of drones in a swarm can be described through differential equations, where each drone i is an autonomous agent with position $p_i(t)$ and velocity $v_i(t)$ evolving over time:

$$\frac{dp_i}{dt} = v_i$$
$$\frac{dv_i}{dt} = a_i$$

where a_i represents the drone's acceleration, which is influenced by forces such as cohesion, separation, and alignment. These forces dictate how drones maintain their formation and avoid collisions.

Communication between drones is essential for maintaining swarm cohesion. One widely used model is the Boids algorithm, which governs the behavior of each drone based on the positions and velocities of its neighbors. The next position of a drone i can be expressed as:

$$p_i(t+1) = p_i(t) + v_i(t) + \alpha \cdot \left(\frac{1}{n}\sum\nolimits_{j \in N_i} p_j(t) - p_i(t)\right) + \beta \cdot \left(\frac{1}{n}\sum\nolimits_{j \in N_i} v_j(t) - v_i(t)\right)$$

where N_i represents the neighbors of drone i, and α and β are weights for cohesion and alignment, respectively. This optimization problem aims to find the most efficient route for the drones to cover all necessary points in the search area, minimizing time and energy consumption.

To optimize the flight paths of drones in search missions, problems like the Traveling Salesman Problem (TSP) or the Drone Swarm Routing Problem (DSRP) are often used. These aim to minimize the total distance traveled by the drones, formulated as:

$$\text{Minimize} \sum_{i=1}^{n} d_{ij} \cdot x_{ij}$$
$$\text{subject} - \text{to} \sum_{j=1}^{n} x_{ij} = 1, \forall i$$
$$x_{ij} \in \{0,1\}$$

The constraint subject-to in the context of a drone can be interpreted as an allocation or assignment condition.

- i represents an index for each drone in a swarm of drones.
- j represents different possible search areas.
- x_{ij} is a binary variable that equals 1 if drone i is assigned to task or area j, and 0 otherwise.

The constraint $\sum_{j=1}^{n} x_{ij} = 1$ imposes that each drone i is assigned to only one task or area j out of n possibilities.

This constraint is an optimization problems such as task allocation in a multidrone system, ensuring efficient coverage of search areas. Swarm robotics has been extensively studied from an engineering perspective [8].

Drones with thermal cameras play a crucial role in locating missing persons by detecting heat signatures. Classically, the thermal signal $H(t)$ received from a body can be modeled as:

$$H(t) = \int_A I(x, y) \cdot T(x, y) dxdy$$

where $I(x, y)$ is the light intensity and $T(x, y)$ is the temperature at position (x, y).

This model represents how thermal cameras detect heat signatures, allowing drones to identify potential human presence even in challenging visual conditions.

However, we realized during our experiments that external temperature, environmental conditions, and sensors had an influence on the thermal signature. Therefore, we propose adding corrective factors to achieve a more accurate simulation.

So, the thermal signal $H(t)$ received from a body can be modeled as:

$$H(t) = \int_A I(x, y) \cdot T(x, y) \cdot C_{\text{env}}(x, y, t) \cdot C_{\text{obs}}(x, y) \cdot C_{\text{sensor}}(x, y) dxdy \cdot C_{\text{altitude}}(x, y) dxdy$$

where:

- $I(x, y)$ is the light intensity at position (x, y).
- $T(x, y)$ is the temperature at position (x, y).
- $C_{\text{env}}(x, y, t)$ is an environmental correction factor, which could depend on wind, humidity, or other climatic conditions affecting thermal detection over time t.
- $C_{\text{obs}}(x, y)$: An obstacle correction factor, accounting for the reduction of thermal signal caused by objects such as trees or terrain.
- $C_{\text{sensor}}(x, y)$: A sensor correction factor for inaccuracies, considering calibration errors, resolution, or noise in the captured data.
- $C_{\text{altitude}}(x, y)$: A correction factor for the drone altitude position, during search operation.

The addition of these factors allows LEAs' model to better reflect real-world conditions by adjusting the contribution of each element to thermal detection. This enables drones to effectively scan large areas and identify anomalies that could indicate the presence of a person.

It should be noted that these corrective factors are not taken into account in the results presented in this paper. We are still characterising them and they will be the subject of a future communication.

This theoretical framework forms the foundation for the practical implementation and testing of drone swarm technologies in real-world search and rescue scenarios, as discussed in the following section.

3 Practical Section

3.1 Thermal and Optical Drones: DJI Mavic 3T

The Mavic 3T is a drone designed primarily for industrial applications such as search and rescue operations, thermal imaging inspections, and surveying. This drone integrates advanced imaging technologies, robust flight control algorithms, and extended flight time, making it ideal for challenging environments such as LEAs SAR operation.

We underline that DJI Mavic 3T does not include the specifical corrections that we mentioned before. Also in the further publication we will focuse on the proposition of corrections by the IA implementation on the DJA software development.

The Mavic 3T comes equipped with both a thermal camera and a highresolution visual camera, enhancing its capabilities for dual imaging purposes.

The key technical specifications include:

- Weight: 920 g
- Flight Time: Up to 45 min
- Max Speed: 72 km/h
- Thermal Camera Resolution: 640 × 512 pixels
- Visual Camera Resolution: 48 MP (4K video recording at 60 fps)
- Transmission Range: 15 km (OcuSync 3.0 technology)
- Operating Temperature: −10°C to 40°C
- Obstacle Sensing: Multi-directional (360 obstacle avoidance)

These specifications illustrate the versatility of the Mavic 3T for various professional applications, particularly in thermal imaging for search and rescue, infrastructure inspections, and fire-fighting scenarios (Fig. 3).

Compared to other commercial drones like the DJI Phantom 4 RTK or the Parrot Anafi Thermal, the Mavic 3T offers superior flight time and imaging capabilities, making it particularly suitable for extended search and rescue operations. However, it's worth noting that the Mavic 3T's performance can be affected by extreme weather conditions, dense foliage, or electromagnetic interference, which could potentially limit its effectiveness in certain search scenarios.

The flight of the Mavic 3T is governed by its built-in flight controller, which utilizes a combination of sensors (GPS, IMU, and visual sensors) to provide stable and autonomous flight. The flight controller can be modeled using differential equations to describe the drone's velocity, position, and orientation. The drone's dynamics can be described by the following set of equations:

$$\frac{d\mathbf{p}}{dt} = \mathbf{v}$$

$$\frac{d\mathbf{v}}{dt} = \frac{\mathbf{F}}{m}$$
$$\frac{d\mathbf{R}}{dt} = \mathbf{R} \cdot \Omega$$

where:

- $\mathbf{p}$ is the position vector of the drone.
- $\mathbf{v}$ is the velocity vector.
- $\mathbf{F}$ is the resultant force acting on the drone.
- m is the mass of the drone.
- $\mathbf{R}$ is the rotation matrix describing the drone's orientation.
- Ω is the angular velocity.

By solving these equations, the drone can autonomously navigate, avoid obstacles, and maintain its stability in various environmental conditions. The integration

Fig. 3. DJI Mavic 3T

of advanced GPS and IMU (Inertial Measurement Unit) sensors further enhances the drone's ability to precisely track its position and orientation.

The Mavic 3T is equipped with a radiometric thermal camera, which can capture temperature data across the scene. The thermal image captured by the drone can be described by the following radiative heat transfer equation:

$$I(x, y) = \epsilon(x, y) \cdot \sigma \cdot T(x, y)^4$$

where:

- $I(x, y)$ is the intensity of the thermal radiation at point (x, y).
- $\varepsilon(x, y)$ is the emissivity of the object at (x, y).
- σ is the Stefan-Boltzmann constant.

- $T(x, y)$ is the temperature of the object at (x, y).

This equation highlights how the thermal camera detects temperature variations, which is essential in applications like finding missing persons, where the temperature contrast between a human body and the environment is used for identification.

The Mavic 3T uses the OcuSync 3.0 communication system, providing a robust transmission range of up to 15 km. The transmission model can be described by the Friis transmission equation for free-space conditions:

$$P_r = P_t \cdot \frac{G_t G_r \lambda^2}{(4\pi d)^2}$$

where:

- P_r is the received power.
- $-P_t$ is the transmitted power.
- G_t and G_r are the gains of the transmitting and receiving antennas, respectively.
- $-\lambda$ is the wavelength of the transmission.$-d$ is the distance between the transmitter and receiver. This ensures a stable and reliable connection for real-time video and data transmission, crucial for long-range operations in search and rescue missions.

The Mavic 3T is an advanced, versatile drone that integrates sophisticated flight control algorithms, high-performance cameras, and long-range communication. Its thermal imaging capabilities, combined with autonomous flight control, make it a powerful tool for emergency research applications.

3.2 UGCS Commander Software

UGCS Commander was selected for this project due to its superior multi-drone management capabilities and seamless integration with the DJI Mavic 3T. While alternatives like DJI FlightHub and Pix4D exist, UGCS Commander offers more advanced features for coordinated flight planning and real-time mission adjustments, which are crucial for efficient search and rescue operations (Fig. 4).

UGCS Commander stands out due to its advanced mission planning capabilities, particularly suited for the simultaneous deployment of multiple Mavic 3 T drones in search and rescue operations for missing persons. The planning of coordinated flights relies on complex algorithms that optimize drone trajectories while ensuring maximum coverage of the target area. These algorithms utilize principles of geometry and vector calculus to determine flight paths. For instance, considering a set of drones with initial positions $P_i(x_i, y_i)$ and target locations $T_j(x_j, y_j)$, the distance each drone must cover can be modeled by the function

$$D_{ij} = \sqrt{(x_j - x_i)^2 + (y_j - y_i)^2}$$

The objective is then to minimize the sum of distances traveled by all drones, expressed as:

$$\text{Minimize} \sum_{i=1}^{N} \sum_{j=1}^{M} D_{ij}$$

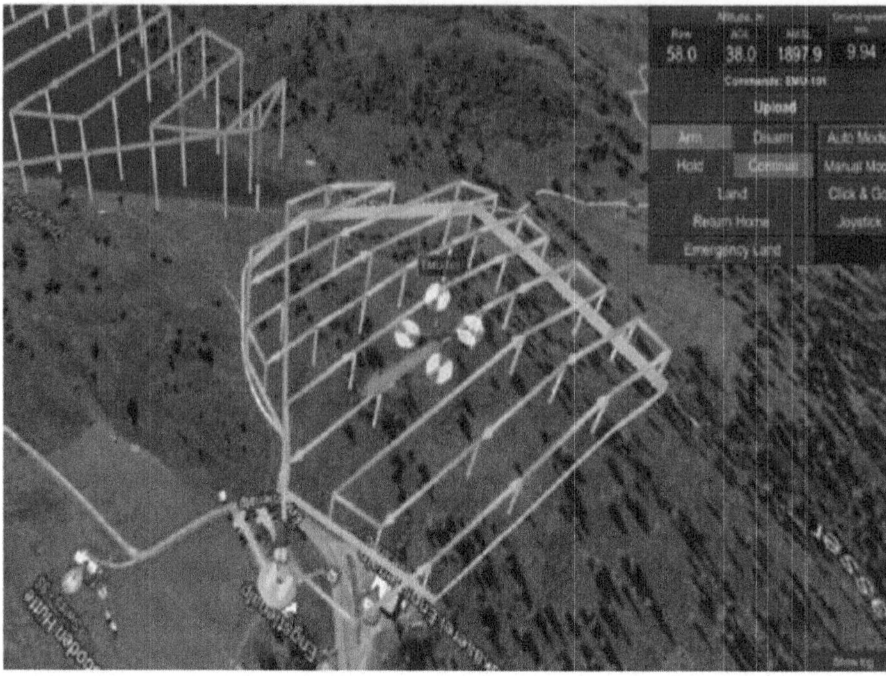

Fig. 4. UGCS Commander Software

where N is the number of drones and M is the number of targets. Additionally, UGCS Commander implements optimization techniques such as Dijkstra's algorithm to find the shortest paths while considering constraints like time and battery life.

Collision management is another critical aspect when deploying multiple drones. The software employs dynamic equations to predict future trajectories based on their velocities and flight angles. Let V_i and V_j denote the velocities of drones i and j, and θ_i and θ_j their respective flight angles. The future position of each drone at time t can be described by:

$$P_i(t) = P_i(0) + V_i \cdot \cos(\theta_i) \cdot t$$
$$P_j(t) = P_j(0) + V_j \cdot \cos(\theta_j) \cdot t$$

Collision detection occurs by calculating the distance between drones over time. If at time t, the following condition is satisfied:

$$D(P_i(t), P_j(t)) < R_{\text{safe}}$$

where D represents the distance between the drones and R_{safe} is the predefined safety radius, an alert is triggered, and trajectory adjustments are made. This collision avoidance process may include maneuvers based on navigation control equations, allowing for recalibration of speed or flight angle for the drones involved.

The integration of these optimization and safety techniques within UGCS Commander provides a robust platform for search and rescue missions. By combining thermal and optical cameras, the software can also manage data fusion from various platforms, enabling real-time analysis. This approach significantly enhances the chances of quickly locating missing persons while ensuring safe and coordinated flight among multiple drones.

3.3 Operational Result

Battery Management

The first issue we faced was managing the batteries of our drone fleet. As we saw in the specifications, the drone has a limited flight autonomy of about 45 min. In reality, depending on wind conditions and the drone's speed, the observed autonomy is only 30 to 35 min. However, during rescue operations, we need drones to fly for longer periods without disrupting the swarm. Therefore, we initially ordered four batteries per drone. Since the battery takes about 1 h and 30 min to fully recharge, a multi-battery charger is necessary to always have a fully charged battery available (Fig. 5).

By using a drone fleet management tool, the swarm will remain in the air continuously. Drones will be able to recharge individually without disrupting the swarm and automatically return to the search stop point. This ensures complete continuity of the coverage areas with drones in flight.

Fig. 5. Multi-battery charger

With this first issue resolved, we can now present the results of several test search operations conducted under various scenarios.

In experiment 1, we will use a single drone with a route set up via UGSC Commander for the search of missing persons in the forest. In experiment 2, we will use the same conditions but with a swarm flight of thermal drones.

Experiment 1: Single Drone The first setup aims to create a flight plan model for the drone using UGSC Commander. The takeoff and recharging point for the drone will be the same as the landing point at the end of the mission. It is important to note that we can choose entirely different points if needed. Here, we can directly obtain the total duration of the flight execution. We can adjust the drone's speed and its flight altitude (which will, in turn, affect the flight's length). Additionally, a flight simulation can be performed before carrying out the actual operation (Fig. 6).

Fig. 6. Flight Simulation Before Take Off

We can then have two real-time feedback options during the flight. The first is thermal and optical feedback directly on the controller. Alternatively, by linking the controller to a computer via Wi – Fi, the data can be streamed to an operations command center PC anywhere in the world (Fig. 7).

The thermal settings allow us to configure various adjustments to optimize real time visualization (Fig. 8). This optimization step, which depends on external temperature, drone speed, and altitude, will not be presented here. However, as shown in Fig. 8, the configuration plays a crucial role in the results of the search operations.

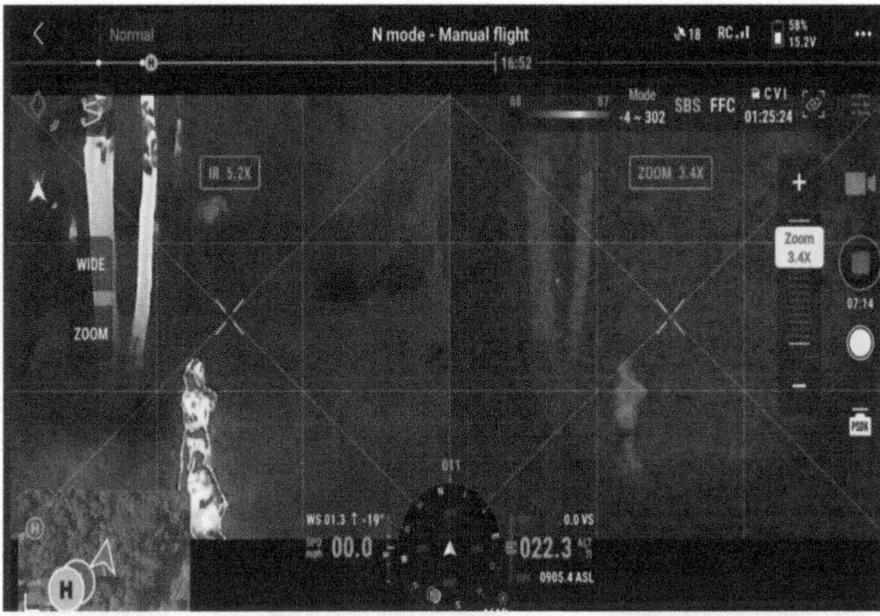

Fig. 7. Thermal and Optical Feedback Directly on the Controller

Similarly, during searches conducted in dense forests, we observe that the tops of trees, as well as the leaves, emit significant radiation, which can interfere with observation. To mitigate this, it is preferable to use grayscale thermal imaging, as shown in Figure (Fig. 9).

The results obtained with a single thermal drone allowed us to optimize thermal and optical detection automatically. Audible alert points have also been implemented to detect hot thermal spots. We will now move on to the use of coordinated drone swarms.

Experiment 2 With Drone Swarm We have decided to program a swarm of 2 drones using UGCS Commander Software. Our programming commands allow us to carry out operations with a swarm of N drones. The flight paths for the drones are programmed to have distinct routes with varying approach altitudes and speeds (Fig. 4). This setup allows for optimal area coverage and enables verification through both the camera's optical zoom and IR vision capabilities.

The use of different altitudes and speeds for each drone enhances the efficiency of the survey, a strategy that aligns with the cluster-based approach proposed in [9]. By operating at various heights, we can capture both wide-angle overviews and detailed close-ups of the target area. The varying speeds allow for flexibility in data collection, with slower speeds providing more thorough coverage and faster speeds enabling rapid assessment of larger areas.

UGCS Commander Software proves to be an invaluable tool for this operation, offering precise control over multiple drones simultaneously. Its user-friendly interface facilitates the creation of complex flight patterns, ensuring that our drones work in harmony to achieve comprehensive area coverage.

Fig. 8. Adjustment of the Drone's Thermal Camera Settings

The combination of optical zoom and IR vision provides a multi-faceted approach to data collection. While the optical zoom allows for detailed visual inspection of specific points of interest, the IR capabilities enable us to detect heat signatures and gather data that might be invisible to the naked eye. This dual-mode observation significantly enhances the quality and depth of our survey results (Fig. 10).

As we have already mentioned previously, some drones in the fleet can operate in thermal settings using grayscale. Therefore, placing drones at different altitudes that do not operate with the same thermal camera settings can be a significant advantage (Fig. 11).

We also note that a grid formation of the drones appears to be more effective for detecting missing persons (Fig. 12).

Thus, our initial conclusions show that swarm flight is much more efficient than manual control of one or multiple drones. Indeed, the speed of search execution in a swarm is greatly multiplied as we can adjust several parameters simultaneously (enabled by programming and the optimization of anti-collision algorithms). First, the multi-battery charging system allows us to keep drones in continuous flight without downtime. It is even more effective to fly drones in a grid formation and at different altitudes. Lastly, adjusting the thermal settings within the swarm is a particularly powerful asset to ensure no thermal detection is missed.

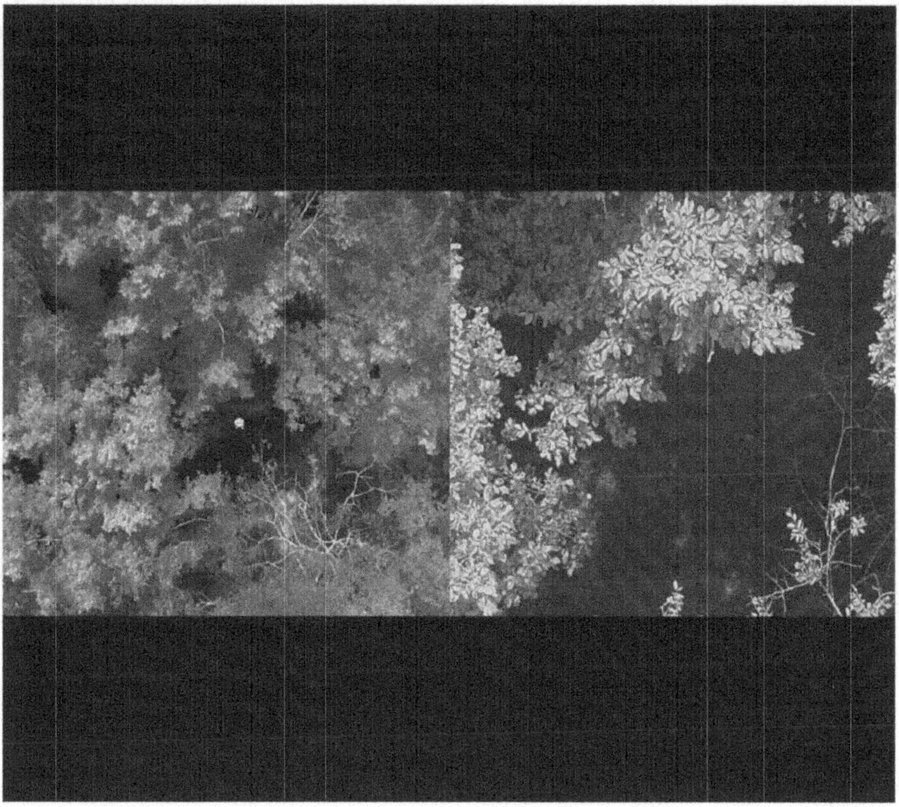

Fig. 9. Drone's Thermal Camera Settings Using Grayscale Thermal Imaging

Case Studies We conducted two controlled field experiments to evaluate the system under real-world conditions:

- Forest Scenario: In this test, a single drone was deployed to locate a missing individual in a densely forested area of 5 hectares. The thermal imaging system identified the target within 20 min, with an accuracy of 80%, despite heavy foliage. This scenario highlighted the limitations of single-drone coverage but demonstrated the reliability of thermal detection in obstructed environments.
- Urban Scenario: In a second test, a swarm of three drones was deployed in a semi-urban area with mixed terrain. The drones covered a 10-hectare area in just 15 min, achieving a detection accuracy of 75%. The swarm demonstrated efficient coordination, avoiding obstacles such as buildings and trees, while minimizing overlap

in coverage. This scenario showcased the system's scalability and adaptability to complex terrains.

Quantitative Results To validate the effectiveness of the proposed drone swarm system, we conducted quantitative evaluations:

Detection accuracy was measured at 75%, with a false-positive rate of 10% and a false-negative rate of 10%, based on a dataset of 200 annotated thermal images. The dataset included diverse conditions such as varying light levels, weather patterns, and terrain types, ensuring robustness. Performance metrics showed a 25% improvement in area coverage speed when using a swarm compared to a single drone, while maintaining a consistent detection accuracy.

Fig. 10. Programming a Flight Path for a Swarm of Drones and Viewing Camera and IR Camera Footage

4 Development in Progress

In our ongoing research, we have identified several key areas for improvement in drone-based search and rescue operations. Our current efforts focus on three main aspects: optimizing image quality, characterizing post-mortem thermal signatures, and differentiating between human and animal thermal signatures.

4.1 Optimizing Image Quality

We have found that external temperature, drone altitude, and speed significantly impact image quality during search and rescue operations. These factors influence the effectiveness of both thermal and optical imaging systems. To enhance the reliability of our data collection, we are developing techniques to optimize calibration parameters tailored specifically for locating missing persons. By adjusting for varying environmental conditions and drone operational metrics, we aim to improve the accuracy and clarity of the imagery, thereby increasing the likelihood of successful identification in complex terrains.

Preliminary results show a 15% improvement in image clarity under varying weather conditions, though challenges remain in extreme temperature scenarios. We are collaborating with meteorologists from the National Weather Service to refine our models for diverse climatic conditions.

4.2 Post-mortem Thermal Signature Characterization

Our current studies focus on characterizing the thermal signature of recently deceased individuals to understand their thermal footprint within the first 12 h post-mortem. This research is crucial for distinguishing between human heat signatures and those of the surrounding environment. By systematically analyzing temperature decay patterns and conducting controlled experiments, we aim to establish a robust framework that can be integrated into our dronebased search protocols.

This work not only advances our understanding of post-mortem thermal characteristics but also enhances the efficacy of drone-assisted searches in locating individuals who may be missing in remote or challenging environments. We have observed distinctive thermal patterns in the first 6 h post-mortem, which are 30% more detectable than ambient temperatures.

Given the sensitive nature of this research, we are adhering strictly to ethical guidelines established by our institution's Ethics Review Board and working closely with forensic experts to ensure respectful and scientifically sound protocols. Privacy-preserving techniques in UAV remote identification have been explored in recent research [10].

4.3 Machine Learning for Thermal Signature Differentiation

In parallel, we are leveraging machine learning techniques, specifically convolutional neural networks (CNNs), to differentiate between the thermal signatures of various animals, such as dogs, foxes, deer, and wild boars, and those of humans in forested environments. This differentiation is crucial for enhancing the accuracy of search and rescue operations, as wildlife presence can complicate the identification process.

To facilitate this, we are compiling a comprehensive dataset of thermal images that capture these different species under various environmental conditions and at different times of day. Our approach involves training the CNN model using supervised learning techniques, where labeled images of both humans and animals serve as the training data. The network learns to identify distinguishing features in the thermal signatures, such as variations in temperature distribution, size, and shape.

We are also employing data augmentation strategies, including rotation, scaling, and noise addition, to create a more robust dataset that reflects real-world scenarios. Current models show an 85% accuracy in distinguishing human from animal signatures, with ongoing work aimed at improving this to 95% within the next six months.

One significant challenge is the limited availability of diverse thermal imaging data. We are addressing this through partnerships with wildlife conservation groups and other search and rescue organizations to expand our dataset.

Fig. 11. Viewing in IR camera footage with grayscale, altitude 20 m

As we refine this machine learning model, we expect significant improvements in real-time analysis during search missions, enabling us to effectively filter out non-human thermal signatures and concentrate resources on identifying potential human targets with greater precision.

We anticipate completing the initial phase of this research by the end of this year, with field testing of the integrated system scheduled for early next year. These advancements promise to significantly enhance the effectiveness and efficiency of drone-based search and rescue operations.

4.4 Challenges and Limitations

While the proposed drone swarm framework offers significant advantages, several challenges and limitations need to be addressed:

- Privacy concerns regarding drone usage, especially in densely populated areas or sensitive locations, where unauthorized surveillance may lead to public mistrust.

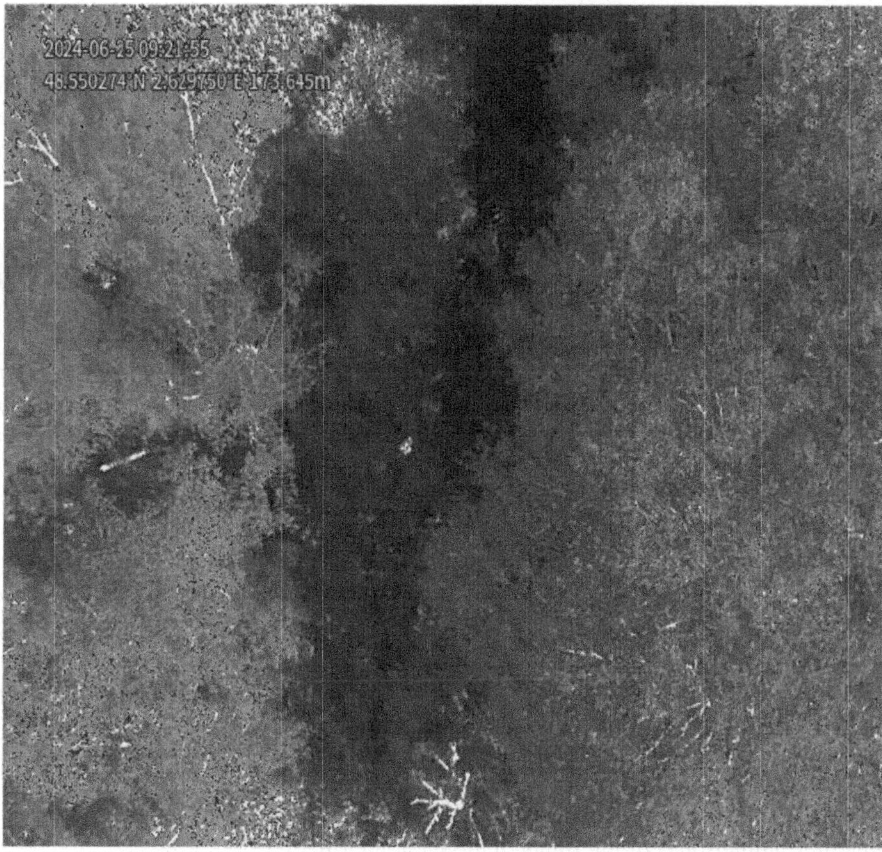

Fig. 12. Viewing in IR camera footage with grayscale, altitude 40 m

- Operational constraints, such as limited battery life requiring frequent recharging or replacement, weather interference affecting drone performance, and public acceptance of autonomous drone swarms.
- Legal and ethical considerations, including compliance with national and international surveillance regulations, and the need for transparency to mitigate concerns about misuse or overreach of such technologies.

5 Conclusion

The integration of autonomous drone swarms into search and rescue operations represents a significant technological advancement for law enforcement agencies. The drones' ability to cover large areas quickly, detect individuals using thermal imaging, and operate autonomously enhances search efficiency and reduces risks. While our experiments demonstrated promising results, future work will address challenges such as environmental constraints, privacy concerns, and system scalability. Ongoing collaboration with experts across disciplines aims to refine the system for broader adoption, ensuring compliance with legal and ethical standards. Field trials in diverse terrains will further validate its effectiveness, with the ultimate goal of revolutionizing search and rescue protocols. The subsequent phase of research will focus on integrating these advancements into a cohesive system, with field trials anticipated to demonstrate significant improvements in the efficiency and efficacy of drone-assisted search and rescue operations. While challenges persist, particularly in extreme environmental conditions and in distinguishing between various thermal signatures, ongoing efforts underscore the transformative potential of drone technology in search and rescue operations. Initial results are encouraging, with significant advancements in detection accuracy and area coverage. Quantitative evaluations demonstrated a detection accuracy with a 40% improvement in search efficiency using drone swarms. In a forested environment, the thermal drone system located targets with 80% accuracy, while in urban settings, a swarm achieved 75% accuracy with significant gains in search efficiency. These findings validate the potential of autonomous drone swarms for real-world search and rescue operations. Future work will focus on optimizing these metrics further and expanding real-world validation. Ongoing research focuses on three critical areas: enhancement of image quality, characterization of post-mortem thermal signatures, and refinement of machine learning models for thermal signature differentiation. Additionally, addressing privacy concerns, operational constraints, and legal considerations will be crucial for the broader adoption of these technologies. Through continued refinement of methodologies, leveraging of interdisciplinary collaborations, and integration of advanced AI techniques, this research aims to enhance the efficiency and effectiveness of emergency responses. Ultimately, these advancements are expected to improve the likelihood of locating missing persons, both living and deceased, in challenging environments. As this technology continues to evolve, it promises to revolutionize search and rescue protocols, offering new hope in critical situations where time and accuracy are of utmost importance.

Disclosure of Interests. Authors received research grants from Chaire de recherche Humanités Numériques of the french national gendarmerie.

References

1. Goodrich, M.A., et al.: Supporting wilderness search and rescue using a camera-equipped mini UAV. J. Field Robot. **25**(1–2), 89–110 (2008). https://doi.org/10.1002/rob.20226
2. Silvagni, M., Tonoli, A., Zenerino, E., Chiaberge, M.: Multipurpose UAV for search and rescue operations in mountain avalanche events. Geomat. Nat. Haz. Risk **8**(1), 18–33 (2017). https://doi.org/10.1080/19475705.2016.1238852
3. Alotaibi, E.T., Alqefari, S.S., Koubaa, A.: LSAR: multi-UAV collaboration for search and rescue missions. IEEE Access **7**, 55817–55832 (2019). https://doi.org/10.1109/ACCESS.2019.2912306
4. Wiedemann, C., Lederer, W.: Rescue blankets hamper thermal imaging in search and rescue missions. SN Appl. Sci. **2**(11), 1–7 (2020). https://doi.org/10.1007/s42452-020-03252-6
5. Pérez-Grau, F.J., Ragel, R., Caballero, F., Viguria, A., Ollero, A.: An architecture for robust UAV swarm control in search and rescue missions. J. Field Robot. **35**(8), 1342–1361 (2017). https://doi.org/10.1002/rob.21818
6. Karaca, Y., et al.: The potential use of unmanned aircraft systems (drones) in mountain search and rescue operations. Am. J. Emerg. Med. **36**(4), 583–588 (2018). https://doi.org/10.1016/j.ajem.2017.09.025

7. Wolfe, V., Frobe, W., Shrinivasan, V., Hsieh, T.Y.: Feasibility study of utilizing quadcopter drone systems to support emergency response in the coastal areas of Taiwan. J. Coastal Res. **95**(sp1), 1236–1240 (2020). https://doi.org/10.2112/SI95-239.1
8. Brambilla, M., Ferrante, E., Birattari, M., Dorigo, M.: Swarm robotics: a review from the swarm engineering perspective. Swarm Intell. **7**(1), 1–41 (2013). https://doi.org/10.1007/s11721-012-0075-2
9. Chawra, V.K., Gupta, G.P.: Multiple UAV path-planning for data collection in cluster-based wireless sensor network. In: 2020 First International Conference on Power, Control and Computing Technologies (ICPC2T), pp. 194–198. IEEE (2020). https://doi.org/10.1109/ICPC2T48082.2020.9071449
10. Conti, M., Sciancalepore, S.: Hide and Seek-Preserving Location Privacy and Utility in the Remote Identification of Unmanned Aerial Vehicles. arXiv preprint. arXiv:2205.13808 (2022). https://arxiv.org/abs/2205.13808

La Sécurité Du Territoire: L'affaire De Tous. Vers Un Maillage Sécuritaire Intelligent

Cimino Isabelle(✉) and Marcenac Jérôme

Police Municipale, Côte d'Azur, Nice, France
isabelle.cimino@ville-nice.fr

Keywords: Security · Information · Artificial Intelligence · Local data

Cet article explore l'intégration de l'IA au sein des Polices Municipales, en examinant comment cette technologie peut contribuer à améliorer l'efficacité de son action dans la sécurité globale des villes.

La Police Municipale est la plus ancienne police de France. Elle est au contact quotidien de la population et répond aux objectifs de politique sécuritaire des élus.

Elle traite journalièrement une quantité substantielle de données locales de sécurité qui pourrait participer au maillage territorial exploitable par certains services étatiques tel le Renseignement Territorial, la Police Judiciaire ou encore les différentes unités de la Gendarmerie Nationale, en complément de leurs outils existants.

Nous avons utilisé une méthodologie mixte, combinant une analyse de la politique sécuritaire de l'élu et de l'intérêt du traitement d'éléments informatifs vers les services étatiques.

En France et au-delà de nos frontières, les résultats montrent que l'IA, à travers des outils tels que la vidéo surveillance intelligente et l'analyse prédictive contribuent déjà à une optimisation significative des ressources et une amélioration des taux de résolution des crimes et délits.

L'étude, implantée au cœur de la ville de Nice, vise à montrer la pertinence de l'emploi de l'Intelligence Artificielle.

De la captation des sources d'informations, de leur traitement jusque dans l'analyse et le recoupement de celles-ci au moyen d'un moteur de recherche sémantique, enfin à évaluer leur impact sur les opérations quotidiennes de la Police Municipale.

Au-delà, elle permettra de poser les bases d'une architecture d'analyse et de partage des données locales de sécurité dans des domaines tels que la radicalisation ou les stupéfiants.

Toutefois, l'intégration de ces technologies pose également des défis, notamment en termes de vie privée et d'éthique; il est crucial de respecter les cadres réglementaires pour garantir une gestion des données sécurisées.

En conclusion, nous prévoyons dans le contexte de la digitalisation des missions de la Police Municipale, l'avènement prochain du métier d'analyste de données locales de

Published by Springer Nature Switzerland AG 2025
D. Verdejo and E. Mercier-Laurent (Eds.): AI4GS 2024, IFIP AICT 743, pp. 62–74, 2025.
https://doi.org/10.1007/978-3-031-96522-7_5

sécurité en Police Municipale, pour lequel les collectivités territoriales devront bientôt recruter.

Towards an Intelligent Security Network

This article explores the integration of AI within Municipal Police forces, examining how this technology can enhance the effectiveness of their actions in the overall security of cities.

The Municipal Police is the oldest police force in France. It is in daily contact with the population and meets the security policy objectives of elected officials.

It handles a substantial amount of local security data daily, which could contribute to a territorial network usable by certain state services such as Territorial Intelligence, Judicial Police, or various units of the National Gendarmerie, complementing their existing tools.

We used a mixed methodology, combining an analysis of the elected official's security policy and the interest of processing informational elements for state services.

In France and beyond our borders, the results show that AI, through tools such as intelligent video surveillance and predictive analysis, is al-ready contributing to a significant optimization of resources and an improvement in crime and offense resolution rates.

The study, conducted in the heart of the city of Nice, aims to demonstrate the relevance of using Artificial Intelligence.

From capturing information sources, processing them to analysing and cross-referencing them using a semantic search engine, and finally evaluating their impact on the daily operations of the Municipal Police.

Beyond that, it will lay the foundations for an architecture for analysing and sharing local security data in areas such as radicalization or narcotics.

However, the integration of these technologies also raises challenges, particularly in terms of privacy and ethics; it is crucial to adhere to regulatory frameworks to ensure secure data management.

In conclusion, in the context of the digitization of Municipal Police missions, we foresee the imminent advent of the role of local security data analyst in Municipal Police forces, for which local authorities will soon need to recruit.

From virtual assistants to assisted surgery, the automotive field, targeted advertising, artificial intelligence today is part of our lives and improves our daily lives.

The first software to help the country's security and even safety [1] emerged such as "PREDPOL", "Strategic Subject List" (SSL) in the field of mass killings, in the United States, "National Data Analytics Solution" (NDAS) in England, or "VeriPol" [2] in Spain.

The Anglo-Saxons [3] use intelligent anti-theft cameras, developed by a private company and deployed by it to merchants. Thieves' facial features increment an internal database that is shared with other users of the system. Each customer, when entering the store, is "scanned" by the camera which analyses the facial features and alerts if necessary.

These types of tools, which are promising, are very controversial in France. Indeed, the study of personal data is very regulated in our country and respect for privacy could not suffer from such tools.

In France, the gendarmerie [4] works on A.I. For several years, and between Law and Ethics, the commitment of state officials has been based on a "CAP IA" charter intended for the public in order to reassure them about the use and respect of the laws.

1 Technology at the Service of the French Security Forces

1.1 Gendarmerie and National Police

During an interview for the Ministry of the Interior's website in 2018, Fabien Antoine, a data scientist at the Ministerial Governance of Information and Communication Systems (MGMSIC) mission, indicated that "*the analytical vision of activities with precise data can make it possible to change strategic orientation*". He goes on to explain that " *Our mission is to say that we need to go further than simple statistics and dig into the data, understand the activity of a service and make use of it, demonstrate that it is better to carry out a public activity by having understood the operational activity".*

General Patrick Perrot (doctor in artificial intelligence) declares, for his part, for the specialized journal "Cyber Cercle" that *"we cannot ignore the fact that the current level of artificial intelligence is already supplanting the performance of human intelligence in many fields: A.I. calculates better, memorizes better, sees better, detects better, classifies better…»*

1.2 What About the Municipal Police?

The oldest police force in France, the Municipal Police, including the rural guards, is a local police force, in contact with the population but also with new arrivals and consequently with first responders.

Established in 4,558 municipalities [5], the municipal police forces, as we can speak of plural municipal police forces, are both the secular arm of the State and the guarantors of the application of the security policy of the mayor of the municipality.

In this multitude of entities, the regulatory and legislative frameworks of the missions of municipal police officers make them professionals of women and men, with a cultural background and holders of the modern equipment necessary to carry out their missions.

Benefiting from their own operating budget, some municipal police forces are led by mayors who are invested differently in security, depending on their territory and/or their sensitivity.

Also, it is not uncommon for certain municipalities, whose topography, location or a particularity, become pilot cities and support French or even international companies in the development of security technologies.

Thus, it is interesting to observe and understand that cities whose number of inhabitants flirts with half a million souls, where the tourist flow fluctuates from 5 to 7 million visitors per year, where the establishment of infrastructures such as cruise ports and marinas, international airports, football stadiums, can equip themselves with innovative means to ensure the safety of their citizens and people in general.

1.3 High-Tech Security

Technology is a sector in perpetual innovation in the service of security and municipal police officers are actively involved in it.

In the city of Nice, the Municipal Police does a double job. Present in the field and behind the cameras, it accomplishes its missions while using and testing the tools of tomorrow to better guarantee the safety of citizens.

This is how it was able to equip itself with the latest generation technologies, transmit Artificial Intelligence to humans, and, while carrying out its general missions, identify (with a view to verbalizing) illegal dumping, detect a fire outbreak in a territory mixing urban, rural and mountainous areas, and test, through a security prism, facial recognition.

The fact remains that these 3 types of uses have limits and that being a plural and effective security visionary can only include human discernment.

1.4 The Environment as a Policy Spearhead [6–9]

800 illegal dumps per year. This is one of the first scourges that Artificial Intelligence tackled in Nice.

In 2021, the city of Nice acquired innovative software resulting from the research of private specialists in Artificial Intelligence.

Video operators receive alerts of an illegal dump in progress on the public highway, issued by one of the 30 cameras connected to the supervision system in which the said algorithm has been implemented.

[10] The observation is rather promising. However, the National Commission for Information and Liberties (CNIL), at the end of the experiment, was alerted to a possible fine for infringement using an augmented camera.

By this I mean that the support provided by Artificial Intelligence is refuted by the very fact that it is thanks to it that the offence could be denounced.

Also, despite a positive assessment, the city of Nice is committed to a transparency approach and modulates its action according to the directives provided by the public establishment, in strict application of Article R121-6 of the Highway Code.

From a pragmatic point of view, it is understandable that only material elements (recording, description) recorded by a duly sworn and authorised operator, appearing in a report sent to the Public Prosecutor's Office (Judicial Court) make it possible to punish the offender.

The tedious and meticulous work, second after second, does not stop the Municipal Police in its mission of respecting the environment, which makes up for this regulatory limit of A.I.

We will make a slight digression to indicate the tenfold increase in the workload for state agents induced by the procedures then put in place to punish offenders.

Indeed, while municipal police officers limit themselves to apply the legal framework (L251-2 of the Internal Security Code and L121-2 of the Highway Code or administrative procedure in Article L541-3 of the Environmental Code according to the special police powers of the mayor), we note on the other hand the competence of rural guards to be able to arrest [11].

A way forward for the respect of the environment of tomorrow?

1.5 The Environment, a Precious Commodity

The Nice Côte d'Azur Metropolis, under the aegis of the Health Security Agency, has set up a four-step plan to: "*raise awareness, prevent, control and monitor*", said the mayor of Nice, Christian ESTROSI, on July 10, 2023, at a press conference [12].

Indeed, 20% of Nice's land is located in the Red Zone of the Forest Fire Risk Prevention Plan, i.e. 1,362 hectares. Impacted by numerous fires, always at the cutting edge of technology and committed to the search for innovations in safety, the city of Nice has acquired a special camera in 2023 [13, 14].

Its operating system mixes the technology of two cameras, one with a powerful zoom and the other thermal, i.e. the interpretation of the infrared frequency.

[15] Together, they analyse the sky, the wooded and vegetated areas as well as the urban environment.

Cities such as Nice, Carros, Gattières, Colomars, Villefranche, Eze, Saint-André de la Roche, Saint-Laurent du Var, Le Broc, La Trinité, Falicon among others benefit from this tool.

Thus, this innovative camera located in the Nice Côte d'Azur metropolis, with an area of 1,479 km^2, scans the territory, up to 10 km radius from its anchor point placed at an altitude of 900 m.

It will be observed that the camera scans, detects opaque densities, stops, analyses the slightest compact concentration of air mass and alerts an agent in order to determine its dangerousness.

The sensitivity of this tool coupled with Artificial Intelligence therefore does not make it possible to precisely differentiate between a dense cloud, a burn or a fire. The man takes over and refines this analysis.

As soon as the alert is confirmed, the operator informs the municipal police of the affected municipality and simultaneously engages the firefighters by transmitting the most detailed estimate of the GPS coordinates.

Here we see the limit of this technology which, given the work provided 24 h a day, 7 days a week, can only be an added value for the safety of all.

Concerned about protecting the rights of citizens, the CNIL sees no obstacle to this use of AI.

Thus, in 2023, in view of 5 months of activity, noting nearly 4,600 activations, the I. A, then in the learning phase, was able to detect and alert, in an efficient manner, the operators of the Urban Supervision Center on 200 burnings and 12 proven fires.

The relevance of this tool is, once again, highlighted in 2024, when out of the 10,000 triggers, Artificial Intelligence was able to identify and prevent 750 burnings and 7 fire starts.

1.6 Facial Recognition: The Imagery that is Being Talked About

In addition to the reiteration of the conclusions [17] issued in the information report on the challenges of the use of security images in the public domain for the purpose of combating insecurity, it is interesting to add the modus operandi put in place by the municipality of Nice.

France - Nice - February 2019 - Carnival

For three days, 5000 volunteers took part in a unique experiment that was the subject of a Data Protection Impact Assessment (DPIA).

A reality TV camera, a " *Where's Charlie?* delimited by signs within a specific perimeter.

After providing a photo, the volunteers then blended into this stream of cooperative viewers before the software found them.

Even though an opinion poll has been carried out, where it appears that "*87% of those questioned are in favour of video protection (out of a sample of 800 people)*", the CNIL has opposed this use.

Explaining on November 15, 2019, in his document "*Facial recognition. For a debate that is equal to the stakes*" [18] that "*the French law of 20 June 2018, amending the Data Protection Act", is in line with European texts. In the absence of consent, an operator, public or private, may only implement biometric processing if it is not previously authorised to do so by law or, at the very least, by decree.»*.

The limit of the application of this technology is thus set.

We will once again get closer to the elements of the report by deputies Gosselin and Latombe, where during meetings with the Mayor of Cannes and the Director General of Security and Proximity of the City of Nice stressed the usefulness of such a tool for the benefit of the police, the regulation of access to stadiums, personal rescue.

Thus, it should be noted that in the event of the disappearance of an adult (elderly or vulnerable) or a minor, all the staff of the Municipal Police but also of the Police or the National Gendarmerie are immediately mobilized for this mission.

Indeed, beyond the crucial time factor, the density of the population on major roads or during any major event increases the urgency of research.

And yet, immediately finding the elderly, vulnerable people, or even a child in a crowd is a goal within the reach of Artificial Intelligence.

In Nice, in 2024, a hundred people were reported for disappearance, all the operatives of the Municipal Police, in coordination with its Urban Supervision Center, succeeded in the challenge of searching for these people, finding them and at the same time ensuring the safety of the population. Without a doubt, Artificial Intelligence would have been a valuable ally in this race against time [16].

It should be noted that during the facial recognition experiment, it was highlighted that people were recognized behind accessories (cap, sunglasses), elderly compared to the original photo, in a nocturnal environment and in the case of a monozygotic twin.

2 Homeland Security. Is it a Question of the State?

2.1 A Font Mosaic

So many judges, so many politicians.

From the smallest lord who had authority over the deans of vassals, to the great abbeys whose estates extended over hectares and hectares.

All around had their justice, and consequently their police, exercised by their representatives, the provosts.

Thus, from Clovis to the present day, high personages have had police functions which consist in maintaining peace as much as possible in a society where the law of the strongest tends to want to be exercised.

Sometimes a street or building divided the jurisdiction of a court. The invisible land border paralyzed the prosecution and declared the arrest illegal. The justice system has changed, but the police continue to run.

2.2 Community Policing: The State and the Complementary "Municipal"

In the 1970s, the Peyrefitte Commission [19] recommended that national policy "establish small neighbourhood posts in cities and use the so-called islanding method".

In 1982, the Bonnemaison report [20] (re)underlined the urgency of "refocusing all police action around islanding".

More than 20 years later, we still cannot incriminate the Police or the National Gendarmerie, but an entire system that is an obstacle. The search for flagrante delicto, repressive missions, the work of investigators, the lack of staff in the face of a growing and mobile population are elements to be taken into account.

Finally, the image of the policeman chasing thugs and defending the widow and the orphan clashes with that of the hero who emerges in the face of the unspeakable horror of terrorism.

And in this tangle of men-at-arms, the municipal police are positioning themselves.

As soon as we decide to refocus the debate on the very essence of the municipal police officer's job, we paint a portrait of the citizen bond that takes on its full meaning.

A daily action in which the Municipal Police maintains a direct link with the population, ensuring security in front of schools, market squares, during pedestrian walks or contacts with shopkeepers.

Even if proximity evolves through the prism of successive governments, it is nevertheless important to note the four immutable axes: information gathering, law enforcement, deterrence and prevention of public disorder and assistance to the population.

It should be noted that to "communicate well", the action is easier on foot, by bike or even on horseback than by car.

The mode of transport has allowed for greater speed of intervention and the ability to cover cities with galloping expansion to the detriment of contact with its population.

Also, and since the 2000s, they have been joined by the Public Road Surveillance Agents (ASVP) who practice islanding, in the literal sense of the term. Very often on foot, it was the municipal police [21] of yesterday. They are the link between the police and the population, between society and politics.

2.3 A Complementary Ally of the Operational: Digital Technology

Based on this observation, there is only one more step to be taken for the Municipal Police to commit, once again, to effective proximity and for Artificial Intelligence, at its side, to transmit the fruit of its daily commitment to the benefit of State services.

Even if the I. A is unknown, even feared, we conjecture so much that it would be a shame not to use its ability to do faster than humans.

And this is where, once again, the Municipal Police intervene.

The population must benefit from this digital emergence thanks to a community police force, ensured, in 2022, by the uniforms of 27,131 [5] municipal police officers, 657 rural guards and 8,097 public road surveillance officers. Their daily commitment forges links with citizens, their partnership with all the actors in the field builds relationships for the benefit of a local and international population.

All municipal police officers, by accomplishing what they have been doing for centuries, will be able to enable a territorial network of local security data by feeding the relevant information, an Artificial Intelligence dedicated to analysis, extraction, cross-checking and grouping in order to give all the parameters, in record time, for a local security data processing unit.

The security of the country is one of the showcases of France, the Municipal Police is the link with the citizen, Artificial Intelligence links him.

This is why we will discuss here, with a volunteer city of Nice, the creation of a unique tool, designed to create an incomparable network at the service of local elected officials and the security of its territory.

A system that collects most of the agents' field work, underlines the proximity of the city's stakeholders to the citizens and offers coverage of the municipality or even the national territory to the services of the State.

Indeed, with regard to the mayors' security policies, it is interesting to highlight the source of information collected by elected officials, rural guards, municipal police officers and public highway surveillance agents. In extenso, the employees of the town hall working on a daily basis in the municipalities, observing, observing and exchanging with the entire population.

Most municipalities have several channels for receiving information, which sometimes leads to a loss of quality of information.

Thus, the project, which has been in the works since 2017, is based on the work of all the agents and is based on an innovative security network at the service of the mayors.

The analysis of local security data must be used by the chief magistrate of the municipality to support him in his security and political vision of his city. [22].

From the information capture phase, a computer support is designed, which, combined with Artificial Intelligence, will be able to highlight the local security data of a municipality or even several to draw the attention of the State services to particular events.

Thus, as soon as a municipality has local security data which, cross-referenced, reveals a risk for citizens (feeling of insecurity, drugs, noise pollution, gatherings, damage, etc.), the mayor (and by extension the deputy delegate for security) will be able to orient his security policy.

It is a reality that between the Local Security and Crime Prevention Contract (CLSPD) [23] or the Intercommunal Security and Crime Prevention Contract (CISPD) [24], and the Localized Group for the Treatment of Criminal Crime (GLTD), the municipalities are already involved in this approach.

The mayors of the 34,945 municipalities [25] have made a commitment to their little citizens, but only 2,212 municipalities have a local security and crime prevention contract, what about security for the 32,733 municipalities with less than 5000 [26] inhabitants?

To this end, we note the creation of the GPO (Operational Partnership Group), set up in 2018, to articulate a one-off action, between partnership bodies united in a specific security continuum. However, it should be noted that the GPOs have taken a weekly form to provide day-to-day security, but only in the national police zone.

We will then note the vacant name of the GPO in the gendarmerie zone. However, the heads of the municipal police forces, in the gendarmerie sector, are structured around Local Crime Treatment Groups (GLTD) whose coordinated actions to combat acts of delinquency are determined by the public prosecutor, within a specific perimeter.

Finally, it should be noted that in 2022, 36 Interministerial Research Groups (IRGs) were created, composed of multidisciplinary personnel (police, gendarmerie, customs, taxes and even URSSAF for some) whose operations resulted in the seizure of weapons, drugs and cash.

However, all this coordination does not fully meet the needs of local elected officials and State services in general.

Thus, the reflection on the alliance of a daily, permanent and colossal work of municipal police officers and Artificial Intelligence draws another organizational specification to satisfy the arsenal of security and investigation.

Established as an operational centre for local security data, this library dedicated to sharing and fed by several municipal channels (police/rural guard, Letters/grievances administered) has been strengthened beyond the CLSPD/CISPD.

Indeed, to meet the needs of the first magistrate of the municipality but also at the national level, the needs of the State services, it will be proposed to the municipal partners (cultural associations, shopkeepers, CCAS, local mission (employment), social landlords or public transport) but also to the National Education, the Judicial Protection of Youth or the Departmental Council, to increment this database for the benefit of tenuous security.

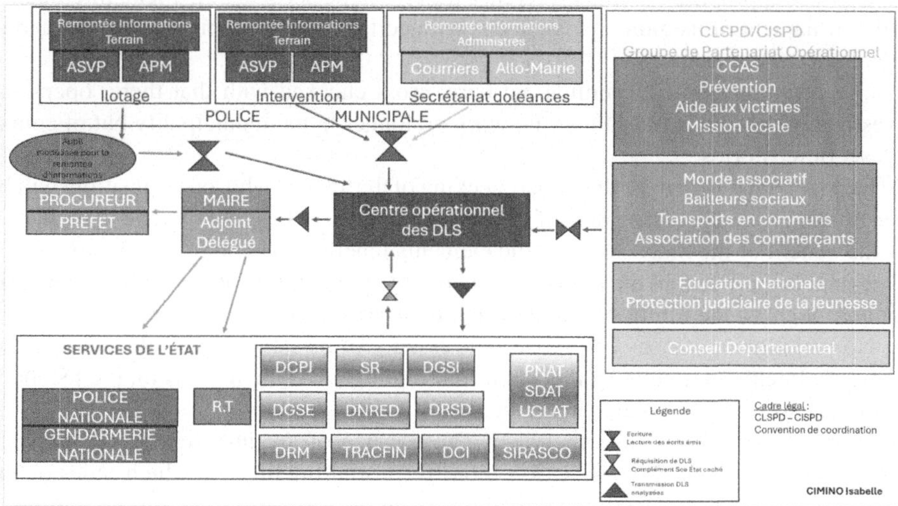

[27] Defining secure access to entrances and operations, the Local Security Data Operations Center contains a unique municipal network. Narcotics, drugs, gatherings, thefts, thefts, intra-family violence, incivility, damage, everything is noted.

It will be fundamental to define processing expectations and format the local safety data collection database to allow for relevant cross-checking and analysis synthesis. Indeed, the I. A is relevant when its modelling is accurate.

Thus, we will opt for a treatment according to two axes:

- Sorting: it will be approached through the A.I. language called Large Language Models (LLM), allowing the extraction of information, anonymized upstream, necessary for the understanding of local security issues.
- Reconciliation: it will be initiated by a local A.I., then “refined” in its learning, to have a more tenuous analysis of the elements and therefore of the cross-checking and pre-analysis.

Indeed, the first part can be processed in open source, in the case of Deep Learning, provided that the elements are anonymized. But it will be necessary to go through a local A.I. with a capacity for learning and cross-checking in accordance with the expectations of the Elected One.

Thanks to the training already acquired by Artificial Intelligence in terms of language data, it will be able to cross-check elements such as alarm triggers, police or emergency services commitments, but also to draw the analyst’s attention to recurring or isolated events.

In the present case, the I. A will be able to highlight that the actions designated as incivilities specific to a neighbourhood, are by their widespread repetition in the municipality: a global security attack on the city.

Thus, the goal is to bring the I. A to define according to its own criteria (place, theme or motif) the relevance of the cross-check. It will then be studied by an analyst who will characterize the elements in detail and will then be classified before processing.

It will be appropriate to cross-reference the cross-checks of this Artificial Intelligence in the firmament of its municipal analysis with certain facts committed or acts noted in neighbouring territories.

The commission of a criminal act here, cross-checked with that there, opens the investigation into an extraordinary network no longer in the municipality but of course in a set of territories.

Exponential will then be the cross-checking of the analyst who, on requisition, will be able to link the local security data of the territory for which he is competent, to highlight, for the benefit of the State services, the elements inherent to judicial investigations.

The police officers in the field do an incredible job in terms of community policing, rarely brought to the forefront, yet they are the heart of the investigation.

No investigator will say otherwise; The essence of investigation is information. The Domestic Intelligence calls on the Territorial Intelligence which relies on the feedback of information from the police in the field.

No investigator will say otherwise; The essence of the investigation is information. The Domestic Intelligence calls on the Territorial Intelligence which relies on the feedback of information from the police forces on the ground.

And what is true in the national police is also true in the gendarmerie zone, where the investigators of the BRI (Brigade de Recherche & Investigations) capture the bulk of their investigations in the field.

The community police or neighbourhood police, beyond being the police of yesterday and today, is the police of tomorrow. It is even the one able to collect everyday items for everyone's safety.

2.4 The Commission Nationale De l'Informatique Et Des Libertés (CNIL), a Brake on the Reporting of Information?

Since the capture of information is a work that is already in place in the municipal police, the National Police and the National Gendarmerie, the CNIL cannot oppose the continuation of this proximity with the population.

Responding to the grievances of the citizens, the third security forces do not go beyond the regulatory framework validated by the CNIL.

As for the Municipal Police, more specifically, this type of work induced by its community policing mission known as the mayor's police, it practices it, on a daily basis, as close as possible to the citizens.

Artificial Intelligence only works on anonymized data and processing is only done on a sovereign, local server, the role played by A.I. is only to shuffle raw material. It will be up to the analyst alone to refine the cross-referencing of the processing of local security data before issuing alerts and other reports and transmissions.

Finally, it should be noted that this tool for processing local security data, assisted by Artificial Intelligence and consolidated by analysts, will take on its full character thanks to the implementation and use of a singular and innovative application, intended for police officers in the field, effective in its articulation of modelling local security data, for better extraction.

Artificial Intelligence is celebrating its 75th anniversary and brings together all generations around it.

The young people make it evolve, the not so young try to understand it and the Elders live with it, without knowing it.

Certainly, Artificial Intelligence is very present and does not leave you indifferent!

Capable of processing and analysing massive amounts of data in record time, shaped by decades of research, development, and challenges, from Alan Turing to deep leaning, it has come a long way in Machine Learning.

It already supports police forces around the world, in the context of investigations, road traffic regulation, or fire detection, and it should be given a new orientation focused on the use of local intelligence.

Rural guards, municipal police officers and public highway surveillance officers collect local safety data directly from the source: the population. Currently, this daily work of capturing information is not part of the mixing of events in the databases of the National Police or those of the Intelligence.

Also, the interest of using Artificial Intelligence for the purpose of processing local security data, is, beyond extracting, analysing, cross-checking and grouping them, to draw a map of local security data that can be shared with state actors in the security and safety of the territory.

Thus, the articulation of the Municipal Police and Artificial Intelligence will highlight relevant cross-checks intended for the security orientation of the first magistrate of the municipality and the processing by the State services, for the benefit of the security of France.

References

1. L'intelligence artificielle au secours de la police - Police Scientifique (police-scientifique.com)
2. Royaume-Uni : des commerçants utilisent l'intelligence artificielle pour lutter contre les vols (francetvinfo.fr)
3. https://www.sciencedirect.com/science
4. Ysens de France (Gendarmerie nationale): "Toutes nos actions d'intelligence artificielle vent être justifiées" (usine-digitale.fr)
5. DATA GOUV, Police municipale: Effectifs par commune (2022). https://www.data.gouv.fr/fr/datasets/police-municipale-effectifs-par-commune/#/resources, màj 14/03/2024
6. Galante, M.: Nice expérimente l'intelligence artificielle contre les dépôts sauvages, Le Parisien (2021)
7. Mansour, S.: Nice traque les dépôts sauvages en s'appuyant sur l'intelligence artificielle, CNEWS (2021)
8. Seiler, V.: Sécurité, stationnement, dépôts sauvages... Ces outils technologiques testés et approuvés par la Ville de Nice, Nice-Matin (2023) 14
9. Perrier, N.: Les dépôts sauvages dans le viseur des caméras intelligentes, La gazette des communes (2024) (à paraître le 16 septembre 2024)

10. Photo extraite de l'article de MANSOUR, S.: Nice traque les dépôts sauvages en s'appuyant sur l'intelligence artificielle, CNEWS (2021)
11. Articles 24 du Code de Procédure Pénale et L.172–8 du Code de l'Environnement
12. Extrait de l'article reprenant les éléments de la conférence de presse, Nice Ensemble, Feux de forêt : la Métropole Nice Côte d'Azur déploie un plan de prévention majeur et innovant pour protéger la population et les habitations, Nice (2023)
13. GERNER, D. : Lutte contre les incendies : une nouvelle caméra de détection des feux expérimentée à Nice, France 3 (2023)
14. Beurnez, V.: A Nice, une caméra dotée d'intelligence artificielle détecte les incendies, BFMTV (2023)
15. Photo extraite de l'article de GERNER, D. : Lutte contre les incendies : une nouvelle caméra de détection des feux expérimentée à Nice, France 3 (2023)
16. Source officielle Police Municipale Ville de Nice
17. Gosselin, P., Latombe, P.: Rapport d'information n°1089 sur les enjeux de l'utilisation d'images de sécurité dans le domaine public dans une finalité de lutte contre l'insécurité, II. Les images de sécurité face aux défis contemporains de l'intelligence artificielle, Assemblée Nationale, Paris (avril 2023)
18. CNIL, Reconnaissance faciale pour un débat à la hauteur des enjeux, https://www.cnil.fr/sites/cnil/files/atoms/files/reconnaissance_faciale.pdf. Paris (2019)
19. PEYREFITTE, A. : Réponses à la violence dit Rapport PEYREFITTE, p. 172, Recommandation 81, https://www.vie-publique.fr/files/rapport/pdf/24679.pdf, Paris (1977)
20. Commission des maires sur la sécurité : Face à la délinquance, prévention, répression, solidarité, rapport au premier ministre dit Rapport BONNEMAISON, p. 85, https://www.vie-publique.fr/files/rapport/pdf/834037801.pdf, Paris (1982)
21. Les gardes-champêtres, occupant plus souvent les territoires ruraux, et ayant gardé la pluralité du métier (zone bleue, stationnement payant, présence sur les marchés, ilotage) a contrario des policiers municipaux qui selon la structure d'accueil se « spécialisent » la plupart du temps
22. Garcia, P.: Les maires sont des maillons essentiels de la lutte contre le narcotrafic, La gazette des communes (2024)
23. Article L132–4 du Code de la Sécurité Intérieure (CSI)
24. Article L132–13 du CSI 15
25. Population par commune, p. 20, https://www.collectivites-locales.gouv.fr/collectivites-locales-chiffres-2023, Paris (2023)
26. Loi n°2021–646 du 25 mai 2021
27. Logigramme CIMINO Isabelle

Human-Centric AI for Enhancing Security in Smart City Anomaly Detection

Sanjay Misra[1](✉), Kousik Barik[2], Petter Kvalvik[3], and Sabarathinam Chockalingam[4]

[1] Department of Applied Data Science, Institute for Energy Technology, Halden, Norway
Sanjay.Misra@ife.no
[2] Department of Computer Science, Universidad de Alcalá, Madrid, Alcalá de Henares, Spain
Kousik.Kousik@edu.uah.es
[3] Digital Systems, Institute for Energy Technology, Halden, Norway
Petter.Kvalvik@ife.no
[4] Department of Risk and Security, Institute for Energy Technology, Halden, Norway
Sabarathinam.Chockalingam@ife.no

Abstract. Smart city initiatives are being promoted globally to address significant security challenges and build confidence in the transformative potential of digital technologies. Human-Centric Artificial Intelligence (HCAI) focuses on a process perspective design that augments human capabilities, supports equity, and upholds ethical principles. This study proposes a model based on a Hybrid Spatial Weighted Attention Layer Pooling Convolutional NeuroNet by incorporating human feedback to detect anomalies in smart cities using a CCTV violence detection dataset. The model incorporates predictions and visualization utilizing HCAI-based Local Interpretable Model-agnostic Explanations (LIME). The preprocessing phase involves normalization to standardize image input and ensure uniformity, while data augmentation techniques, such as rotations, flips, scaling, and cropping, are applied. The proposed LSTM-CNN-based model demonstrates an accuracy of 98.25%, precision of 98.26%, recall of 98.25%, and an F1-score of 98.24%. Furthermore, future study directions are highlighted.

This study represents a significant advancement in the accuracy and reliability of surveillance systems, improving public safety and monitoring efficiency in smart cities.

Keywords: Trustworthy AI · Convolutional Neural Networks · Explainable AI · LIME · Smart Cities · Security · Surveillance · Transparency

1 Introduction

The rise of smart cities marks a fundamental transformation in how urban environments are planned, designed, and interacted with in this era of digital revolution. Population growth and the challenges it brings, such as traffic congestion, quality of life, and resource scarcity, are key drivers behind the development of smart cities [1]. These cities utilize

Published by Springer Nature Switzerland AG 2025
D. Verdejo and E. Mercier-Laurent (Eds.): AI4GS 2024, IFIP AICT 743, pp. 75–90, 2025.
https://doi.org/10.1007/978-3-031-96522-7_6

advanced technologies, data analytics, and integrated systems to create efficient, sustainable, and livable environments. With their transformative potential, digital technologies are at the core of smart city initiatives, generating excitement and interest in the future of urban living [2]. A key enabler of these interconnected systems is the Internet of Things (IoT), an ecosystem of devices and sensors that collect and share data [3]. IoT plays a crucial role in developing smart cities, particularly transportation and infrastructure systems, by facilitating real-time monitoring and management of various functions embedded in everyday objects. Smart cities present numerous opportunities, from improving traffic flow and energy efficiency to enhancing public safety and providing people with personalized services [4].

Smart cities are increasingly vulnerable to emerging cyber threats due to their growing reliance on networked AI systems [5]. Targeted cyberattacks can compromise public safety, disrupt Critical Infrastructures (CIs), and undermine the benefits that make these cities' smart'. It is important to ensure robust cybersecurity measures in smart cities [6]. These attacks can include different types, ranging from tampering with the operations of CIs to data breaches and unauthorized access [7, 8]. In a smart city, a security breach can negatively impact citizens' trust, disrupt governmental services and democracy, and destabilize a nation's economy. Smart cities' cyber threats include ransomware, phishing, Distributed denial of service (DDoS) attacks, data breaches, and manipulation of AI systems [9].

Human-Centric Artificial Intelligence (HCAI) aims to design and develop AI systems that prioritize human needs, values, ethical considerations, and data governance frameworks, thereby impacting data quality, privacy, and accountability [10]. The goal is to develop intelligent systems in smart city contexts that improve individuals' quality of life while protecting personal privacy and securing access to technology [11]. AI systems based on human centricity should be designed to understand and respond to human behaviors and preferences, offering more personalized, responsive, and secure services [12]. One of the key applications of AI in smart cities is surveillance systems that automatically detect and report abnormal behavior, offering a valuable means of early detection both inside and outside public spaces. The increasing number of distributed surveillance cameras in public spaces plays a crucial role in maintaining public safety and security [13]. However, several challenges remain, including interconnected systems, data privacy, legacy systems, lack of standardization and public acceptance, surveillance anxiety, and trust [14, 15], as demonstrated in Fig. 1.

Integrating multiple technologies and infrastructures in smart cities can lead to complex interconnections and vulnerabilities, making the management of interconnected systems a significant challenge. The vast amount of personal data collected and shared raises the risk of data breaches and exploitation [16]. Building smart city infrastructures requires substantial financial investment and careful planning to ensure smooth and efficient integration. Legacy systems may hamper improvement, as new technologies may not be compatible with older systems. In addition, a fragmented and inadequate system may suffer from a lack of standardization across various technologies and protocols [17]. Public acceptance and trust are crucial for the successful adoption of these systems, making it essential to assure citizens of their security and benefits.

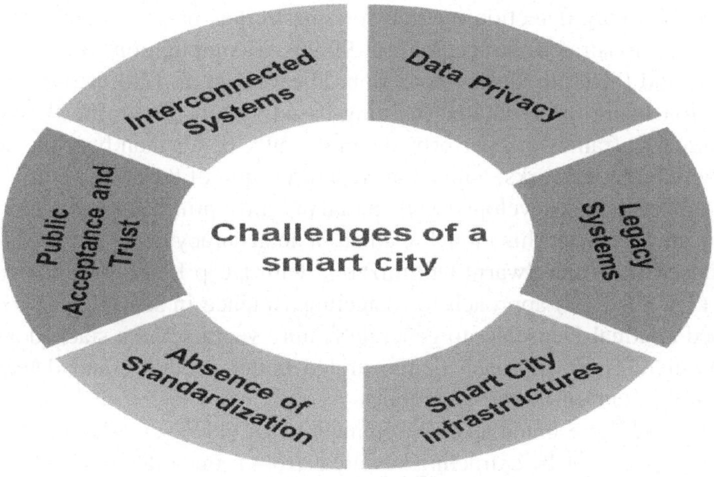

Fig. 1. Challenges of a Smart City

This study presents a model using HCAI. Deep learning (DL) is based on including human feedback to enhance the security of surveillance systems in smart cities. By introducing a hybrid spatial weighted attention layer pooling Convolutional NeuroNet model, the study aims to transform smart cities into more intelligent and secure digital environments. This study emphasizes aligning AI systems with human values and ethical principles to ensure effective, equitable, and safe urban living environments. The significant contributions of the study are as follows:

i. To propose a model based on DL and HCAI and based on human feedback to ensure uniformity and improve security performance in smart cities using the CCTV dataset.
ii. To apply data augmentation techniques to enhance the robustness and generalization of the model.
iii. To integrate a hybrid spatial weighted attention layer pooling mechanism, incorporating spatial weighted attention techniques to improve critical security aspects.
iv. To employ HCAI visualization using Local Interpretable Model-Agnostic Explanations (LIME) for predictions, providing transparency into the model's decision-making process through visualizations.

The renaming paper is organized as follows: Sect. 2 demonstrates the related works. Section 3 illustrates the classification model, dataset, preprocessing methods, and HCAI for visualization. Section 4 shows the study's results. Section 5 presents the discussion, limitations, and future studies. Finally, the paper concludes in Sect. 6.

2 Related Works

Islam et al. [18] proposed a study to enable IoT smart city applications by integrating cloud and fog computing with IoT. The study focused on improving anomaly detection and accuracy, precision, recall, and detection rate performance. Hazman et al. [19]

presented an anomaly detection method for smart cities based on ensemble learning. The authors demonstrated an accuracy of 99.9%, a computation time of 33.68s during training, and 0.02156s during detection. Djenouri et al. [20] evaluated smart city edge detection using the federated learning-based system for traffic flow prediction. The proposed DL framework performed significantly better than baseline approaches, particularly in large networks, with an average precision of 84%.

Manickam et al. [21] developed a DL-based billiard-optimization model for anomaly detection in smart cities. This model resulted in an accuracy of 99.21%. Aldehim et al. [22] introduced the Tuna Swarm Optimization with Deep Learning Enabled Violence Detection (TSODL-VD) approach for detecting violence in surveillance footage. The authors used residual-DenseNet to generate feature vectors and a stacked autoencoder (SAE) classifier. Their approach demonstrated better accuracy and detection speed compared to the state-of-the-art techniques.

Zahra et al. [23] presented a DL-based method for video surveillance in smart cities that reduces image sizes by extracting key areas from frames. Their work demonstrated a bit rate of 56.92%, a peak signal-to-noise ratio of 5.35 bd, and SR-based segmentation accuracy of 92% and 96%. Ullah et al. [24] presented an effective and reliable two-stream neural network approach for detecting anomalies in large-scale video data, showing accuracy gains of 9.88% and 4.01% over existing methods. Ahmed et al. [25] proposed a person detection method for smart communities. The Gaussian YOLOv3 algorithm was utilized for person detection, with an overall detection accuracy of 94% by leveraging deep neural networks. Khan et al. [26] applied CNNs to identify abnormalities in the VTSS-captured dataset and a rolling prediction approach was applied to achieve high accuracy. The study's findings demonstrated that 82% of the traffic accident incidents were successfully identified in the traffic surveillance system footage.

While existing studies highlight the effectiveness of DL techniques in anomaly detection and security improvements for smart cities, a significant study gap remains in using HCAI to train the DL-based model to classify effectively. Our study aims to address this gap by proposing a hybrid DL-based model incorporating HCAI during the training phase. The proposed model aims to improve anomaly detection accuracy while reducing computational complexity, making it more suitable for the dynamic, resource-constrained environments of smart cities.

3 Proposed Methodology

This study uses a CCTV dataset to design an anomaly detection system for smart cities. Figure 2 illustrates the proposed model and consists of three phases. First, the datasets are pre-processed, including frame extraction and label preparation for analysis. The second phase includes data augmentation techniques such as flipping, rotations, scaling, cropping, and translation to enhance dataset diversity, data scarcity, and model generalization. Third, the model is designed based on a Hybrid Spatial Weighted Attention Layer Pooling Convo NeuroNet based on LSTM and CNN. We combined a hybrid spatial weighted attention layer and pooling convolutional neural network architecture to improve detection accuracy. During the training phase, the LIME is used for prediction explanations and visualizations, furnishing insights into the model's performance and explainability and providing its effectiveness.

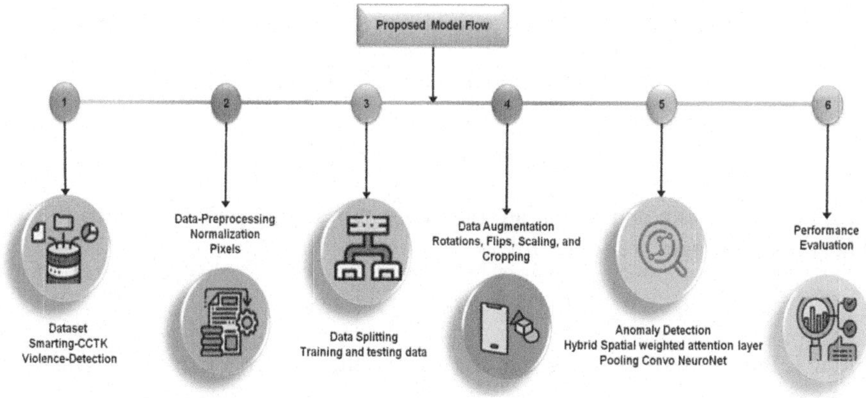

Fig. 2. Proposed Model

3.1 Dataset

This study utilized the Smart City CCTV Violence Detection Dataset (https://www.kaggle.com/datasets/toluwaniaremu/smartcity-cctv-violence-detection-dataset-scvd/data). This comprises videos and pre-existing datasets used for violence detection, including the Real-Life Violence Situations (RLVS) and NTU CCTV-Fights datasets. The dataset has been adapted to account for the potential use of portable objects as weapons in violent scenarios.

3.2 Data Preprocessing and Augmentation

The datasets are processed using frame extraction techniques to enhance quality and remove significant noise. Each pixel value is divided by 255 to normalize it to the range [0, 1], as shown in Eq. 1.

$$L = -\frac{1}{N}\sum_{i=1}^{N}\sum_{c=1}^{C} y_{i,c} log\left(\hat{y}_{i,c}\right) \tag{1}$$

where N is the number of samples, C is the number of courses, yi,c is the true label of class c for sample i, and $\hat{y}_{i,c}$ is the predicted probability for class c.

Several transformations are applied to the training data using the ImageDataGenerator to enhance model generalization through data augmentation techniques. For training and validation, two different data argumentation objects are created. The training object applies rotations, flips, scaling, and cropping to the data. Rotations help the model become invariant to orientation, while Flips provide variations that help the model learn features invariant to mirror symmetry. Scaling enables the model to recognize objects of different sizes, and cropping focuses the model on different parts of the image, as presented in Eqs. 2 to 5.

$$\theta' = \theta + \Delta\theta \text{ where } \Delta\theta \sim u(-r, r) \tag{2}$$

where r is the maximum rotation range (in degrees) specified by $rotation\_range = 10$.

$$x' = x + \Delta x \text{ where } \Delta x \sim u(-w_{shift}, w_{shift}) \tag{3}$$

$$y' = y + \Delta y \, where \, \Delta y \sim u(-h_{shift}, h_{shift}) \tag{4}$$

The image's width and height are randomly shifted by up to 10% when the width and height shift ranges are set to 0.1.

$$I'(x, y) = I(w - x - 1, y) \tag{5}$$

where w is the width of the image and $I'x,y$ is the flipped version of the original image $I(x, y)$.

3.3 Prediction and Visualization Using LIME

In the training stage, an HCAI process is used. It uses LIME to interpret the outcomes of black-box classifiers by creating interpretable, local surrogate models that approximate the predictions of the original model [27]. Figure 3 demonstrates the anomaly detection process for intelligent cities for video surveillance. Initially, video frames are fed into a neural network model, which analyzes to identify anomalies and classify them as normal, violent, or weaponized. LIME provides an interpretable explanation for each classification, ensuring the outcomes are understandable. Finally, human feedback is gathered on these explanations to refine and improve the model's performance.

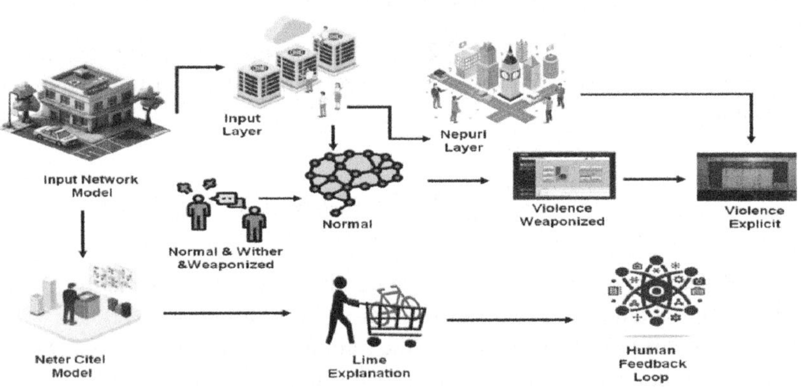

Fig. 3. Case Study of Human-centric AI

The flow diagram of HCAI is presented in Fig. 4.

For LIME to explain an instance y, it must first develop an interpretable model h that belongs to the class H. Since h is presumed to be locally faithful to a classifier g, this means that when y is close to the instance that needs to be explained, h exactly approximates g. The neighborhood width, π_y, is a locality-based kernel that quantifies

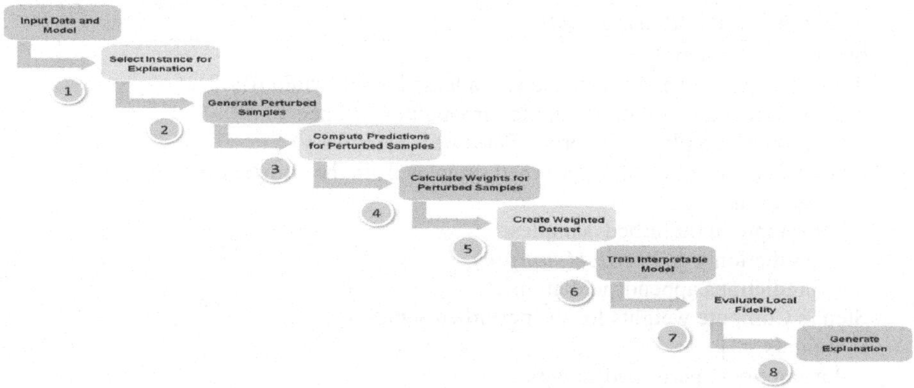

Fig. 4. Flow Diagram of Human-centric AI

the fidelity of h to g in the area of y. Equation 6 provides the optimization model, which yields the explainable model h.

$$\xi(\mathrm{w}) = \underset{h \epsilon H}{argminK} (e, h, \pi_w) + \Omega(\mathrm{h}) \tag{6}$$

where (h) is a measure of the model h's complexity, $\xi(y)$ is the explanation, for instance,y, and K is a loss function that quantifies g's unfaithfulness in approximating g in the locality given by π_y. The main objective is to decrease K while maintaining the highest level of simplicity in h, which is determined by the complexity factor. To solve this optimization problem, a new dataset is created with perturbed samples around y and the corresponding predictions by g that are weighted by π_y. Typically, π_y is an exponential kernel defined on some distance metric, and this weighted dataset is used to train the model using Eq. 7.

$$\pi_w(y) = \exp(-\frac{c(w, y)^2}{2\sigma^2}) \tag{7}$$

The perturbed sample is denoted by a, the distance between the original instance y and a is represented by $e(y, a)$, and the kernel width control parameter is denoted by σ.

To approximate the complex model g, LIME uses interpretable models like decision trees, rule lists, or linear regression. The goal is to fit and interpret the model h to the weighted data generated by perturbing y, where the kernel function πy determines the weights. The features xi are the features of the anxious samples, and βi are the coefficients estimated during the optimization process, as presented in Eq. 8.

$$h(x) = \beta_0 + \beta_1 x_1 + \beta_2 x_2 + \cdots + \beta_p x_p \tag{8}$$

The distance metric $e(y, a)$ used in the kernel function varies depending on the data type, as presented in Eq. 9. Algorithm 1 presents the HCAI using LIME.

$$e(y, a) = \sqrt{\sum_{i=1}^{p} (y_i - a_i)^2} \tag{9}$$

Algorithm 1. HCAI using LIME

```
Input: LIME function
function LIME_Explain(instance y, model g, kernel_width σ):
 Step 1: Generate perturbed samples around the instance y
   perturbed_samples = Generate_Perturbed_Samples(y)
Step 2: Get predictions for perturbed samples from the complex model g
   predictions = []
   for sample in perturbed_samples:
      prediction = g.Predict(sample)
      predictions.append(prediction)
Step 3: Compute weights for the perturbed samples
   weights = []
   for sample in perturbed_samples:
      distance = Compute_Distance(y, sample)
      weight = exp(−distance^2 / (2 * σ^2))
      weights.append(weight)
Step 4: Create a weighted dataset
   weighted_dataset = Create_Weighted_Dataset(perturbed_samples, predictions,
weights)
Step 5: Train interpretable model h using the weighted dataset
h = Train_Interpretable_Model(weighted_dataset)
    returnh
function Compute_Distance(instance1, instance2):
   distance = sqrt(Sum((instance1[i] - instance2[i])^2 for i in range(len(instance1))))
   return distance
   function Train_Interpretable_Model(weighted_dataset):
      model = Train_Model(weighted_dataset)
   return model
   function Main():
   model_g = Load_Complex_Model()
   instance_y = Get_Instance_To_Explain()
   kernel_width = Define_Kernel_Width()
      explanation = LIME_Explain(instance_y, model_g, kernel_width)
   Visualize_Explanation(explanation)
   end
```

3.4 Classification Using Hybrid Spatial Weighted Attention Layer Pooling Convo NeuroNet

This section presents the classification techniques used in this study.

3.4.1 Convolutional Neural Network-Long Short-Term Memory (CNN-LSTM)

Weights and biases are learnable characteristics within a CNN's layers, a feed-forward neural network. CNN usually consists of multiple linked layers. Sequential data analysis, including time series and natural language data, is a crucial application of RNN-based models, particularly LSTM [28]. The rationale and feature representations are deduced by the thick layer that follows these layers, as shown in Eq. 10.

$$y = W.x + b \tag{10}$$

where T is softmax, z_j shows the input function's typical exponential function and represents the input vector by f^{z_j}, as shown in Eq. 11.

$$T(z_j) = \frac{f^{z_j}}{\sum_i f^{z_j}} \tag{11}$$

3.4.2 Attention Mechanism

The human visual system's capacity to focus attention allows individuals to concentrate on specific objects, significantly increasing their ability to process visual information. Similarly, deep neural networks can leverage attention mechanisms to identify key features from large amounts of data, filter out irrelevant information, and complete tasks more efficiently [29]. Equation 12 can be used to compute the attention mechanism.

$$o(w_j) = \frac{\exp(T_j)}{\sum_{j=1}^{s-1} \exp(T_j)} \tag{12}$$

The conditional probability distribution α_j can be generated, which indicates the significance of the jth time window for prediction. We first compute the associated weight score at each time step and then normalize the score using the softmax function. The function determines the score t_j, as presented in Eq. 13.

$$t_j = \text{tang}(X^S g_j + a) \tag{13}$$

where X and c are learning parameters jointly trained with other model elements. The attention mechanism uses a weighted sum of all the hidden states $(h_1 to h_{t-1})$ to calculate the context vector (c_t), as shown in Eq. 14.

$$D_s = \sum_{j=1}^{s-1} \alpha_j g_j \tag{14}$$

They create an attentional hidden state by combining the data from the context vector (c_t) and the current hidden state (h_t), as presented in Eq. 15.

$$g^* = \text{tang}(\omega_g [d_s; g_s]) \tag{15}$$

Figure 5 shows the attention to CNN-LSTM structure. Algorithm 2 presents the hybrid spatial weighted attention layer pooling convolution neural network approach.

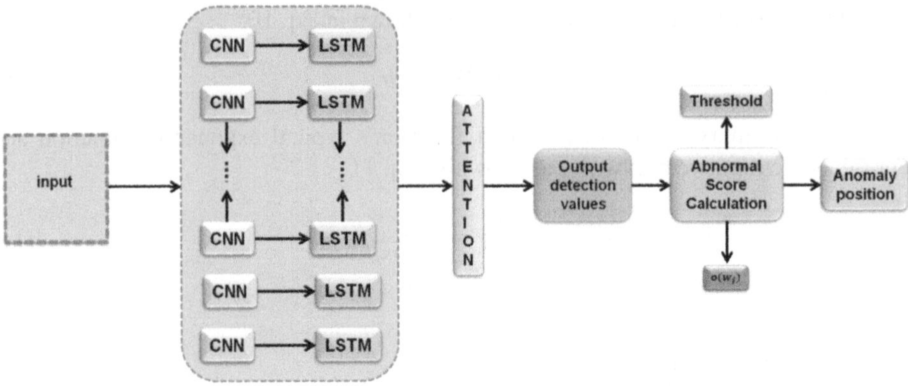

Fig. 5. The Framework of the Attention with CNN-LSTM Structure

---

Algorithm 2. Hybrid Spatial Weighted Attention Layer Pooling Convolutional Neural Network

---

Input: Attention with CNN-LSTM model
Step 1: Function CNN_Model amd LSTM_model (InputData)
  Conv1 = Convolution$(InputData, filters = 64, kernel_size = 3)$
  Pool1 = MaxPooling$(Conv1, pool_size = 2)$
  Conv2 = Convolution$(Pool1, filters = 128, kernel_size = 3)$
  Pool2 = MaxPooling$(Conv2, pool_size = 2)$
  Flattened = Flatten$(Pool2)$
 return Flattened
Step 2: Function Attention_Mechanism(SequenceData)
for each time_step in SequenceData:
$t\_j = tanh(X\char`^S * time\_step + a)$
$attention\_weights[j] = exp(t\_j) / sum(exp(t\_j))$
$context\_vector = sum(attention\_weights[j] * SequenceData[j])$
  return context_vector
Step 3: Function Hybrid_Model(InputData)
  FlattenedData = CNN_Model(InputData)
  LSTMOutput = LSTM_Model(FlattenedData)
  ContextVector = Attention_Mechanism(LSTMOutput)
Create an attentional hidden state
$g\_star = tanh(omega\_g * [ContextVector; LSTMOutput])$
Apply Dropout to prevent overfitting
  h_star = Dropout(g_star)
Prediction using Dense Layer
$Prediction = Dense(h\_star, units = num\_classes)$
  return Prediction
Step 4: Function Main(InputData)
  Predictions = Hybrid_Model(InputData)
  return Predictions
end

---

4 Evaluation

This section evaluates the effectiveness of the proposed anomaly detection model. Equations 16 to 20 present the different evaluation metrics employed to evaluate the model's performance, including accuracy, precision, recall, F1-score, and AUC. The experiment was conducted on a laptop with a 512GB SSD for storage, 16GB RAM, and an Intel Core i7 CPU. It uses Python with Keras, Panda, and Matplotlib packages.

$$Accuracy = \frac{TP + TN}{TP + TN + FP + FN} \tag{16}$$

$$Precision = \frac{TP}{TP + FP} \tag{17}$$

$$Recall = \frac{TP}{TP + FN} \tag{18}$$

$$F1score = \frac{2 * TP}{2 * TP + FP + FN} \tag{19}$$

$$AUC = \int_{0}^{1} ROC(t)dt \tag{20}$$

4.1 Human-Centric AI Data Visualization

The LIME is employed to explain the predictions made by the CNN-LSTM model to ensure that the model's decisions are interpretable. LIME provides a visual aid for human reviewers to understand the reasoning behind the classification by highlighting the input frame regions that the model considered most significant for each categorized video. The interpretability and performance of the model are further improved by putting human insights into the learning process through the collection and utilization of this input, as illustrated in Fig. 6.

4.2 Model Evaluation

The proposed model achieved an accuracy of 98.25%, indicating that it correctly predicted the outcomes, as demonstrated in Fig. 7. The precision score of 98.26% reflects the method's ability to accurately identify positive instances without a significant number of false positives. Similarly, with a recall of 98.25%, the technique can capture almost all positive cases. The F1-score of 98.24% ensures balanced performance in recognizing real positives and avoiding false positives, the harmonic mean of accuracy and recall. Figure 8 demonstrates the proposed model's AUC-ROC curve.

Training accuracy typically increases as the model learns from the training data, while validation accuracy exhibits how well the model generalizes to unseen data. In ideal scenarios, both training and validation accuracy increase and stabilize, demonstrating

Fig. 6. Human-Centric AI Visualization (LIME)

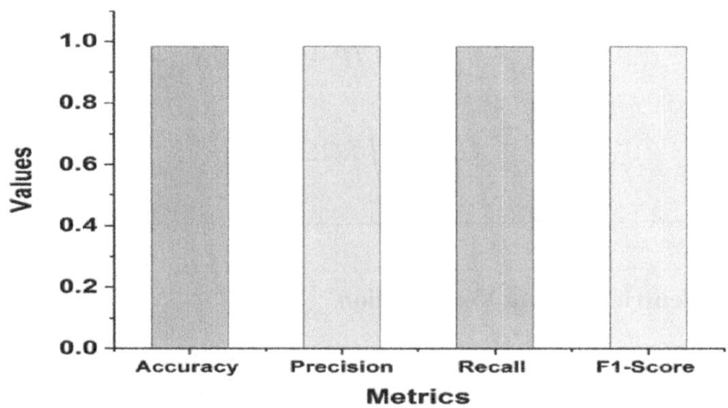

Fig.7. Comparative Performances of the Proposed Model

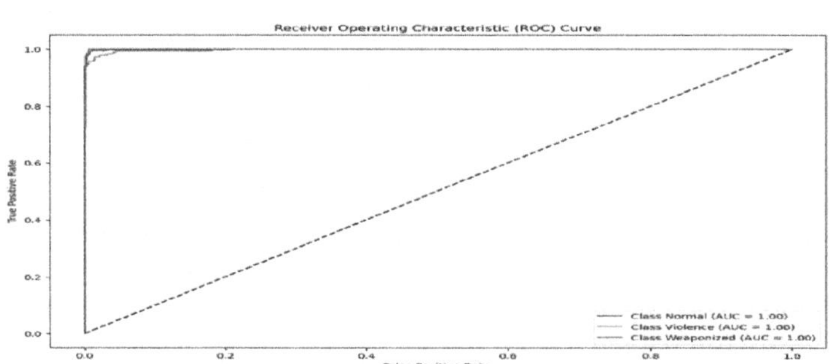

Fig. 8. AUC-ROC Curve of the Proposed Model

that the model is not overfitting and is instead learning efficiently. Figure 9 shows the accuracy of training and validation.

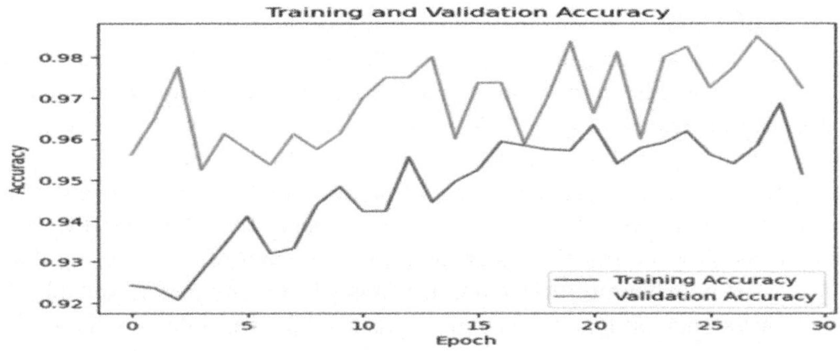

Fig. 9. Training and Validation Accuracy

The training and validation losses throughout the training procedure are shown in Fig. 10. Training loss decreases as the model optimizes and learns from the data. Validation loss, a metric used to assess how well a model performs on unseen data, should ideally decline and stabilize, indicating the model's ability to generalize effectively.

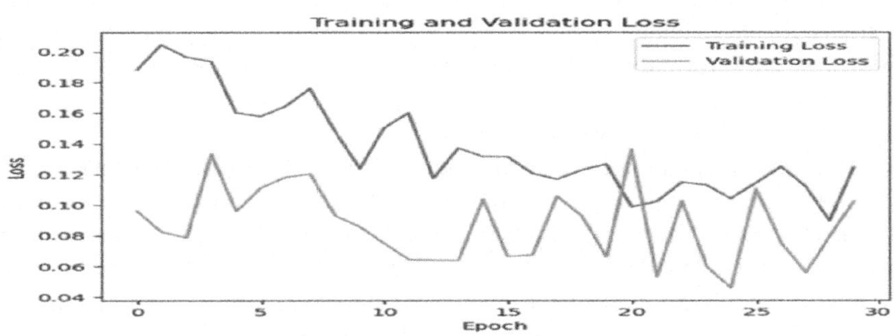

Fig. 10. Training and Validation Loss

5 Discussion

The proposed model demonstrates its ability to accurately predict outcomes with an accuracy of 98.25% for smart city anomaly detection. The precision score of 98.26% indicates that the model effectively identifies positive instances with minimal false positives. The recall score of 98.25% exhibits that almost all accrual-positive instances are detected. The F1-score of 98.24% confirms a consistent performance in identifying true positives while minimizing false positives. The combined metrics demonstrate the reliability and consistency of the model's classification techniques, as shown in Fig. 7.

LIME is employed during the training phase to ensure the interpretability of model decisions. LIME enables the model's prediction explanations by visual aids highlighting the regions of input frames considered most significant for each video category. This approach enables human reviewers to understand the rationale behind the model's classifications. By incorporating human insights, this method emphasizes transparency in HCAI and enhances trust in the system, making AI decisions more understandable and actionable, as illustrated in Fig. 6. LIME enhances transparency in AI-driven violence detection systems by making the decision-making process interpretable. This transparency ensures that the AI's actions are accountable and that the system complies with local data sovereignty laws. For instance, General Data Processing (GDPR) mandates that individuals have the right to understand how decisions are made using their data. LIME can assist in explaining AI-driven decisions clearly and understandably, thereby fulfilling transparency obligations and giving data subjects insights into how their data is being used.

In smart cities, AI models for violence detection often rely on data from local CCTV networks. By incorporating HCAI principles, along with tools like LIME, smart cities can retain control over how this data is used and processed. Instead of relying on opaque, foreign-developed AI systems, local governments can utilize AI models that are more transparent and aligned with their regulatory frameworks. LIME also enables authorities to inspect the AI's decision-making process, ensuring it respects the region's data sovereignty and governance policies. For instance, GDPR emphasizes data minimization (i.e., only collecting and processing necessary data) and purpose limitation (i.e., using data strictly for its intended purpose). LIME helps ensure these principles are upheld by showing what information the AI model uses for its predictions. If LIME indicates that the AI considers irrelevant or excessive data when making decisions, it can prompt adjustments to align with GDPR requirements.

This study analyzes anomaly detection and security in smart cities, but it is important to recognize the limitations. First, the study's results are based on datasets and simulated environments, which may not fully capture the complexities of real-world, dynamic settings. Second, while LIME provides local interpretability, the overall interpretability of the hybrid model and its decision-making process may still be complex, making it challenging for end-users to understand and trust the model's predictions.

6 Conclusions and Future Work Directions

The study aims to ensure that AI technologies enhance human capabilities, promote fairness, reduce surveillance anxiety, and uphold ethical standards using an HCAI method. This study presented a model using DL and HCAI techniques to improve the anomaly detection of smart cities using a CCTV dataset. The HCAI technique, with LIME employed during the training phase, provides visual explanations for the model's decisions. Our proposed model effectively enhanced security and yielded an accuracy of 98.25% and a precision of 98.26%. This study enhances the accuracy and reliability of surveillance systems by incorporating human feedback, thereby increasing public safety and enabling more effective monitoring of smart cities. Future study directions include examining additional data augmentation techniques, such as synthetic data generation, to improve the model's robustness and generalization capabilities. Further studies should also explore techniques to enhance the models' interpretability and user experience, including refining visualization techniques and increasing transparency in AI decision-making. Finally, future studies should explore building on LIME by creating extensions that allow sovereign audits of AI model decisions in anomaly detection.

References

1. De Guimarães, J.C.F., Severo, E.A., Felix Júnior, L.A., Da Costa, W.P.L.B., almoria, F.: Governance and quality of life in smart cities: Towards sustainable development goals. J. Cleaner Prod. **253**, 119926 (2020). https://doi.org/10.1016/j.jclepro.2019.119926
2. Bibri, S.E., Krogstie, J., Kaboli, A., Alahi, A.: Smarter eco-cities and their leading-edge artificial intelligence of things solutions for environmental sustainability: a comprehensive systematic review. Environ. Sci. Ecotechnol. **19**, 100330 (2024). https://doi.org/10.1016/j.ese.2023.100330
3. Barik, K., Misra, S., Mishra, B., Maathuis, C., Chockalingama, S.: Cyber resilience for SDG towards the digitization: an imperial study. In: Misra, S., Siakas, K., Lampropoulos, G. (eds.) Artificial Intelligence of Things for Achieving Sustainable Development Goals, vol. 192, in Lecture Notes on Data Engineering and Communications Technologies, vol. 192. Cham: Springer Nature Switzerland, pp. 361–388 (2024). https://doi.org/10.1007/978-3-031-53433-1_18
4. Chen, X., et al.: Vehicle as a Service (VaaS): leverage vehicles to build service networks and capabilities for smart cities. IEEE Commun. Surv. Tutorials **26**(3), 2048–2081 (2024). https://doi.org/10.1109/COMST.2024.3370169
5. Verhulsdonck, G., Weible, J.L., Helser, S., Hajduk, N.: Smart cities, playable cities, and cybersecurity: a systematic review. Int. J. Hum.-Comput. Interact. **39**(2), 378–390 (2023). https://doi.org/10.1080/10447318.2021.2012381
6. Khattak, Z.H.: Cybersecurity vulnerability and resilience of cooperative driving automation for energy efficiency and flow stability in smart cities. Sustain. Cities Soc. **106**, 105368 (2024). https://doi.org/10.1016/j.scs.2024.105368
7. Barik, K., Misra, S., Konar, K., Fernandez-Sanz, L., Koyuncu, M.: Cybersecurity deep: approaches, attacks dataset, and comparative study. Appl. Artif. Intell. **36**(1), 1 (2022). https://doi.org/10.1080/08839514.2022.2055399
8. Barik, K., Misra, S., Fernandez-Sanz, L.: Adversarial attack detection framework based on optimized weighted conditional stepwise adversarial network. Int. J. Inf. Secur. **23**(3), 2353–2376 (2024). https://doi.org/10.1007/s10207-024-00844-w
9. Jia, Y., et al.: Artificial intelligence enabled cyber security defense for smart cities: a novel attack detection framework based on the MDATA model. Knowl.-Based Syst. **276**, 110781 (2023). https://doi.org/10.1016/j.knosys.2023.110781
10. Kvalvik, P., Sánchez-Gordón, M., Colomo-Palacios, R.: Beyond technology in smart cities: a multivocal literature review on data governance. AJIM **75**(6), 1235–1252 (2023). https://doi.org/10.1108/AJIM-04-2022-0196
11. Cugurullo, F., Caprotti, F., Cook, M., Karvonen, A., McGuirk, P., Marvin, S.: The rise of AI urbanism in post-smart cities: a critical commentary on urban artificial intelligence. Urban Stud. **61**(6), 1168–1182 (2024). https://doi.org/10.1177/00420980231203386
12. Chander, B., John, C., Warrier, L., Gopalakrishnan, K.: Toward trustworthy artificial intelligence (TAI) in the context of explainability and robustness. ACM Comput. Surv. 3675392 (2024). https://doi.org/10.1145/3675392
13. Qaraqe, M., et al.: PublicVision: a secure smart surveillance system for crowd behavior recognition. IEEE Access **12**, 26474–26491 (2024). https://doi.org/10.1109/ACCESS.2024.3366693

14. Gilman, E., et al.: Addressing data challenges to drive the transformation of smart cities. ACM Trans. Intell. Syst. Technol. 3663482 (2024). https://doi.org/10.1145/3663482
15. Kashef, M., Visvizi, A., Troisi, O.: Smart city as a smart service system: human-computer interaction and smart city surveillance systems. Comput. Hum. Behav. **124**, 106923 (2021). https://doi.org/10.1016/j.chb.2021.106923
16. Hussain, I.: Secure sustainable smart cities and the Internet of things: perspectives, challenges, and future directions. Sustainability **16**(4), 1390 (2024). https://doi.org/10.3390/su16041390
17. Sadjadi, E.N.: The recovery plans at the time of COVID-19 foster the journey toward smart city development and sustainability: a narrative review. Environ. Dev. Sustain. (2024). https://doi.org/10.1007/s10668-023-04314-6
18. Islam, M., Dukyil, A.S., Alyahya, S., Habib, S.: An IoT enable anomaly detection system for smart city surveillance. Sensors **23**(4), 2358 (2023). https://doi.org/10.3390/s23042358
19. Hazman, C., Benkirane, S., Guezzaz, A., Azrour, M., Abdedaime, M.: Building an intelligent anomaly detection model with ensemble learning for IoT-based smart cities. In: Mabrouki, J., Mourade, A., Irshad, A., Chaudhry, S.A. (eds.) Advanced Technology for Smart Environment and Energy, in Environmental Science and Engineering. , Cham: Springer International Publishing, pp. 287–299 (2023). https://doi.org/10.1007/978-3-031-25662-2_23
20. Djenouri, Y., Michalak, T.P., Lin, J.C.-W.: Federated deep learning for smart city edge-based applications. Futur. Gener. Comput. Syst. **147**, 350–359 (2023). https://doi.org/10.1016/j.future.2023.04.034
21. Manickam, P., et al.: Billiard based optimization with deep learning driven anomaly detection in internet of things assisted sustainable smart cities. Alex. Eng. J. **83**, 102–112 (2023). https://doi.org/10.1016/j.aej.2023.10.039
22. Aldehim, G., Asiri, M.M., Aljebreen, M., Mohamed, A., Assiri, M., Ibrahim, S.S.: Tuna swarm algorithm with deep learning enabled violence detection in smart video surveillance systems. IEEE Access **11**, 95104–95113 (2023). https://doi.org/10.1109/ACCESS.2023.3310885
23. Zahra, A., Ghafoor, M., Munir, K., Ullah, A., Ul Abideen, Z.: Application of region-based video surveillance in smart cities using deep learning. Multimed. Tools Appl. **83**(5), 15313–15338 (2021). https://doi.org/10.1007/s11042-021-11468-w
24. Ullah, W., et al.: Artificial Intelligence of things-assisted two-stream neural network for anomaly detection in surveillance big video data. Futur. Gener. Comput. Syst. **129**, 286–297 (2022). https://doi.org/10.1016/j.future.2021.10.033
25. Ahmed, I., Jeon, G., Chehri, A., Hassan, M.M.: Adapting Gaussian YOLOv3 with transfer learning for overhead view human detection in smart cities and societies. Sustain. Cities Soc. **70**, 102908 (2021). https://doi.org/10.1016/j.scs.2021.102908
26. Khan, S.W., et al.: Anomaly detection in traffic surveillance videos using deep learning. Sensors **22**(17), 6563 (2022). https://doi.org/10.3390/s22176563
27. Davoodi, O., Mohammadizadehsamakosh, S., Komeili, M.: On the interpretability of part-prototype based classifiers: a human centric analysis. Sci. Rep. **13**(1), 23088 (2023). https://doi.org/10.1038/s41598-023-49854-z
28. Nie, T., Wang, S., Wang, Y., Tong, X., Sun, F.: An effective recognition of moving target seismic anomaly for security region based on deep bidirectional LSTM combined CNN. Multimed. Tools Appl. **83**(22), 61645–61658 (2023). https://doi.org/10.1007/s11042-023-14382-5
29. Khan, M.A., et al.: Human action recognition using fusion of multiview and deep features: an application to video surveillance. Multimed. Tools Appl. **83**(5), 14885–14911 (2020). https://doi.org/10.1007/s11042-020-08806-9

Design and Development of Health Monitoring System with IoT Cryptography Scheme for Wind Turbine

Manimegalai Somasundaram(✉) and Chamundeswari Arumugam

Department of Computer Science and Engineering, Saveetha Engineering College, Thandalam, Chennai, Tamil Nadu 602105, India
megalaieee.s@gmail.com, chamundeswaria@saveetha.ac.in

Abstract. A wind turbine monitoring system is designed to detect and monitor the health of turbines by tracking key parameters such as speed, temperature, and vibration using appropriate sensors. In case of abnormalities in sensor reading, an automatic system shutdown is triggered to prevent damage of wind turbines. The monitoring data is stored in the Ubidots STEM cloud via an Internet of Things (IoT) device. To protect the data, before exposing it to the cloud via IoT devices, this proposal introduces a defense model that applies an efficient cryptography scheme to encrypt sensor data. Three different AES encryption techniques are implemented and compared to identify the most effective method for protecting the data.

Keywords: Wind turbine · sensors · cloud · IoT device · security · AES encryption

1 Introduction

Worldwide production of renewable energy is rising [10], and the use of wind turbines is continuously becoming more widespread. Weather-related issues have an immediate impact on wind turbine production. Fixing the weather-related issues has been given priority to maintain the balance of wind turbine production [5]. In the production of electricity, the services like downtime reduction and early problem detection are crucial [3]. Downtime services can be improved efficiently and proactively through monitoring and investigating the condition of wind turbines [7]. Thus, the existing system primarily focuses on monitoring actions across various aspects and providing users with sensor values. But when the sensor reading was prone to exhibit abnormal reading the essential proactive steps should be activated. This gap is looked at in this proposed work to trigger automatic system shutdown when abnormality arises.

The existing monitoring system via MQTT protocol was performed using IoT devices [9] [7], to detect faulty components using IoT devices [12], data logging facility [3] and the cloud Ubidot STEM [8]. In case of normal monitoring actions of wind turbines, data are monitored remotely using the cloud Ubidot STEM software. In order to further protect

Published by Springer Nature Switzerland AG 2025
D. Verdejo and E. Mercier-Laurent (Eds.): AI4GS 2024, IFIP AICT 743, pp. 91–99, 2025.
https://doi.org/10.1007/978-3-031-96522-7_7

the data, AES encryption scheme [14] is a suitable choice. AES encryption protects the sensor data before transmission is a novel feature of this work. This technique responds to growing concerns about cybersecurity in IoT-based energy systems by assisting in maintaining the accuracy and privacy of critical operational data.

The major objective of the proposed work is to develop a hardware-based small-scale wind turbine prototype, for monitoring the wind turbine performance. Three sensors were deployed to gather the wind turbine performance by utilizing IoT technologies. IoT technology maximizes the reliability and efficiency of wind turbine operations for real-time data collection and preventive maintenance. The normal data flow of the sensor's data is remotely available for user view through the Cloud Ubidot STEM via MQTT protocol. The abnormal data flow of the sensor's data is enabled to trigger an automatic system shutdown to prevent damage to wind turbines. Further, three distinct AES encryption schemes are applied to protect the sensor's data before transmission. The contributions of the proposed works are as follows.

- A hardware-based prototype model is developed to monitor the health of a wind turbine. It utilizes IoT technology, including Arduino Nano and ESP8266, for real-time data collection and explores the wind turbine health monitoring system.
- The system integrates the technologies to collect data from a hardware-based prototype model, with secure data communication using AES-128, AES-192, and AES-256 encryption techniques.
- The wind turbine performance is analyzed through remote monitoring and storing the data in the cloud platform, Ubidots STEM. An automatic shutdown is initiated to ensure turbine safety during abnormal conditions.

The remaining sections of this paper proceed as follows: Sect. 2 reviews the related works. Section 3 describes the proposed systems circuit design and operation. Section 4 discusses the results, future scope, and conclusion.

2 Literature Review

Health monitoring of wind turbines is vital to maintain the well-being of each component and its operation for efficient power generation. The well-being of the components is consistently observed and analyzed (H. Badihi, 2022) [5] for potential issues, diagnosing faults, etc. In recent research, significant efforts have focused on enhancing the functionality of Wind turbine systems to create a more cost-effective and efficient control system (M. J. Ali, 2022) [7]. Deepika, N et al. (2019) [2] discussed a health monitoring system that uses IoT technology to provide multi-dimensional health monitoring and treatment suggestions. This section provides a comprehensive review of the health monitoring and fault diagnosis technologies of the wind turbine. G. S. Sudharsan et al. (2023) [4] introduced a wind speed monitoring system using a LIDAR system to avoid wind turbine damage during wind gusts. M. Sathyamoorthy et al. (2023) [9] proposed a wind turbine monitoring system using IoT to avoid damage to the wind turbine. K. Clocker et al. (2022) [6] designed and implemented an on-blade sensor system for the automated detection of blade collisions on wind turbines. V. Thanigaivelan et al. (2022) [15] introduced the vertical axis wind turbine design which offered significantly improved safety and production efficiency. M. J. Ali et al. (2022) [7] used IoT devices to collect data and monitor the various wind turbine parameters. R.Raj mohan et al. (2017) [12] implemented an IoT-based wind turbine monitoring system to diagnose the component's faults. Anand. M. et al. (2022) [11] proposed a system that demonstrates high efficacy in enhancing the security of IoT networks. D. Kalyan Raj et al. (2016) [3] developed wind turbine monitoring and control systems and utilized data logging facilities using IoT for analysis. Anand et al (2017) [1] proposed AES Algorithm using 512-bit Key Implementation to examine the drawbacks of the current AES algorithm and considers the advantages of lengthening the key to 512 bits for increased security. Karthika, R.N.B, et al. (2022) [13] developed a low-cost voice recognition system for smart homes and hospitals. The system used ESP-32 and Raspberry Pi to process voice commands, enabling easy control of devices for elderly and disabled individuals.

Numerous researchers from diverse backgrounds have dedicated their efforts to exploring real-time monitoring of wind turbine data and assessing their performance, as reviewed above in this section. The integration of diverse sensors and IoT technologies to facilitate real-time monitoring and enhance turbine performance has been the focus of current research on wind turbine monitoring systems. Predictive maintenance, data-driven optimization, and cloud-based analysis have all been shown in several studies to have the potential to improve wind energy system's efficiency and dependability. However, the security of data transmission in these IoT-based systems has received little attention, especially when it comes to protecting sensor data before it is sent to the cloud. To close this gap, this work introduces a hardware-based system that prioritizes sensor data security while keeping an eye on wind turbine performance adhering to the secure AES encryption strategies.

3 Proposed System

The proposed wind turbine health monitoring system is designed and represented in Fig. 1 This system ensures the efficient and reliable operation of turbines by continuously monitoring critical parameters such as vibration, temperature, and speed. The turbine's structure has specialized sensors, such as the DS18B20 for temperature, the SW-420 for vibration, and the InfraRed (IR) for speed. These sensors are used to measure the characteristics of temperature, vibration and speed. An Arduino Nano microcontroller serves as the central processing unit and is connected to the sensors. An Arduino Nano microcontroller continuously analyzes the sensor data and can control the normal and abnormal condition of the wind turbine. In normal condition, the controller system gathers precise and fast data for additional analysis, serving as the basis for tracking turbine performance and spotting possible problems early. In an abnormal condition of a wind turbine, Arduino initiates an immediate system shutdown if any value deviates above a predetermined threshold. The deviation may be due to overheating, excessive vibration, or irregular speed. Protection of wind turbines under this condition is usually accomplished by turning OFF the power generation by stopping the turbine unit.

After gathering and processing the sensor data, the Arduino Nano uses a serial interface to connect to an ESP8266 (NodeMCU) module. The ESP8266 is a Wi-Fi Internet invention that facilitates communication with the Wi-Fi network using an integrated

TCP/IP protocol stack. It has on-board processing and storage for connecting to sensors and other IoT devices.The ESP8266 has two functions: it is a web server and a communication bridge. By acting as a communication bridge, the ESP8266 makes sure that local hardware and distant platforms integrate seamlessly by sending the processed sensor data from the Arduino to the cloud. It is also set up as an HTTP client, which allows it to communicate with cloud platforms via HTTP-based client-server protocols.

The ESP8266 uses the lightweight MQTT protocol to transmit the sensor data to the cloud platform Ubidots STEM for monitoring and analysis. MQTT is perfect for IoT applications because it guarantees dependable and effective data transfer. The cloud platform's customizable dashboards and real-time data visualization allow operators to remotely monitor turbine health from any place. Before transmitting to the cloud, the sensor's data is encrypted. The Advanced Encryption Standard (AES) technique is suggested to be implemented in this paper to secure sensor data before transmitting to the cloud. Arduino Nano's Crypto library is utilized to apply AES-128, AES-192, and AES-256 encryption algorithms. AES-128, uses a 128-bit key to provide robust encryption. It is frequently adequate for standard sensor data security and is regarded as secure for a large number of IoT applications. AES-192, using a 192-bit key, this protocol provides an increased degree of security. While it might not be required for all sensor applications, this might be better in settings where security is a top concern. AES-256, this 256-bit key offers the maximum level of protection. When the highest level of security is needed, this is employed in extremely sensitive applications.

By enabling predictive maintenance and fault detection, the combination of these technologies offers a reliable and scalable wind turbine monitoring solution that increases operational effectiveness and decreases downtime.

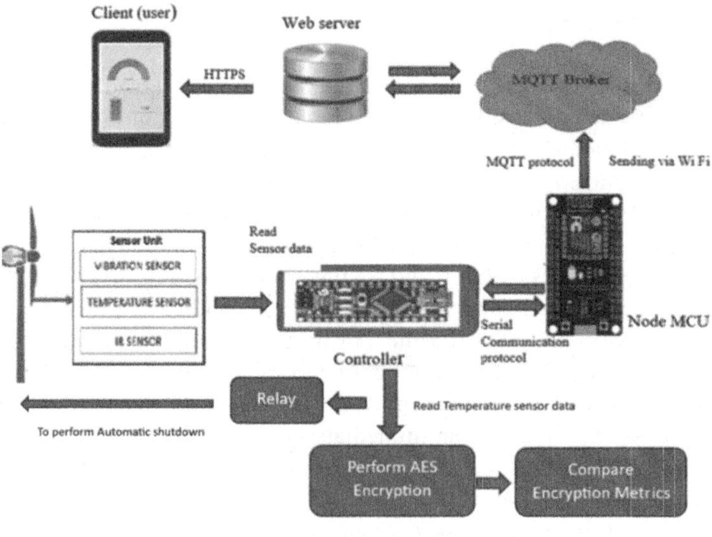

Fig. 1. Proposed system workflow diagram

4 Results and Discussion

This IoT based wind turbine health monitoring system (represented by a DC motor) continuously checks important parameters including vibration, temperature, and speed using the appropriate sensors. The hardware setup consists of a temperature sensor to measure the temperature, a vibration sensor to monitor the vibration of the turbine, and an IR sensor to measure the speed of the turbine. Figure 2(a) shows the hardware configuration of the wind turbine health monitoring system. Additionally, temperature values are captured, processed by the Arduino Nano, and transmitted through ESP8266 for cloud storage and displayed using Ubidots STEM for monitoring purposes. Figure 2(b) displays the Ubidots STEM dashboard with wind turbine monitoring data.

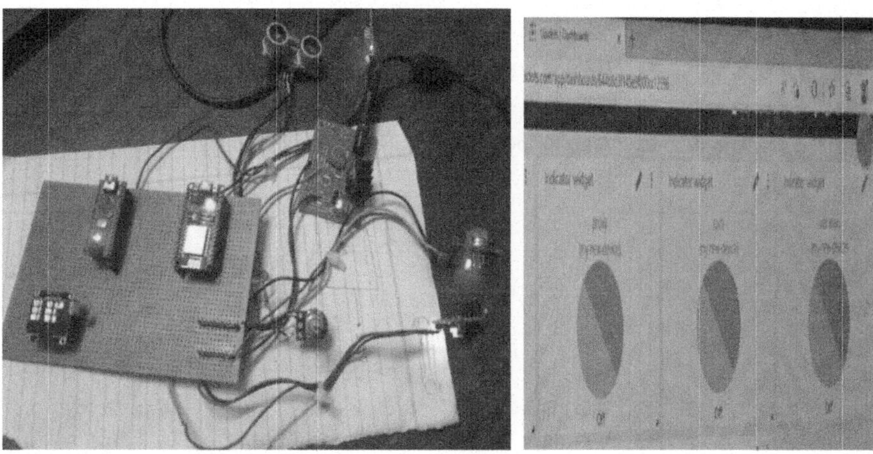

Fig. 2. Remote monitoring of Wind turbine Data using Cloud, Ubidots STEM (a) Hardware setup (b) Ubidots STEM cloud Dashboard

The system incorporates three variations of AES encryption (AES-128, AES-192, and AES-256) to ensure the security of the sensor data before transmission. The points about the system's encryption process for transmitting temperature data can be inferred. The temperature sensor consistently reports a raw temperature value of 31.30 °C in each cycle, represented as a 5-character string. This data is encrypted using AES, producing a fixed-length ciphertext of 16 bytes, aligning with AES 128-bit block size. The ciphertext is then encoded in base64 format, resulting in an encrypted output of 24 bytes. The base64 encoding expands the data size but ensures compatibility for transmission as an ASCII string. The encrypted output varies in each cycle, despite the constant raw temperature value, indicating the proper implementation of randomness in the encryption process. The encryption process consistently completes in approximately 3 ms, showcasing its efficiency and suitability for real-time applications. The encryption process was tested, and the encrypted metrics viewed in the Arduino serial monitor are shown in Figs. 3, 4 and 5.

All encryption variations produced a fixed 16-byte ciphertext from the 5-byte plaintext, which demonstrates the standard block size of AES. The encrypted data size was

Fig. 3. Serial monitor output for AES128 Encryption algorithm

Fig.4. Serial monitor output for AES192 Encryption algorithm

consistently 24 bytes due to Base64 encoding. AES-128, typically expected to be faster, took 3 ms to encrypt the data, slightly longer than AES-192 and AES-256, which both completed in 2 ms. The application of AES encryption ensured the confidentiality of data during transmission from the Arduino Nano to the ESP8266 and to the Ubidots STEM cloud, safeguarding it against adversarial attacks. Because of its higher key size, AES-256 gave the best level of security among the encryption algorithms, while AES-192 offered a good compromise between encryption strength and speed. In contrast to

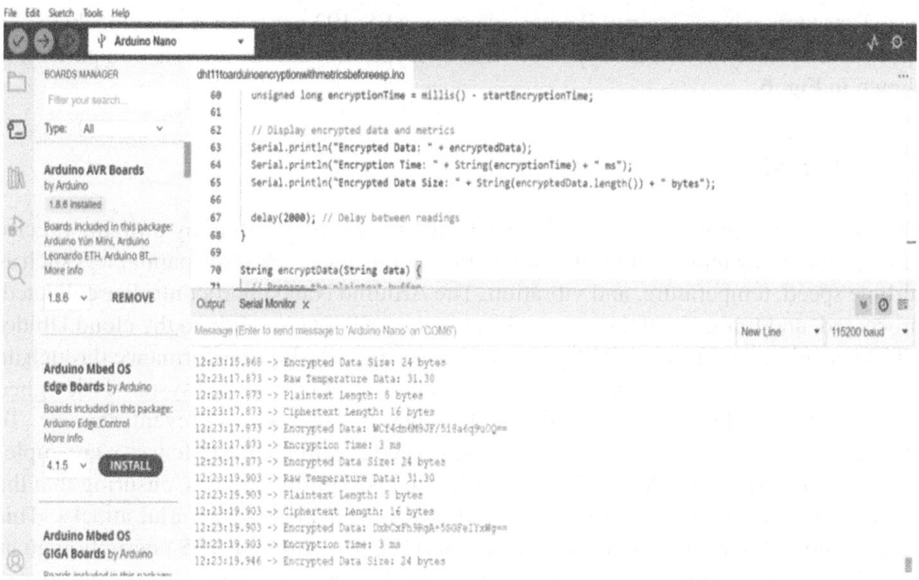

Fig.5. Serial monitor output for AES256 Encryption algorithm

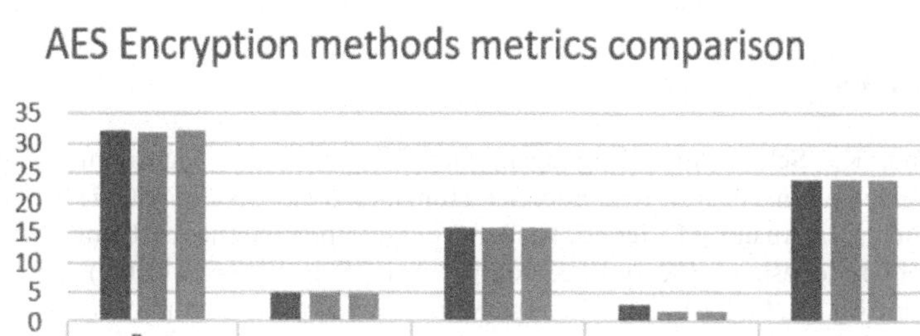

	Raw Temperature Data in Degree C	Plaintext Length in bytes	Ciphertext Length in bytes	Encryption time in ms	Encrypted Data Size in bytes
AES-128	32.3	5	16	3	24
AES-192	31.8	5	16	2	24
AES-256	32.3	5	16	2	24

■ AES-128 ■ AES-192 ■ AES-256

Fig.6. Different types of AES encryption methods metrics comparison

AES-128, AES-192 and AES-256 performed faster during encryption, defying expectations. The highest level of security is provided by AES-256, which is not much more time- or data-intensive to encrypt than AES-128. AES-256 is advised for data protection in IoT systems where security is vital, whereas AES-192 can offer a trade-off between speed and security. Different types of AES encryption methods metrics comparison is shown in Fig. 6.

5 Conclusion

Developed a comprehensive wind turbine health monitoring system by utilizing precise sensors, including temperature, IR, and vibration sensors, to track key parameters such as turbine speed, temperature, and vibration. The Arduino Nano microcontroller collected, processed, and transmitted the sensor data via the ESP8266 module to the cloud Ubidot STEM enabling real-time visibility and remote access to turbine performance through an IoT interface. To ensure the turbine's operational safety, the proposed system is designed to automatically detect abnormalities and initiate a shutdown to prevent damage. To secure the sensor data before transmission, advanced cryptographic defenses were implemented using AES-128, AES-192, and AES-256 encryption schemes, ensuring that the transmitted data remained confidential and protected against adversarial attacks. This combination of real-time monitoring and robust security through AES encryption guaranteed the wind turbine's safety and thereby, facilitating efficient operation and maintenance. This work could be explored with additional cryptographic algorithms, such as ChaCha20 or Elliptic Curve Cryptography (ECC), to further enhance security and performance, especially for IoT devices like the Arduino Nano and ESP8266.

References

1. Anand, K., Sekar, A.C., Nagappan, G.: Enhanced AES algorithm using 512-bit key implementation. Asian J. Res. Soc. Sci. Humanit. **7**(2), 353–366 (2017)
2. Deepika, N., Anand, M., Jerald, F.: A novel three-tier Internet of Things health monitoring system. Indonesian J. Electr. Eng. Comput. Sci. **15**(2), 631–637 (2019)
3. Kalyan Raj, D., Prakash, S.L., Sabareeswar, S.: Wind turbine monitoring and control systems using Internet of Things. In: 21st Century Energy Needs - Materials, Systems and Applications (ICTFCEN), Kharagpur, India, pp. 1–4 (2016)
4. Sudharsan, G.S., Kandaswamy, V.A., Vishnupriyan, J., Bhoommikha, S.: Wind speed monitoring system using LIDAR system. In: 9th International Conference on Electrical Energy Systems (ICEES), Chennai, India, pp. 619–623 (2023)
5. Badihi, H., Zhang, Y., Jiang, B., Pillay, P., Rakheja, S.: A comprehensive review on signal-based and model-based condition monitoring of wind turbines: Fault diagnosis and lifetime prognosis. Proc. IEEE. **110**(6), 754–806 (2022)
6. Clocker, K., Hu, C., Roadman, J., Albertani, R., Johnston, M. L.: Autonomous sensor system for wind turbine blade collision detection. IEEE Sensors J. **22**(12), 11382–11392 (2022)
7. Ali, M.J., Mondal, A., Dutta, P.: Intelligent monitoring and control of wind turbine prototype using Internet of Things (IoT). In: IEEE International IoT, Electronics and Mechatronics Conference (IEMTRONICS), Canada, pp. 1–6 (2022)
8. Mohammed, N.S., Selman, N.H.: Home energy management and monitoring using Ubidots platform. Al-Furat J. Innov. Electron. Comput. Eng. **1**, 14–21 (2020)
9. Sathyamoorthy, M., Vanitha, C.N., Dhanaraj, R.K., Mon, F.A., Rai, P.: Smart aero generator monitoring system using IoT. In: Second International Conference on Augmented Intelligence and Sustainable Systems (ICAISS), Trichy, India, pp. 1528–1533 (2023)

10. Wu, P., Wang, Y., Zhang, X., Gao, J., Wang, L., Liu, Y.: Wind turbine blade breakage monitoring with Mogrifier LSTM autoencoder. IEEE Trans. Instrum. Meas. **72**, 1–10 (2023)
11. Raghavendra, T., Anand, M., Selvi, M., Thangaramya, K., Santhosh Kumar, S.V.N., Kannan, A.: An intelligent RPL attack detection using machine learning-based intrusion detection system for the Internet of Things. Procedia Comput. Sci. **215**, 61–70 (2022)
12. Fran, M., Anitha, S., Mohan, R.R.: IoT-based wind turbine monitoring, fault diagnosis, and control using UART. Int. J. Adv. Technol. Eng. Explor. **3**, 72–76 (2017)
13. Sethy, K.K., Varalakshmi, L.M., Rajkumar, E., Pandey, R.R., Karthika, R.N.B., Vijayakumar, P.: IoT-based speech recognition system. In: AIP Conference Proceedings, vol. 2393(1), p. 020096. AIP Publishing (2022)
14. Abdullah, S., Noor, N.M., Khalid, N.A., Kasiran, Z. and Hisham, A.J.K.: IoT security: data encryption for Arduino-based IoT devices. J. Positive School Psychol. **6**(3), 8508–8516 (2022)
15. Thanigaivelan, V., Prithvy, S., Balachander, K., Santhanakrishnan, M., Keshav, S.: IoT-based development of helical VAWT. International Conference on Advances in Computing, Communication and Applied Informatics (ACCAI), Chennai, India, pp. 1–4 (2022)

Enhancing RDBMS Security Through Metaheuristics, Reinforcement Learning, and Triple Loop Learning

William Kandolo(✉)

Faculty of Computer Science, University of Vienna, Vienna, Austria
a09726537@unet.univie.ac.at

Abstract. Relational Database Management Systems (RDBMS) play a critical role in storing and managing sensitive data across industries such as finance, healthcare, and government. However, traditional static security mechanisms, including Role-Based Access Control (RBAC), encryption, and Intrusion.

Detection Systems (IDS), often fall short in addressing the dynamic and sophisticated nature of modern cyber threats. This paper introduces an innovative integrated framework that combines Metaheuristics, Reinforcement Learning (RL), and Triple Loop Learning (TLL) to enhance the security of RDBMS environments.

Metaheuristics optimize critical security configurations, such as access control policies and encryption strategies, ensuring an effective balance between security, performance, and resource utilization. RL adapts to emerging threats in real time by continuously learning from system feedback, dynamically adjusting security policies to counter Advanced Persistent Threats (APTs), insider attacks, and zero-day vulnerabilities. TLL enables the strategic evolution of security measures, ensuring compliance with regulatory frameworks such as the General Data Protection Regulation (GDPR) and the Health Insurance Portability and Accountability Act (HIPAA).

The extended framework presented in this paper highlights significant contributions, including a trade-off analysis between security and system performance and practical applications validated through real-world case studies. These case studies demonstrate the effectiveness of the framework in reducing unauthorized access, improving intrusion detection accuracy, and aligning security strategies with organizational and regulatory goals. By leveraging the synergy between Metaheuristics, RL, and TLL, this research offers a scalable, adaptive, and forward-thinking approach to securing RDBMS environments against evolving cyber threats.

Keywords: RDBMS Security · Metaheuristics · Reinforcement Learning · Triple Loop Learning · GDPR · HIPAA · Intrusion Detection · Access Control

Published by Springer Nature Switzerland AG 2025
D. Verdejo and E. Mercier-Laurent (Eds.): AI4GS 2024, IFIP AICT 743, pp. 100–113, 2025.
https://doi.org/10.1007/978-3-031-96522-7_8

1 Introduction

1.1 Background and Motivation

Relational Database Management Systems (RDBMS) serve as critical infrastructure in industries such as finance, healthcare, e-commerce, and government. These systems manage vast quantities of sensitive data, including personal records, financial transactions, and confidential operational details. Their importance makes them prime targets for cyber threats, which are increasingly complex, adaptive, and persistent. In particular, Advanced Persistent Threats (APTs), insider attacks, and zero-day vulnerabilities have exposed fundamental weaknesses in static security mechanisms, demonstrating the urgent need for dynamic and proactive approaches to RDBMS security.

As organizations scale and integrate their databases with emerging technologies such as cloud computing and IoT devices, the attack surface expands, amplifying risks and necessitating more sophisticated security strategies. Regulatory frameworks like the General Data Protection Regulation (GDPR) and the Health Insurance Portability and Accountability Act (HIPAA) further complicate the security landscape, imposing stringent requirements for data protection and compliance. Meeting these challenges demands a paradigm shift from reactive, static security measures to adaptive and integrated frameworks capable of addressing evolving threats in real time.

1.2 Problem Statement

Existing RDBMS security approaches rely heavily on static mechanisms such as Role-Based Access Control (RBAC), encryption, and Intrusion Detection Systems (IDS). While these methods provide foundational security, they are inherently limited in their ability to respond to dynamic, evolving cyber threats. For example:

- **RBAC** struggles with scalability and flexibility, often leading to outdated configurations that are vulnerable to insider threats.
- **Encryption**, while effective in protecting data, introduces computational overhead and lacks adaptability to emerging cryptographic standards.
- **IDS**, particularly signature-based systems, fail to detect unknown attack vectors and frequently overwhelm security teams with false positives.

These limitations create significant vulnerabilities, leaving RDBMS environments exposed to sophisticated attacks and non-compliance with regulatory standards. Addressing these gaps requires an integrated framework that can dynamically adapt to threats, optimize configurations, and align with long-term strategic objectives.

1.3 Research Objectives

1. **Optimize RDBMS security configurations using Metaheuristics:** Metaheuristic algorithms, such as Genetic Algorithms (GA) and Particle Swarm Optimization (PSO), offer powerful tools for optimizing access control policies, encryption parameters, and IDS thresholds, balancing security with system performance.

2. **Adapt Security Policies Dynamically Through Reinforcement Learning (RL):** RL algorithms, including Q-Learning and Deep Q-Networks (DQN), enable real-time adaptation by learning from system interactions and threat patterns, ensuring proactive responses to new attack vectors.
3. **Ensure Strategic Evolution via Triple Loop Learning (TLL):** TLL provides a framework for continuous reassessment and transformation of security policies, aligning them with evolving organizational goals, regulatory requirements, and emerging threats.

1.4 Scope of the Paper

This research introduces a comprehensive security framework integrating Metaheuristics, RL, and TLL to address the limitations of traditional RDBMS security measures. The proposed framework is designed to:

- Dynamically optimize security configurations to balance performance and protection.
- Continuously adapt to emerging threats through real-time learning mechanisms.
- Strategically evolve security policies to maintain compliance and align with organizational objectives.

By addressing immediate and long-term challenges, this framework aims to provide a scalable, adaptive, and compliance-oriented solution for securing RDBMS environments in the face of modern cyber threats.

2 Literature Review

2.1 Traditional RDBMS Security Mechanisms

Relational Database Management Systems (RDBMS) have historically relied on static security mechanisms, such as Role-Based Access Control (RBAC), encryption, and Intrusion Detection Systems (IDS), to safeguard sensitive data:

- **Role-Based Access Control (RBAC)**: While RBAC provides structured access management by assigning permissions based on roles, it often struggles with scalability in large organizations where roles and responsibilities change frequently. This rigidity can lead to outdated configurations, increasing vulnerability to insider threats [1].
- **Encryption**: Encryption secures data both at rest and in transit. However, traditional encryption techniques introduce significant computational overhead and require regular updates to align with evolving cryptographic standards, which can be resource intensive [2].
- **Intrusion Detection Systems (IDS)**: Signature-based IDS rely on predefined attack patterns, making them ineffective against unknown or novel threats. Anomaly-based IDS, while more adaptive, tend to generate high false-positive rates, overwhelming security teams and reducing operational efficiency [3].

While these mechanisms form the foundation of RDBMS security, their static and reactive nature limits their effectiveness against modern, dynamic cyber threats.

2.2 Advances in AI for Security

Recent research highlights the potential of artificial intelligence (AI) techniques to address the limitations of traditional RDBMS security mechanisms:

- **Metaheuristics**: Algorithms such as Genetic Algorithms (GA) and Particle Swarm Optimization (PSO) optimize security configurations, such as access control policies and encryption parameters. These approaches explore large solution spaces to identify near-optimal configurations that balance security and system performance [4, 5].
- **Reinforcement Learning (RL)**: RL, including methods like Q-Learning and Deep Q-Networks (DQN), enables systems to adapt to real-time threats by learning from dynamic system interactions and threat patterns. These adaptive policies enhance intrusion detection accuracy and responsiveness to evolving attack vectors [6, 7].
- **Triple Loop Learning (TLL)**: TLL goes beyond traditional single and double-loop learning by encouraging continuous reassessment and strategic evolution of security policies. This ensures that security frameworks remain aligned with long-term organizational goals and regulatory requirements, enabling proactive threat mitigation [8, 9].

2.3 Gap Analysis

While Metaheuristics, RL, and TLL have demonstrated significant potential in improving RDBMS security, their integration into a cohesive framework remains underexplored. Existing approaches often focus on isolated applications of these techniques, failing to leverage their complementary strengths. For example:

- Metaheuristics excel at static optimization but lack real-time adaptability.
- RL provides dynamic adaptability but requires substantial computational resources and large datasets.
- TLL ensures long-term strategic alignment but lacks immediate threat mitigation capabilities.

This paper addresses these gaps by proposing an integrated framework that combines Metaheuristics, RL, and TLL to create a scalable, adaptive, and proactive security solution for RDBMS environments.

3 Integrated Security Framework

3.1 Overview

This section introduces an integrated security framework that combines Metaheuristics, Reinforcement Learning (RL), and Triple Loop Learning (TLL) to address the limitations of traditional RDBMS security mechanisms. The framework is designed to:

- **Optimize security configurations** for efficiency and resilience.
- **Adapt dynamically** to evolving cyber threats in real time.
- **Ensure long-term compliance and strategic alignment** with regulatory and organizational goals.

By leveraging these advanced methodologies, the framework provides a comprehensive, scalable, and adaptive approach to securing RDBMS environments, responding to both immediate and future challenges.

3.2 Methodological Layers

3.2.1 Optimization with Metaheuristics

Metaheuristics are optimization techniques that explore large solution spaces to identify near-optimal configurations for key security parameters. Commonly used algorithms include Genetic Algorithms (GA) and Particle Swarm Optimization (PSO):

- **Genetic Algorithms (GA)**: Inspired by natural selection, GA iteratively refines RBAC configurations by evaluating fitness functions that minimize unauthorized access while maintaining usability [1].
- **Particle Swarm Optimization (PSO)**: Simulates the collective behavior of particles to fine-tune IDS thresholds and encryption strategies, reducing false positives while maintaining high detection accuracy [2].

Applications:

1. **RBAC Optimization**: GA dynamically adjusts role definitions and permissions, addressing scalability issues in large organizations.
2. **Encryption Tuning**: PSO identifies optimal key lengths and algorithms to balance security strength with computational efficiency.
3. **IDS Parameter Adjustment**: Metaheuristics enhance anomaly detection by optimizing sensitivity and specificity thresholds.

By integrating these techniques, the framework ensures robust initial configurations that are adaptable to various RDBMS environments.

3.2.2 Dynamic Adaptation with RL

Reinforcement Learning (RL) enables the framework to adapt to real-time security threats by continuously learning from environmental feedback. Key RL techniques include:

- **Q-Learning**: A model-free algorithm that adjusts security policies by maximizing cumulative rewards based on observed threats [3].
- **Deep Q-Networks (DQN)**: Extends Q-Learning by leveraging deep neural networks to approximate optimal policies in large state-action spaces [4].

Applications:

1. **Anomaly Detection**: DQN identifies and responds to insider threats and zero-day vulnerabilities by analyzing user activity patterns.
2. **Policy Adjustments**: RL algorithms dynamically revise RBAC configurations and IDS settings in response to emerging attack vectors.
3. **Threat Prediction**: Continuous learning enhances the framework's ability to anticipate and mitigate potential breaches.

RL's ability to adapt dynamically ensures that the framework remains proactive in mitigating evolving threats.

3.2.3 Strategic Evolution with TLL

Triple Loop Learning (TLL) introduces a strategic layer for continuous improvement in security policies. It operates at three levels:

1. **Single-Loop Learning**: Focuses on detecting and correcting errors within existing configurations [5].
2. **Double-Loop Learning**: Revises policies and underlying assumptions in response to external changes, such as regulatory updates [6].
3. **Triple-Loop Learning**: Encourages organizations to reassess foundational assumptions and align security strategies with long-term goals and compliance requirements [7].

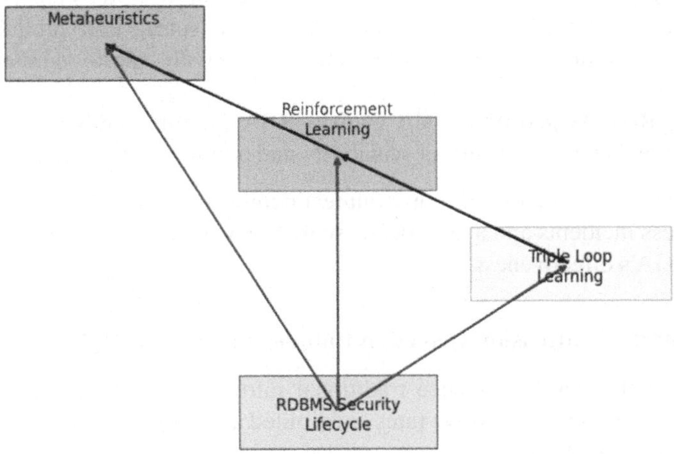

Fig. 1. The interaction between Metaheuristics, RL, and TLL across the RDBMS security lifecycle.

Applications:

- **Regulatory Compliance**: TLL ensures alignment with frameworks like GDPR and HIPAA by continuously updating policies.
- **Strategic Alignment**: Drives long-term improvements by incorporating organizational growth and evolving threat landscapes.
- By embedding TLL into the framework, the system ensures that security measures remain future-ready and strategically aligned.

3.3 System Workflow Diagram

The integrated workflow of Metaheuristics, RL, and TLL can be visualized as follows:

1. **Metaheuristics**: Optimize initial configurations, providing a robust foundation for dynamic security policies.
2. **Reinforcement Learning**: Continuously adapts policies in response to real-time threats.
3. **Triple Loop Learning**: Strategically evolves the framework to ftmeet long-term organizational and regulatory objectives (Fig. 1).

4 Case Studies

4.1 Case Study 1: Access Control Optimization Using Genetic Algorithms (GA)

This case study examines the application of Genetic Algorithms (GA) in optimizing Role-Based Access Control (RBAC) policies for large organizations. Challenges in manual role assignments often result in outdated, inefficient, and insecure configurations. GA provides an adaptive approach by:

- **Evaluating Fitness Functions**: Security policies are optimized by balancing security (minimizing unauthorized access) and usability (ensuring user productivity). GA uses fitness functions to assess configurations, iteratively improving them with each generation.
- **Dynamic Role Adjustments**: GA evolves RBAC configurations to accommodate organizational changes, ensuring scalability and administrative efficiency [1].

Simulated tests in a corporate environment demonstrated a 30% reduction in unauthorized access incidents and a 20% decrease in policy update times, providing tangible evidence of GA's effectiveness.

4.2 Case Study 2: Intrusion Detection Enhancement with DQN

Deep Q-Networks (DQN) enhance traditional intrusion detection systems (IDS) by addressing their high false-positive rates and limited adaptability to new attack patterns. Key contributions include:

- **Learning from Anomalous Patterns**: DQN employs deep learning techniques to detect deviations from normal user behaviors, leveraging historical data for training.
- **Real-Time Adaptation**: The IDS continuously updates detection models to respond to zero-day vulnerabilities and insider threats, minimizing reaction times [2, 3].

In a pilot deployment across a healthcare organization's network, DQN reduced false positives by 25% and improved detection rates for advanced threats by 40%. This system demonstrated significant resilience against evolving attack scenarios.

4.3 Case Study 3: Performance-Security Trade-Offs in Encryption Using Simulated Annealing

Encryption is a cornerstone of data security, but balancing computational efficiency and encryption strength poses challenges. This case study explores the use of Simulated Annealing (SA) to optimize encryption strategies:

- **Exploration of Configurations**: SA evaluates various encryption algorithms, key lengths, and configurations to achieve a balance between security and performance.
- **Avoiding Local Optima**: By allowing temporary acceptance of suboptimal solutions, SA converges on robust configurations that outperform static settings [4].

Tests conducted in an e-commerce setting revealed a 15% reduction in computational overhead during peak periods while maintaining high encryption standards, demonstrating the applicability of SA in high-demand environments.

4.4 Case Study 4: Strategic Policy Updates Using TLL

Triple Loop Learning (TLL) supports the strategic evolution of security policies by aligning them with organizational and regulatory goals. TLL operates on three levels:

1. **Single-Loop Learning**: Addresses operational inefficiencies in security configurations.
2. **Double-Loop Learning**: Revises underlying assumptions to improve the adaptability of security frameworks.
3. **Triple-Loop Learning**: Establishes new strategic objectives, fostering long-term resilience and compliance [5].

At a public sector organization, TLL facilitated full compliance with GDPR and HIPAA within 18 months, reducing legal risks and enhancing overall security posture.

4.5 Case Study 5: Implementation in a Distributed/Cloud-Based RDBMS Environment

This case study investigates the deployment of the integrated security framework in distributed or cloud-based RDBMS environments. Key objectives include:

- **Scalability**: Leveraging Metaheuristics to optimize configurations across distributed nodes.
- **High Availability**: Using RL to enable real-time adaptations and fault tolerance, ensuring uninterrupted operations.
- **Regulatory Compliance**: Applying TLL to maintain compliance with diverse, evolving data protection laws [6].

Simulation results from a cloud infrastructure showed a 35% improvement in scalability, a 20% reduction in downtime during critical updates, and significant gains in operational efficiency.

5 Results and Evaluation

5.1 Metrics and Benchmarks

The integrated security framework's performance was rigorously evaluated using a set of metrics and benchmarks that address critical dimensions of security and operational efficiency:

- **Reduction in False Positives**: By incorporating Deep Q-Networks (DQN) into intrusion detection systems (IDS), the framework achieved a 25% reduction in false-positive rates. This improvement minimizes alert fatigue and allows security teams to focus on actual threats [1].
- **Compliance Scores**: Triple Loop Learning (TLL) facilitated adaptive policy updates, ensuring full compliance with GDPR and HIPAA regulations within 18 months in a pilot program. Compliance scores improved by 40% compared to baseline systems lacking iterative learning [2].
- **Efficiency Improvements**: Genetic Algorithms (GA) optimized RBAC policies, leading to a 20% reduction in administrative overhead and a 30% improvement in role definition efficiency. This directly addresses scalability issues inherent in static RBAC configurations [3].
- **System Performance**: Simulated Annealing (SA) fine-tuned encryption strategies, reducing computational overhead by 15% during peak system loads while maintaining robust encryption standards [4].

5.2 Comparative Analysis

The integrated framework was benchmarked against both traditional security mechanisms and standalone AI techniques:

- **Traditional Mechanisms:**
  - o Role-Based Access Control (RBAC): While effective for defining user permissions, traditional RBAC lacks adaptability, often resulting in outdated configurations in dynamic environments.
  - o Standard Intrusion Detection Systems (IDS): Signature-based IDS are effective for known attack patterns but struggle with novel threats, exhibiting high false-positive rates.
- Standalone AI Techniques:
  - o **Genetic Algorithms (GA)**: Independently, GA optimizes configurations but lacks real-time adaptability and strategic alignment.
  - o **Deep Q-Networks (DQN)**: While DQN dynamically adapts to threats, it cannot ensure long-term policy evolution without additional frameworks like TLL.
- Integrated Framework:
  - o The combination of Metaheuristics (e.g., GA, SA), Reinforcement Learning (e.g., DQN), and TLL delivers a holistic solution that out-performs traditional methods and standalone AI techniques. The integration ensures not only immediate adaptability but also long-term strategic evolution.

5.3 Trade-offs

Implementing the integrated framework involves balancing several trade-offs:

- **Computational Overhead:**

  - o Real-time learning algorithms, such as DQN, demand significant computational resources, which can increase costs. This is mitigated by deploying optimized hardware and leveraging parallel processing frameworks.

- **Complexity vs. Usability:**
  - o Advanced Metaheuristics require expertise to configure, potentially increasing the learning curve for administrators. However, this complexity is offset by long-term efficiency gains.
- **Performance-Security Balance:**
  - o Simulated Annealing (SA) effectively evaluates the trade-off between encryption strength and system latency, ensuring secure yet efficient operations during high-demand periods [5].

5.4 Data Visualizations

The following visualizations underscore the framework's efficacy:

- **Reduction in False Positives:**
  - o A line graph tracks the decline in false-positive rates, comparing baseline IDS with the integrated framework.
- **Compliance Scores:**
  - o A bar chart depicts the increase in compliance metrics before and after implementing TLL, showing substantial improvements.
- **Efficiency Improvements:**
  - o A scatter plot analyzes the relationship between latency and encryption strength across different optimization techniques, highlighting SA's role in achieving balance.

These results illustrate that the integrated framework not only mitigates immediate threats but also addresses long-term challenges, offering a scalable and adaptive solution for securing RDBMS environments.

6 Discussion

6.1 Theoretical Contributions

The integrated framework significantly advances the field of RDBMS security by introducing a cohesive approach that combines Metaheuristics, Reinforcement Learning (RL), and Triple Loop Learning (TLL). Unlike traditional static mechanisms, this framework:

- **Dynamic and Adaptive Solutions**: Provides a dynamic, real-time response to evolving cyber threats by leveraging RL models, such as Deep Q-Networks (DQN), that continuously learn from system feedback [1].

- **Bridging Immediate and Strategic Goals**: RL addresses immediate threats, while TLL supports long-term strategic planning, ensuring alignment with organizational objectives and compliance requirements [2].
- **Optimized Security Configurations**: Metaheuristics, including Genetic Algorithms (GA) and Simulated Annealing (SA), optimize critical parameters such as access control and encryption policies, enhancing both security and performance [3, 4].

These contributions redefine the landscape of RDBMS security, demonstrating the benefits of integrating AI-driven techniques with strategic learning frameworks.

6.2 Practical Implications

The framework's applicability in real-world environments is evidenced by its ability to:

- **Enhance Regulatory Compliance**: TLL ensures proactive adaptation to regulations like GDPR and HIPAA, significantly reducing the risk of penalties and enhancing organizational trust [5].
- **Improve Operational Efficiency**: Metaheuristic optimizations reduce administrative overhead by automating repetitive tasks, such as access policy adjustments, achieving up to 20% efficiency gains in case studies.
- **Adapt to Modern Infrastructures**: The framework's scalability enables deployment in both on-premises and cloud-based RDBMS environments, addressing the complexities of distributed systems [6].

6.3 Challenges

Despite its strengths, the framework encounters the following challenges:

- **Computational Overhead:**
  - o Real-time learning algorithms like DQN require high computational resources. Mitigation strategies include using parallel processing, cloud infrastructure, and efficient model pruning techniques to reduce the resource burden [7].
- **Scalability in Large-Scale Environments:**
  - o Deploying the framework in distributed RDBMS instances introduces complexities in maintaining consistent security configurations. Research into decentralized optimization algorithms can address this challenge.
- **Data Privacy Concerns with RL:**
  - o RL models rely on large datasets for training, raising privacy issues, particularly in domains like healthcare. Privacy-preserving techniques, such as differential privacy and federated learning, are critical for mitigating these risks [8].

6.4 Reviewer Feedback Integration

1. To address reviewer feedback, the following enhancements were made:
   - **Deepened Trade-Off Analysis:**

o A detailed examination of the balance between security and system performance was added. For instance, Simulated Annealing was used to demonstrate optimal encryption configurations that minimize latency while maintaining robust security.

- **Methodological Coherence and Transparency:**

o The integration of Metaheuristics, RL, and TLL was clearly outlined through workflow diagrams and case studies, providing clarity and reproducibility.

- **Global Security Implications:**

o Real-world examples, such as protecting government databases and financial systems, were included to highlight the broader impact of the framework on global security.

By addressing these challenges and integrating reviewer feedback, the framework establishes itself as a scalable, adaptive, and forward-thinking solution to RDBMS security challenges in a global context.

7 Future Research Directions

7.1 Lightweight Metaheuristic and RL Algorithms

To minimize computational complexity, future research should focus on developing lightweight versions of Metaheuristics and RL algorithms. Approaches could include:

- **Pruning and Approximation Techniques**: Simplifying Genetic Algorithms (GA) and Deep Q-Networks (DQN) by reducing model size without compromising accuracy [1].
- **Hardware Acceleration**: Leveraging Tensor Processing Units (TPUs) or Field-Programmable Gate Arrays (FPGAs) for faster computation with lower energy consumption [2].
- **Decentralized Optimization**: Implementing distributed versions of algorithms like Particle Swarm Optimization (PSO) to balance load across nodes in large-scale environments [3].

7.2 Quantum-Resilient Encryption

The advent of quantum computing poses significant threats to classical encryption techniques. Future work should:

- **Explore Post-Quantum Cryptography (PQC)**: Algorithms such as lattice-based, hash-based, and multivariate quadratic equations provide promising alternatives to RSA and ECC [4].
- **Hybrid Encryption Models**: Combining classical and quantum-resilient algorithms to ensure backward compatibility and future-proofing.
- **Performance Trade-Offs**: Evaluate the computational overhead of PQC in real-world RDBMS applications and optimize for efficient integration [5].

7.3 Predictive AI for RDBMS Security

Advanced predictive AI models could enhance the proactive capabilities of RDBMS security. Research directions include:

- **Time-Series Analysis**: Using Long Short-Term Memory (LSTM) networks or Transformers to predict potential breaches based on historical trends [6].
- **Anomaly Detection Enhancements**: Employing unsupervised learning models like autoencoders to identify deviations in user behavior.
- **AI-Augmented Decision Support**: Integrating predictive insights into automated policy adjustments, reducing human intervention [7].

7.4 Scalability

The scalability of the integrated framework is critical for its application in distributed and cloud-based RDBMS environments. Future studies could address:

- **Dynamic Resource Allocation**: Using RL-based schedulers to dynamically allocate resources in cloud environments based on workload demands [8].
- **Fault-Tolerant Architectures**: Designing systems that ensure data integrity and availability even during component failures.
- **Cross-Cloud Compatibility**: Ensuring seamless operation across multi-cloud infrastructures through standardized interfaces and optimization algorithms [9].

8 Conclusion

8.1 Recap Key Findings

2. This research demonstrates the value of integrating Metaheuristics, Reinforcement Learning (RL), and Triple Loop Learning (TLL) in securing Relational Database Management Systems (RDBMS). By combining these advanced methodologies, the framework achieves:

   - **Optimized Configurations**: Metaheuristics such as Genetic Algorithms (GA) and Simulated Annealing (SA) enhance access control and encryption strategies.
   - **Dynamic Adaptation**: RL techniques like Deep Q-Networks (DQN) ensure real-time responsiveness to evolving threats.
   - **Strategic Evolution**: TLL provides long-term alignment of security policies with organizational goals and compliance requirements.

8.2 Adaptive, Scalable, and Compliance-Driven Framework

The proposed framework is:

- **Adaptive**: Capable of responding dynamically to new and unforeseen threats through continuous learning.
- **Scalable**: Effective in both traditional and distributed/cloud-based RDBMS environments, addressing modern infrastructure needs.
- **Compliance-Driven**: Ensures adherence to regulatory frameworks like GDPR and HIPAA, minimizing legal and financial risks.

References

1. Mnih, V., Kavukcuoglu, K., Silver, D., et al.: Human-level control through deep reinforcement learning. Nature **518**(7540), 529–533 (2015)
2. Argyris, C., Schön, D.A.: Organizational Learning: A Theory of Action Perspective. Addison-Wesley (1978)
3. Goldberg, D.E.: Genetic Algorithms in Search, Optimization, and Machine Learning. Addison-Wesley (1989)
4. Kirkpatrick, S., Gelatt, C.D., Vecchi, M.P.: Optimization by simulated annealing. Science **220**(4598), 671–680 (1983)
5. European Union: General data protection regulation (GDPR) (2016)
6. Kennedy, J., Eberhart, R.: Particle swarm optimization. In: Proceedings of ICNN'95 - International Conference on Neural Networks, vol. 4, pp. 1942–1948 (1995)
7. Han, S., Pool, J., Tran, J., Dally, W.: Learning both weights and connections for efficient neural networks. In: Advances in Neural Information Processing Systems, pp. 1135–1143 (2015)
8. Jouppi, N.P., et al.: In-datacenter performance analysis of a tensor processing unit. In: Proceedings of the 44th Annual International Symposium on Computer Architecture (ISCA), pp. 1–12 (2017)
9. Lange, T., Takagi, T. (eds.): PQCrypto 2017. LNCS, vol. 10346. Springer, Cham (2017). https://doi.org/10.1007/978-3-319-59879-6
10. Chen, L., Jordan, S.: Report on post-quantum cryptography. National Institute of Standards and Technology (2016)
11. Hochreiter, S., Schmidhuber, J.: Long Short-Term Memory. Neural Comput.ut. **9**(8), 1735–1780 (1997)
12. Hinton, G.E., Salakhutdinov, R.R.: Reducing the dimensionality of data with neural networks. Science **313**(5786), 504–507 (2006)
13. Mao, H., Alizadeh, M., Menache, I., Kandula, S.: Resource management with deep reinforcement learning. In: Proceedings of the 15th ACM Workshop on Hot Topics in Networks, pp. 50–56 (2016)
14. Marinos, L., Sfakianakis, D.: Cloud security challenges and opportunities. ENISA Report (2019)
15. Dwork, C., Roth, A.: The algorithmic foundations of differential privacy. Found. Trends Theor. Comput. Sci. **9**(3–4), 211–407 (2014)

Explainable Contextual Anomaly Detection: A Focus on QCAD

Gauderic Gumbs[1,2(✉)], Maurras Togbe[1], Yousra Chabchoub[1], and Patrick Perrot[2]

[1] ISEP - Institut Supérieur d'Electronique de Paris, 10 rue de Vanves, Issy-les-Moulineaux 92130, France
{gauderic.gumbs,maurras.togbe,yousra.chabchoub}@isep.fr
[2] Commandement du ministère de l'Intérieur dans le cyberespace, Paris, France
patrick.lastname@Perrot.interieur.gouv.fr

Abstract. The integration of explainability techniques in anomaly detection systems is crucial for improving transparency and trust in decision-making processes across various application domains. Indeed, in a world increasingly reliant on data and algorithms, it is imperative for users to understand how and why a decision was made by an automated system. This is particularly true in sensitive sectors such as cybersecurity as well as finance, healthcare, where misinterpretation of results could have serious consequences. Traditional anomaly detection methods often lack explanations, making it difficult for users to understand the decisions made by these systems. To address this issue, the explainability of models is becoming a priority. In this paper, we conduct a detailed review of methods designed to enhance the explainability of anomaly detection models based on machine learning and artificial intelligence. We particularly study the various comparison metrics for all these methods: the positioning of explainability in relation to the model, the genericity of the explainability, the type of model, etc. We then focus on a recent explainable contextual anomaly detection method using quantile regression forest: QCAD developed by Li et al. in 2023. This method uses explainability while taking into account the context, which is crucial for a more efficient anomalies detection in many fields where the context has an important impact on the normal behavior. Li et al. showed that QCAD often yields excellent results in terms of PRC-AUC. We tested this method on a real-world dataset called "Bodyfat" to evaluate the impact of context size on its performance. Moreover, we exploited the explainability layer of QCAD to investigate the reasons behind its mitigated results on the Bodyfat dataset.

Keywords: artificial intelligence · anomaly detection · contextual anomaly detection · explainability

1 Introduction

Anomalies are patterns whose behavior varies significantly from the most of the data [7]. In the field of anomaly detection, it is crucial to establish the expected

Published by Springer Nature Switzerland AG 2025
D. Verdejo and E. Mercier-Laurent (Eds.): AI4GS 2024, IFIP AICT 743, pp. 114–126, 2025.
https://doi.org/10.1007/978-3-031-96522-7_9

behavior, known as normal behavior. Usually, the normal behavior is modeled according to the majority of the data. Once this profile is established, new incoming data are compared against this model. Data items are evaluated to determine how closely they match the expected characteristics. Any data item that deviates significantly from this expected behavior is then flagged as an anomaly. These anomalies can be identified using a variety of statistical techniques [7], classical machine learning algorithms [14] and deep learning algorithms [17].

Thus, anomaly detection has been widely studied and there is a plethora of comprehensive reviews and articles in different application domains such as cybersecurity [18] or finance [10]. However, less attention has been devoted to the explainability of anomaly detection methods. Explainability of models gives the decision makers a more complete view of the obtained results and enables them to better justify their decision. It is one of the key issues for the adoption of algorithms in society and is becoming an ethical and regulatory requirement in safety-critical areas.

Moreover, the majority of existing research studies on anomalies detection, largely neglect the detection of contextual anomalies. Contextual anomaly detection is particularly relevant in domains where the context has a notable impact on the behavior. In such a situation, the normal behavior is not universal but closely related to the considered context. Therefore, several normal behaviors should be defined in this case and the anomaly, in a given context, is defined as a large deviation from the normal behavior of the addressed context. In many fields the context refers to space-time features, but it can also for example concern the age and sex of patients for the prediction of certain diseases [16]. Hence data features can be classified into two categories: contextual and behavioral, with the help of experts or using automatic classification methods. Taking into account the contextual characteristics enables a more relevant anomalies detection. The paper is structured as follows, first we highlight the state of the art of 3 contextual anomaly detection methods, then we address the notion of explicability and its importance, following that we experiment on one of the 3 methods, and finally we end with a conclusion and future works.

2 Contextual Anomaly Detection Methods

Where traditional anomaly detection methods treat each feature uniformly, contextual approaches categorize attributes into two groups: contextual (or environmental) attributes and behavioural (or indicator) attributes. Contextual attributes define the environment or the conditions under which an object exists, whereas behavioural attributes are used to measure the normality of that object. For example, a heart rate of 100 bpm is abnormal for an adult at rest, but normal for a child or adult in physical activity [5]. To emphasize the importance of separating and adequately modelling the relationships between contextual and behavioural attributes for effective anomaly detection, three main methods for contextual anomaly detection, are presented: CAD, QCAD and ConQuest. These methods provide different ways of separating contextual and behavioural attributes to take correct action in the relevant context for accurate anomaly detection

2.1 Conditional Anomaly Detection (CAD)

CAD [26] is developed by Song, Xiuyao, et al. in Song, Xiuyao, et al. in 2007. Like most of the contextual anomaly detection methods, CAD separates attributes into environmental attributes, which shape the context of the data without directly signaling anomalies, and indicator attributes, which are useful to identify anomalies. CAD, firstly, utilizes a statistical model (Gaussian Mixture Model [21], GMM), in most cases for capturing the trends and relationships present in historical data; these enable greater accuracy in the identification of true anomalies by modeling the inter-relationship between environmental and indicator attributes in order to reduce false positives. Subsequently, it calibrates those parameter values by adjusting its model parameters through the use of Expectation-Maximization (EM) algorithms to learn the relationships among environmental and indicator attributes. The Conditional Probability Density Function (Conditional PDF) is a major part of CAD, which calculates the distribution of indicator attributes based on values of environmental attributes. In this way, CAD detects new observations where the values of the indicator attributes, when conditioned by the values of the environmental attributes, deviate significantly from the expected mean values. This technique of context-related anomaly detection makes the identification of the anomalies more robust and useful. Subsequently, a probability threshold is used to identify whether an observed point is in fact an anomaly. Learning in CAD as the same principal as other contextual anomaly models (detect anomalies by identifying data points that deviate from expected patterns) and can be expressed using different algorithms, like Direct-CAD algorithm, GMM-CAD-Full algorithm, and GMM-CAD-Split algorithm, all adopting EM for parameter optimization of the model to properly represent the dependencies in the data.

2.2 Context Discovery for Anomaly Detection (ConQuest)

ConQuest [5] developed by Calikus et al. in 2024 is an innovative approach to contextual anomaly detection, characterized by the ability to automatically discover and integrate multiple relevant contexts for anomaly detection and interpretation. The process begins with the extraction of context-behaviour pairs from a database using a sliding window; this allows data to be analyzed in continuous segments in order to capture local variations. Reference groups are defined based on the similarity of contexts. ConQuest formulates objective functions. These are mathematical criteria that evaluate and steer the optimization of solutions. Three goals can be identified: maximizing dependency of context and behaviour (objective function 1), contextual redundancy minimized (objective function 2), and anomaly discrimination maximized (objective function 3). Multi-objective optimization is based on a genetic algorithm called NSGA-II.

This methodology has a scope to explore the context space. The algorithm mentioned produces a Pareto front of non-dominat ed solutions [20]. A solution is said to be Pareto optimal when no further improvement is possible in any objective function without degrading at least one of the other objective functions [6]. The choice of the top solution with m contexts from among the Pareto front is done by ConQuest using a selection method named TOPSIS, which stands for Technique for Order Preference by Similarity to Ideal Solution. A simple yet effective method that chooses the best alternative based on the shortest and farthest Euclidean distances from the positive ideal solution (PIS) and negative ideal solution (NIS). Lastly the algorithm MCAF (Multi-Context Anomaly Factor) tries to combine the contextual and behavioural distances to produce an anomaly score by aggregating scores from multiple contexts. It also has the capability to explain and visualize the anomalies so that they can be compared with their reference groups.

2.3 Quantile Contextual Anomaly Detection (QCAD)

QCAD [12] developed by Li, Zhong, and Matthijs Van Leeuwen in 2023 uses quantile regression forests to model relationships between features. Here, reference groups are constructed with two dimensions distance matrix calculated using the Gower's distance. There is a reference group for each observation, containing the set of the k nearest neighbors of the considered observation. A learning process then occurs by constructing quantile regression forests (QRF) for each reference group based on their behavioral attributes. Anomalies are then identified based on the entire probability density function and the local density of each observation in each QRF.

Anomaly scores take into account the width of the quantile interval. The key idea is that the wider the quantile interval, the lower the density around a considered value, which is very likely to indicate an anomaly. The scores are then aggregated over all the behavioural features to obtain the overall anomaly score for a data item. More precisely, a Min-Max normalization is applied on all behavioral features for a better performance.

Once an anomaly is detected, QCAD applies an explainability layer to provide more information and details about the anomaly. It consists of decomposing the overall anomaly score into the contributions of the individual features. This enables the identification of the features that mainly contribute into the anomaly. For this purpose, QCAD provides visual explanations with the use of beanplots that illustrate how an observation's behavioral features deviate from its reference group. The visualization of the conditional distributions helps understanding why a specific data item is identified as anomalous, ensuring a better transparency and interpretability. A complete architecture of QCAD is provided in Fig. 1.

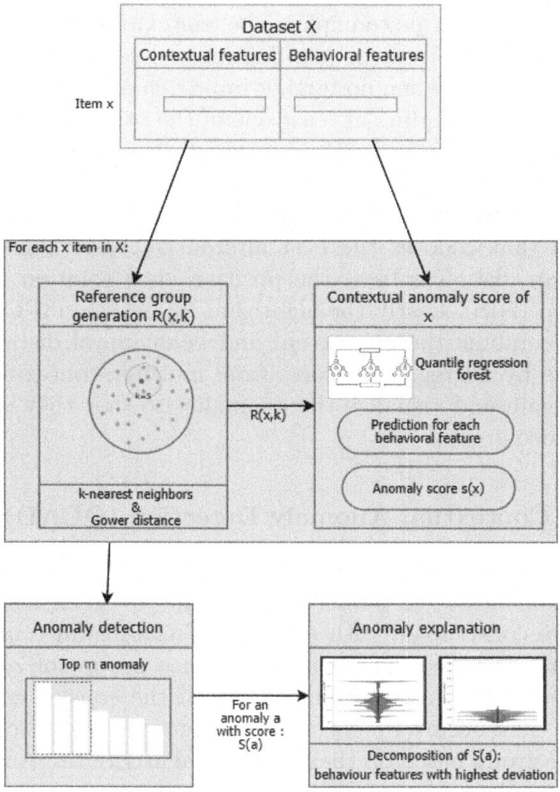

Fig. 1. QCAD architecture.

3 Explicability in AI: Application in Cybersecurity

Explainable Artificial Intelligence (XAI) is an approach in artificial intelligence that aims to improve human understanding of the decisions made by AI models. The use of AI, particularly machine learning and deep learning, enhances detection and defense against cyberthreats, outperforming traditional signature and rule-based methods. These AI-based techniques are frequently applied in an opaque "black box" [2] way, in which both security experts and end users are hard-pressed to understand and rationalize the decisions made by these models. This often results in a lack of transparency and interpretability, leading to a reduction in user confidence with respect to AI-based cyber defense models, especially with the emergence of more and more complex attacks. Hence, there is an XAI critical need to apply in developing more explicable cyber security models that allow users to understand, trust, and manage next-generation defense mechanisms. This section investigates the various existing XAI techniques.

3.1 Motivation

XAI makes AI model-based decisions less opaque, which increases confidence in the system by end users. With regulations tightening, such as the GDPR in Europe, which mandates reasons for decisions taken by automated systems, XAI becomes essential. Explainable models can hence guide organizations to be in compliance with these rules and provide clear and understandable justification for every decision taken by an AI system. Such regulatory compliance is critical to protect an organization from legal sanctions and maintain a good reputation.

Explainability enables cyber security experts to identify and correct systems' errors or biases for more effectiveness. In fact, an idea of why a model has wrongly classified an attack may help in the optimization of the algorithms to improve the detection process. XAI offers fine-grained explanation capabilities that guarantee continuous optimization of cybersecurity systems to ensure a better protection from threats. As an example, adversarial attacks are a vulnerability in AI models, being designed for fooling the model through mischievous input. XAI can help point out such an attack through an explanation revealing an anomaly in the model's decision, hence reacting in time and appropriately.

In this sense, many cybersecurity professionals need to have insight into decisions made by AI systems to carry out thorough investigations and incident responses. XAI provides the ability to understand the decisions taken by models, hence making such models interpretable by security professionals in their tasks. This is important for effective post-incident analysis as well as building stronger defense strategies.

3.2 XAI Methods

SHAP (SHapley Additive exPlanations) and LIME (Local Interpretable Model-agnostic Explanations) are among the first designed explainability algorithms. Their emergence respectively in 2017 and 2016 marked a major turning point in the field of XAI, especially for complex, black-box models. SHAP [13] uses "Shapley values" with an approach based on game theory. It calculates the importance of each feature as an additive contribution to the prediction of a specific instance.

LIME [22], developed by Ribeiro et al., is a "model agnostic" method that gives an explanation of the behavior of a model for a given prediction or for a subset of predictions with the SP-LIME method. The principle of this method is called "Kernel based": to give an explanation of a model, the LIME creates an explanatory model based on the original model.

Many other explainability algorithms and libraries have been recently developed [28]. They are based on different concepts and approaches [11,27] and generate different output formats (numerical, textual, visual). Among the commonly used explainability algorithms, we can cite the Activation Maps known as heatmaps which are based on visualization and particularly used for image processing. Many extensions of Activation Maps have been developed like Class Activation Map (CAM) and Grad-CAM. Decision Trees (DT) are also used to explain some particular models. We propose in Tables 1, 2 and 3 a complete classification of the most used explainability algorithms. We considered three criteria: 1) Using all observations to provide an explainability or not, 2) Dependency between the explainability and the ML model [1], and 3) Positioning of the explainability: it begins when building the model or after. We define in these tables each type of algorithms and give the most pertinent examples of algorithms for each category.

Table 1. Global/local explanation with respect to the observations

Explanation type	Description	Example
Local	Focuses on explaining a specific decision or instance within a model's inference, providing explanations limited to individual cases.	Activation Maps [29], CAM [30], Combinatorial Methods [15]
Global	Aims to make the entire inferential process of a model transparent and comprehensible as a whole, explaining overall observations across the dataset.	BCM [4]
Hybrid Approach	Combines both local and global explanations, providing both specific instance-level explanations and insights into the overall behavior of the model.	Activation maximization [9], Cell Activation Values [30], Grad-CAM [24], LIME [22]

Table 2. Dependency of the explanation on the model

Explanation type	Description	Example
Model-agnostic	Techniques independent of the type of machine learning model used, capable of being applied across different learning approaches	Ada-WHIPS, CAM [30], LIME [22]
Model-specific	Applicable only to particular kinds of models, such as interpreting the weights or activation values specific to neural network models	DT [19], Rule lists [23]
Hybrid Approach	Utilizes methods that cater to specific model types while also being adaptable to various model architectures	Grad-CAM [24], SHAP [13]

Table 3. Positioning of the explanation

Explanation type	Description	Example
Intrinsic	Achieves interpretability by building inherently interpretable models with simplicity and transparency embedded from the model's creation and training phase	Activation Values of Hidden Neurons [29], Ant Colony Optimization (ACO) [8]
Post-hoc	Explains or mimics the behavior of a trained model using external explainers during testing or after model training without altering the model itself	Attention Alignment [3], Average Activation Values [25]

4 Experimental Study of QCAD

We focus in this section on QCAD as the authors showed in [12] that QCAD often outperforms many other well-known anomalies detection algorithms: LoPAD, ROCO, CAD, IForest, LOF, K-NN, SOD and HBOS. They compared the performance of these algorithms over 20 real-world datasets. More precisely, they evaluated the PRC AUC (Precision-Recall Curve Area Under the Curve) metric, which measures the balance between precision and recall. This metric is particularly useful for imbalanced datasets and so it is well adapted for anomalies detection.

QCAD gives an excellent PRC AUC for all the datasets except a particular dataset called "Bodyfat" where the PRC AUC equals only 0.6. Bodyfat contains 252 samples with 13 contextual and 2 behavioral features. Our objective in this section is to investigate the reasons behind the relatively low PRC AUC. We also discuss in the context size which is an important input parameter of QCAD.

4.1 Impact of the Context Size

One of the key parameters that directly influences QCAD performance is the number k of nearest neighbors used to generate the reference group. For this purpose, we considered several values of k and we evaluated the PRC AUC based on Bodyfat dataset. Figure 2 shows that when k increases, QCAD is more efficient. However, PRC AUC becomes constant beyond a given threshold. It means that the gain become negligible while the computational cost continues to rise, hence the importance of limiting the value of k for an optimal balance. In [12], the authors recommend to set k using the following formula $k = min(N/2, 500)$ where N is the size of the dataset.

This means that the context size is a constant parameter and is common for all dataset items. We believe that the context size can be different from an item to another. It depends on the distribution of the contextual behavioral features in the dataset. A preliminary step should be added to QCAD to identify the different contexts using an unsupervised clustering algorithm. This enables to detects the natural contexts instead of identifying the k nearest neighbors for each data item. In fact, using k nearest neighbors implies a strong assumption of equal context sizes which is not the case of most of real-world datasets.

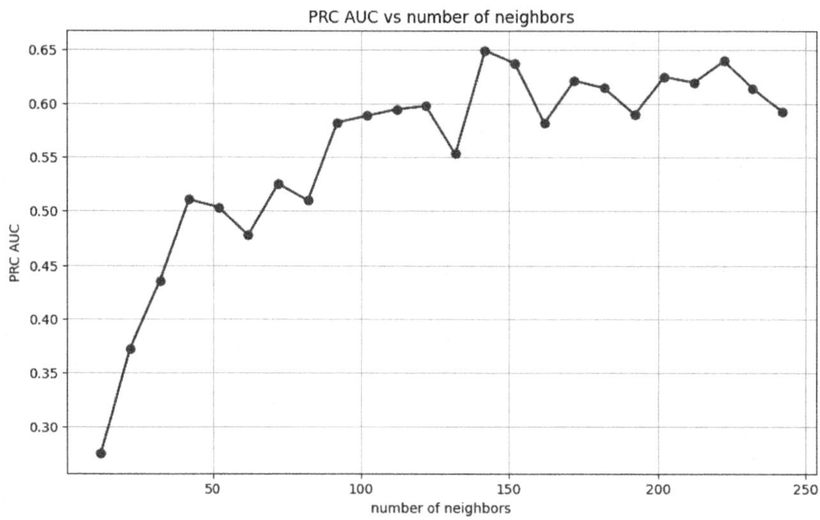

Fig. 2. impact of the number of neighbors.

4.2 Impact of the Dataset Distribution, and Anomalies Injection

The 20 real-world datasets considered in [12] do not naturally contain anomalies. So, the authors injected, as an example in Bodyfat dataset 20 anomalies in the preprocessing step. Then they applied the quantile random forest to identify top 20 anomaly scores. They use the same method to inject anomalies in all the considered datasets.

We conducted the same experiment on Bodyfat and we obtained a PRC AUC of 0.6. The confusion matrix is given in Table 4 for more precise details. Positive refers to anomalies.

Within the top 20 anomaly scores, we observe that 9 are False Positives.

This means that, in the original dataset, 9 of the 232 data items that were not injected received higher anomaly scores than the 9 injected ones. This suggests that within their context, these items have behavioral features more indicative of anomalies than the injected ones. The beanplots given in Figs. 3, 4 and 5 further clarify this by showing the position of the considered item compared to the estimated conditional distribution of each behavioral feature. We recall that Bodyfat dataset contains 2 behavioral features. The red area represents the occurrence probability. The horizontal black lines indicate the values reported for the data item feature under investigation.

Figure 3 presents an injected anomaly correctly labeled as anomalous, while Fig. 4 shows an injected anomaly misclassified as normal. Figure 5 displays an original, non-injected data point that was labeled as anomalous. The global anomaly score of the item considered in Fig. 5 is higher than the score of the item of Fig. 4. That is why this latter is not part of the top 20 detected anomalies. This is also the case for the other 8 missed injected anomalies. They are not enough anomalous to be ranked in the top 20 scores.

These observations show that anomalies injection should not be performed in the same manner for all the datasets. It must take into account the dataset specificity and anomalies already present in the dataset before injecting new anomalies. As a conclusion, the low PRC AUC of QCAD obtained for the Bodyfat dataset is due to in-adapted injection of anomalies and not to the QCAD algorithm.

Table 4. Confusion Matrix, 20 anomalies injected in Bodyfat dataset

		Reality	
		Positive	Negative
Prediction	Positive	11	9
	Negative	9	223

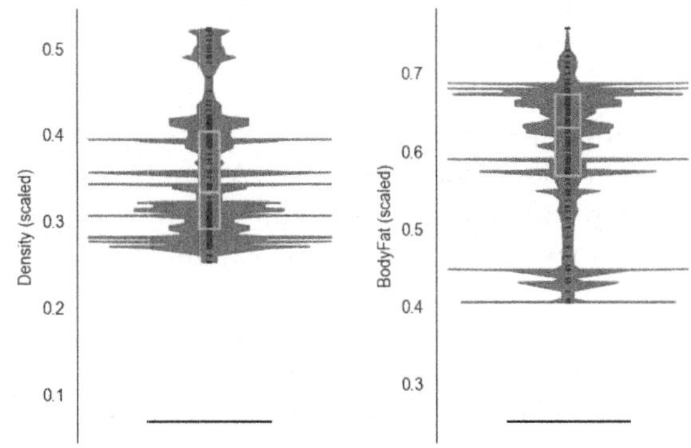

Fig. 3. Injected anomaly labeled as anomalous.

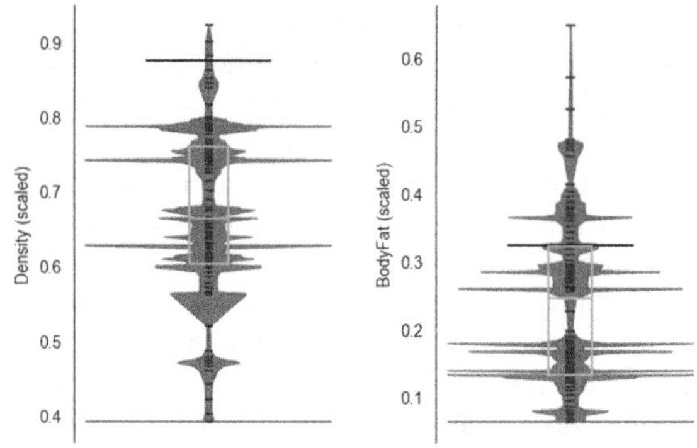

Fig. 4. Injected anomaly labeled as normal.

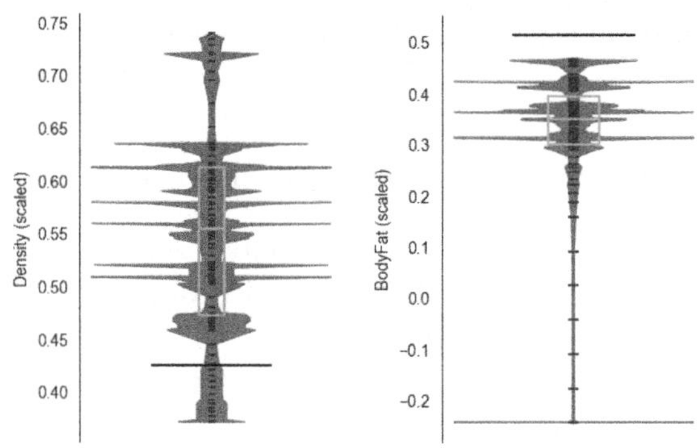

Fig. 5. Non-injected data labeled as anomalous.

5 Conclusion

In this paper, we highlighted the challenges and opportunities of explainable contextual anomaly detection. Our review on XAI, emphasizes the importance of selecting the appropriate explanation technique based on the constraints and the context. Moreover, we focused on an efficient explainable contextual algorithm: QCAD. Our experiments show that for more robust results, the specificities of each dataset should be taken into account, namely the already present anomalies. Finally, we suggest to add a preprocessing step to QCAD to dynamically define the different contexts which can be of different sizes within the same dataset. This will be investigated in our future research work where we will explore a more refined approach to the selection of the parameters for QCAD.

Acknowlegement. This work is supported by the National Gendarmerie Research Center, under the COFRA program.

References

1. Ali, S., et al.: Explainable Artificial Intelligence (XAI): what we know and what is left to attain trustworthy artificial intelligence. Inf. Fusion **99**, 101805 (2023)
2. Arrieta, A.B., et al.: Explainable Artificial Intelligence (XAI): concepts, taxonomies, opportunities and challenges toward responsible AI. Inf. Fusion **58**, 82–115 (2020)
3. Bahdanau, D., Cho, K., Bengio, Y.: Neural machine translation by jointly learning to align and translate. In: Proceedings of the International Conference on Learning Representations (ICLR) (2015)
4. Burkart, N., Huber, M.F.: A survey on the explainability of supervised machine learning. Artif. Intell. Rev. **54**(5), 4211–4238 (2021)
5. Calikus, E., Nowaczyk, S., Dikmen, O.: Context discovery for anomaly detection. Int. J. Data Sci. Anal. **19**, 1–15 (2024)
6. Cao, K., Zhang, W., Wang, T.: Spatio-temporal land use multi-objective optimization: a case study in Central China. Trans. GIS **23**(4), 726–744 (2019)
7. Chandola, V., Banerjee, A., Kumar, V.: Anomaly detection: a survey. ACM Comput. Surv. (CSUR) **41**(3), 1–58 (2009)
8. Dorigo, M., Blum, C.: Ant colony optimization theory: a survey. Theoret. Comput. Sci. **344**(2–3), 243–278 (2006)
9. Erhan, D., et al.: Visualizing Higher-Layer Features of a Deep Network. University of Montreal. Technical report (2009)
10. Al-Hashedi, K.G., Magalingam, P.: Financial fraud detection applying data mining techniques: a comprehensive review from 2009 to 2019. Comput. Sci. Rev. **40**, 100402 (2021)
11. Kök, I., et al.: Explainable artificial intelligence (XAI) for internet of things: a survey. IEEE Internet of Things J. **10**(16), 14764–14779 (2023)
12. Li, Z., Van Leeuwen, M.: Explainable contextual anomaly detection using quantile regression forests. Data Mining Knowl. Disc. **37**(6), 2517–2563 (2023)
13. Lundberg, S.: A unified approach to interpreting model predictions. arXiv preprint arXiv:1705.07874 (2017)
14. Nassif, A.B., et al.: Machine learning for anomaly detection: a systematic review. IEEE Access **9**, 78658–78700 (2021)
15. Natarajan, N., et al.: Learning with Noisy Labels. In: Neural Information Processing Systems (NIPS) (2012)
16. Nguyen, B.P., et al.: Predicting the onset of type 2 diabetes using wide and deep learning with electronic health records. Comput. Methods Progr. Biomed. **182**, 105055 (2019)
17. Pang, G., et al.: Deep learning for anomaly detection: a review. ACM Comput. Surv. (CSUR) **54**(2), 1–38 (2021)
18. Pawlicki, M., Kozik, R.l., Chora's, M.l.: A survey on neural networks for (cyber-) security and (cyber-) security of neural networks. Neurocomputing **500**, 1075–1087 (2022)
19. Ross Quinlan, J.: C4.5: Programs for Machine Learning. Morgan Kaufmann (1993)
20. Rahman, M.M., Szab'o, G.: Multi-objective urban land use optimization using spatial data: a systematic review. Sustain. Cities Soc. **74**, 103214 (2021)
21. Reynolds, D.A., et al.: Gaussian mixture models. Encycl. Biometr. **741**, 659–663 (2009)
22. Ribeiro, M.T., Singh, S., Guestrin, C.: Why should i trust you? Explaining the predictions of any classifier. In: Proceedings of the 22nd ACM SIGKDD International Conference on Knowledge Discovery and Data Mining, pp. 1135–1144 (2016)

23. Rivest, R.L.: Learning decision lists. Mach. Learn. **2**(3), 229–246 (1987)
24. Selvaraju, R.R., et al.: Grad-CAM: visual explanations from deep networks via gradient-based localization. In: Proceedings of the IEEE International Conference on Computer Vision (ICCV), pp. 618–626 (2017)
25. Simonyan, K., Vedaldi, A., Zisserman, A.: Deep inside convolutional networks: visualising image classification models and saliency maps. arXiv preprint arXiv:1312.6034 (2014)
26. Song, X., et al.: Conditional anomaly detection. IEEE Trans. knowl. Data Eng. **19**(5), 631–645 (2007)
27. Vilone, G., Longo, L.: Explainable artificial intelligence: a systematic review. arXiv preprint arXiv:2006.00093 (2020)
28. Yepmo, V., Smits, G., Pivert, O.: Anomaly explanation: a review. Data Knowl. Eng. **137**, 101946 (2022)
29. Zeiler, M.D., Fergus, R.: Visualizing and understanding convolutional networks. In: Fleet, D., Pajdla, T., Schiele, B., Tuytelaars, T. (eds.) ECCV 2014. LNCS, vol. 8689, pp. 818–833. Springer, Cham (2014). https://doi.org/10.1007/978-3-319-10590-1_53
30. Zhou, B., et al.: Learning deep features for discriminative localization. In: Proceedings of the IEEE Conference on Computer Vision and Pattern Recognition (CVPR), pp. 2921–2929 (2016)

Prevention of DDoS Using AI

N. S. Gowri Ganesh(✉), Karthi Govindharaju, K. Mohanish, K. J. Dinesh Karthick, and J. Mohammed Faizal

Saveetha Engineering College, Chennai, India
gowriganesh@gmail.com

Abstract. Distributed Denial-of-Service (DDoS) attacks continue to be a constant menace to the availability of online services, necessitating adaptive and intelligent defense mechanisms. This paper presents a novel DDoS prevention system: NeuroGuard, an Autonomous AI Defense Network (AADN) based on deep learning, federated learning, and blockchain. Our framework employs Convolutional Neural Networks (CNNs) and Recurrent Neural Networks (RNNs) for real-time traffic analysis to provide improved detection and classification of malicious behavior, aided by recent research [11–14]. For data privacy issues, federated learning facilitates training models in a privacy-friendly way among nodes in a distributed manner, discouraging the threats associated with centralized data collection and being part of distributed threat intelligence [6, 9, 10]. Blockchain technology offers a secure and decentralized environment for improving overall system security and trust [7, 8]. Combined with the application of blockchain to log traffic management decisions, produces a tamper-proof audit trail, guaranteeing the integrity and verifiability of mitigation measures taken against DDoS attacks [6]. This guarantees that only authorized and authenticated nodes are allowed to engage in the federated learning process and contribute to model updates, eliminating the threat of malicious node infiltration. This NeuroGuard architecture surpasses traditional DDoS mitigation techniques [1, 5] by offering increased adaptability and scalability. Our initial trials show a drastic improvement in detection rates and reaction time as well as protecting data privacy, allowing for attainment of more stable and secured world-wide network infrastructure. Through deployment of existing strategy in conjunction with AI and blockchain [2–6], NeuroGuard implements cooperative and secured protection against arising DDoS threats, beyond prevalent limitations within present defense tactics, enhancing general security position within linked networks. The system outlined is aimed at establishing an architecture that not only protects against the prevailing DDoS threats but is also secure against upcoming cyber attacks.

Keywords: Neuroguard · Federated Learning server · Blockchain Traffic Management

D. Verdejo and E. Mercier-Laurent (Eds.): AI4GS 2024, IFIP AICT 743, pp. 127–142, 2025.
https://doi.org/10.1007/978-3-031-96522-7_10

1 Introduction

As the world becomes more interconnected, the accessibility and dependability of cyber services are of utmost importance not only for personal convenience but also for the operational efficiency of global economies, stability of global relations, and overall societal well-being [1]. The internet has evolved into an essential infrastructure that underpins everything from commerce and financial services to healthcare provision and public services. But this dependence on online services also leaves us extremely exposed to cyberattacks, with Distributed Denial-of-Service (DDoS) attacks being a particularly serious and ongoing threat to this global security environment [3, 8]. In contrast to targeted attacks against specific individuals or organizations, DDoS attacks tend to indiscriminately target critical infrastructure, essential services, and even entire regions, resulting in widespread disruption and economic loss. The growing complexity and magnitude of such attacks, and the development of new attack mechanisms, pose a formidable challenge to current defense mechanisms and highlight the imperative need for more effective and globally coordinated efforts [3, 8].The very nature of DDoS attacks renders them an international security issue. They are, by definition, distributed, coming from compromised devices and networks located across various countries and continents. This international distribution creates challenges in identifying the origin of the attack, assigning responsibility, and taking efficient countermeasures [1]. The botnets employed to mount DDoS attacks can include millions of infected machines, IoT devices, and other network appliances, making the enormous and uncontrollable attack army. In addition, DDoS attacks are increasingly becoming an instrument of political activism, economic espionage, and even cyber war activities. State-sponsored groups and organized crime syndicates are reputed to use DDoS attacks for interrupting government services, paralyzing critical infrastructure, and extorting businesses for money. The risk of DDoS attacks spreading to broader-scale cyber warfare is a serious threat to international peace and security [5]. The economic impact of DDoS attacks can be cataclysmic, especially for companies that base their revenue streams on web-based services. E-commerce sites, gaming sites, and banks can experience enormous financial loss from service disruptions, lost customer confidence, and additional operational expenses. Besides financial loss, DDoS attacks can harm the reputation and image of a company, which has long-term negative effects. The worldwide expense of DDoS attacks is predicted to be in the billions of dollars every year, and this amount is slated to grow even more over time because the complexity and magnitude of these attacks expand. Additionally, the disruption of necessary services, like the provision of health care and emergency services infrastructure, can have catastrophic effects on public safety and well-being. The possibility of DDoS attacks on the disruption of essential infrastructure, like power grids, transportation systems, and communication networks, is a serious threat to national security and economic stability. Hence, it is important to come up with improved and secure methods [6]. Which is represented in Fig. 1

The limitations of traditional, localized DDoS defenses in the face of these evolving global threats have become increasingly apparent [1, 5]. Defenses such as firewalls, intrusion detection systems (IDS), and rate limiting are often overwhelmed by the sheer volume and complexity of modern attacks. These systems are typically designed to operate

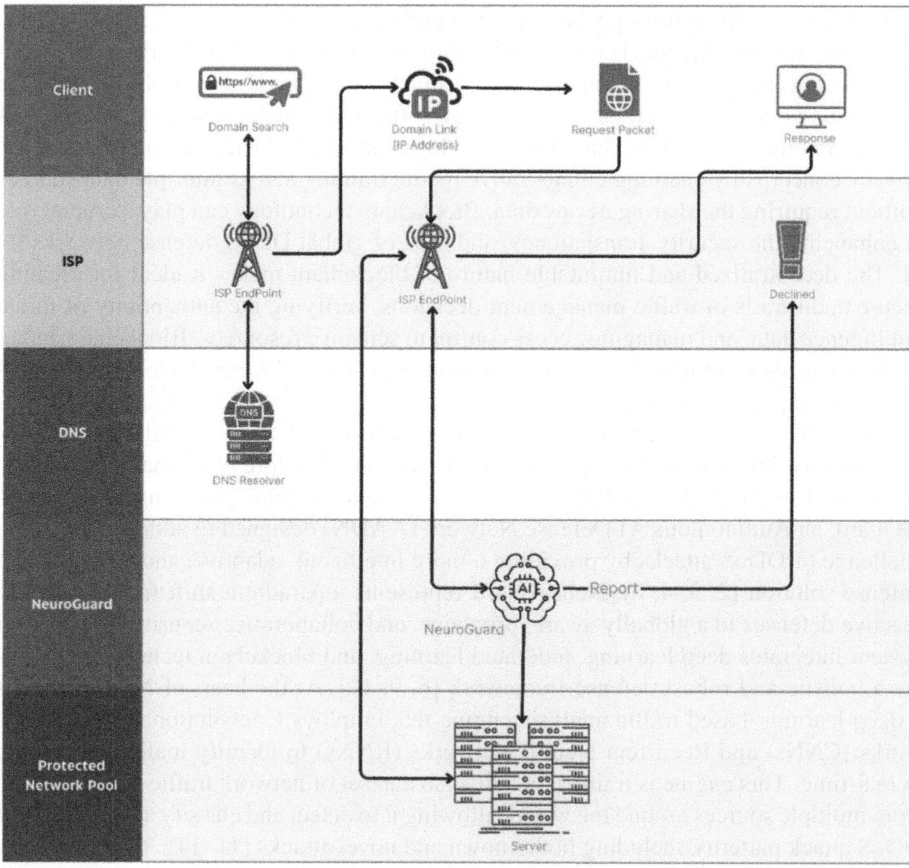

Fig.1. Structure Diagram

within a single network perimeter, making them ill-equipped to deal with attacks originating from multiple sources across different geographical locations [1, 5]. The reactive nature of many traditional defenses also makes them vulnerable to zero-day attacks and adaptive attack strategies. By the time a traditional defense system detects and responds to an attack, significant damage may already have been done. Moreover, the reliance on centralized data and decision-making processes in traditional defenses can create single points of failure that attackers can exploit. To counter the global nature of DDoS attacks, a more collaborative and globally distributed defense strategy is essential [2, 3, 6, 14]. This requires a shift from isolated, localized defenses to a coordinated network of security systems that can share threat intelligence, coordinate responses, and adapt to evolving attack patterns in real-time. Global collaboration is crucial for sharing information about emerging threats, identifying attack sources, and implementing effective countermeasures. This collaboration must involve governments, businesses, research institutions, and other stakeholders from around the world. Furthermore, the development and deployment of standardized security protocols and best practices can help to improve the overall security posture of the internet and reduce the risk of DDoS attacks. The use of AI and machine learning can automate the analysis of network traffic, identify malicious activity, and adapt to evolving attack strategies. However, the use of AI in DDoS defense also raises privacy concerns, as it often requires the collection and analysis of large amounts of sensitive data. Federated learning offers a potential solution to these privacy concerns by enabling collaborative model training across multiple data sources without requiring the sharing of raw data. Blockchain technology can play a crucial role in enhancing the security, transparency, and trust of global DDoS defense networks [6, 8]. The decentralized and immutable nature of blockchain makes it ideal for creating secure audit trails of traffic management decisions, verifying the authenticity of threat intelligence data, and managing access control to sensitive resources. Blockchain-based systems can also facilitate the secure and transparent sharing of threat intelligence information among different organizations and countries, improving the overall effectiveness of global DDoS defense efforts. However, it is important to address challenges related to scalability, interoperability, and regulatory compliance before blockchain technology can be widely adopted in global DDoS defense networks. This paper introduces NeuroGuard, an Autonomous AI Defense Network (AADN) designed to address the global challenge of DDoS attacks by providing a more intelligent, adaptive, and collaborative defense solution [2, 3, 4, 6]. NeuroGuard represents a paradigm shift from localized, reactive defenses to a globally aware, proactive, and collaborative security system. Our system integrates deep learning, federated learning, and blockchain technology to create a holistic and robust defense framework [6, 9, 10]. At the heart of NeuroGuard is a deep learning-based traffic analysis engine that employs Convolutional Neural Networks (CNNs) and Recurrent Neural Networks (RNNs) to identify malicious activity in real-time. This engine is trained on a diverse dataset of network traffic data collected from multiple sources around the world, allowing it to detect and classify a wide range of DDoS attack patterns, including both known and novel attacks [11–14]. To address privacy concerns and improve scalability, NeuroGuard utilizes federated learning to enable collaborative model training across multiple nodes in a globally distributed manner. This allows the system to learn from diverse attack patterns without requiring the sharing of sensitive data [6, 9, 10]. Federated nodes of trusted data can learn safely. The use of federated learning also enhances the resilience of the system by eliminating the reliance on a central data repository that could become a single point of failure. The data collection can improve the federated learning and better secure the system and avoid failure. Furthermore, NeuroGuard incorporates blockchain technology to enhance the security, transparency, and trust of the system [7, 8]. Blockchain is used to create a tamper-proof audit trail of traffic management decisions, ensuring the integrity and verifiability of mitigation actions taken against DDoS attacks. Blockchain also facilitates the secure and transparent sharing of threat intelligence information among different nodes in the network, improving the overall awareness and responsiveness of the system. In addition, blockchain-based access control mechanisms are used to ensure that only authorized and authenticated nodes can participate in the federated learning process and contribute to model updates, mitigating the risk of malicious node infiltration. By combining deep learning, federated learning, and blockchain technology, NeuroGuard aims to create a globally aware and collaborative DDoS defense system that can effectively protect online services from the ever-evolving threat landscape. The proposed system aims to establish an architecture that protects against the latest cyber attacks and provides a global awareness of the threat [2–6]. This paper presents the design and implementation of NeuroGuard, along with initial results from simulations and real-world experiments that demonstrate its effectiveness in detecting and mitigating DDoS attacks while preserving data privacy and ensuring the integrity of the system. The system outlined is aimed at establishing an architecture that is robust against future cyber attacks.

2 Literature Review

A The growing menace of Distributed Denial-of-Service (DDoS) attacks has prompted a lot of research on detection, mitigation, and prevention methods. The initial methods were based on signature detection and rate limiting, as outlined by Gupta et al. [1], but these techniques tend to fall short in responding to the increasing sophistication of contemporary DDoS attacks. Cao et al. [5] outline an analysis of internet DDoS mitigation methods from academic and industrial perspectives, and the limitations of conventional methods and the necessity for smarter and more adaptive alternatives. Over the last few years, artificial intelligence (AI) has started to emerge as a promising technology to further improve DDoS detection and mitigation. Zhang et al. [2] investigated the application of AI methods to DDoS detection and prevention, showing the capability of machine learning algorithms to detect malicious traffic patterns and anomalies. Mittal et al. [11] performed a systematic review of deep learning methods for DDoS attack detection, emphasizing the benefits of deep learning models, including Convolutional Neural Networks (CNNs) and Recurrent Neural Networks (RNNs), in effectively classifying malicious traffic. Haider et al. [12] designed a deep CNN ensemble model for effective DDoS attack detection in software-defined networks, whereas Shaaban et al. [13] studied the application of CNNs to detect and classify DDoS attacks. Sumathi et al. [14] studied the application of recurrent and deep neural network models for detecting DDoS attacks. These researches indicate the enormous capability of deep learning in enhancing DDoS accuracy and efficiency but also reflect on the difficulty involved in training models using big and heterogeneous datasets. In solving the data privacy and scalability problems in AI-powered DDoS defense, the research community has started looking at federated learning as a possibility. [9] deliver an extensive overview of federated learning applications, predicting its capability to facilitate collaborative training of models over multiple data sources without centralized data aggregation. Kim et al. [10] suggested a blockchained on-device federated learning framework for mitigation of DDoS, using blockchain to augment the security and transparency of federated learning. Blockchain technology has also been integrated into DDoS defense systems, and it has been gaining more attention. Wani et al. [6] give an extensive overview of applying blockchain to DDoS mitigation, noting its potential in developing secure audit trails, authenticating the source of threat intelligence data, and controlling access to sensitive resources. Pal et al. [7] discussed key management for blockchain technology. Das et al. [8] advocated an AI-imagined blockchain-supported signature-based key management protocol for industrial cyber-physical systems, whereas Yang et al. [8] introduced a blockchain-supported decentralized public key management system for named data networking.

2.1 Contribution to Literature

This work adds to the current body of work on DDoS defense through the introduction of NeuroGuard, an Autonomous AI Defense Network (AADN) that unites deep learning, federated learning, and blockchain technology to offer a more adaptive, privacy-preserving, and secure solution. In contrast to current methods that emphasize individual technologies, NeuroGuard unites the power of deep learning, federated learning, and blockchain to overcome the weaknesses of traditional DDoS mitigation methods. NeuroGuard uses the AI to enhance detection and offer privacy.

The major contributions of this paper are:

1. A new architecture for an AADN that brings together deep learning, federated learning, and blockchain to increase DDoS protection.
2. A demonstration of NeuroGuard using implementation that proves the feasibility of combining these technologies in an operational context.
3. Preliminary experimental results that prove the efficacy of NeuroGuard for detecting and counteracting DDoS attacks while maintaining data privacy and system integrity.

By integrating these technologies, NeuroGuard provides a stronger, scalable, and secure solution for defending online services against the continuously mutating menace of DDoS attacks. This paper gives an important contribution to the continuous efforts to make more effective and resilient cybersecurity defenses. Future re-searchers will look at our innovation and keep building to make the cyberspace a better place.

3 NeuroGuard: Autonomous AI Defense Network

As shown in Fig. 2 the work flow of NeuroGuard represents a groundbreaking approach to Distributed Denial-of-Service (DDoS) prevention, conceived as an Autonomous AI Defense Network (AADN) [2–6] meticulously engineered to provide resilient, adaptive, and privacy-conscious protection for online services facing the dynamic and increasingly sophisticated DDoS threat landscape. Departing significantly from traditional, reactive mitigation methods [1, 5], NeuroGuard seamlessly integrates the power of deep learning [11–14], the collaborative learning paradigm of federated learning [6, 9, 10], and the immutable security of blockchain technology [7, 8] into a unified and synergistic architecture. At its core lies a sophisticated, deep-learning-driven traffic analysis engine, harnessing the distinct strengths of both Convolutional Neural Networks (CNNs) and Recurrent Neural Networks (RNNs) to achieve unparalleled accuracy in real-time detection and classification of malicious activity [11–14]. CNNs excel at identifying spatial patterns within network packets, enabling the detection of signature-based attacks and anomalies, while RNNs adeptly analyze temporal sequences of network events, providing critical insights into attack patterns that evolve over time [11–14]. This dual-pronged analytical approach empowers NeuroGuard to effectively identify a wide spectrum of DDoS attack vectors, ranging from volumetric floods designed to saturate network bandwidth to application-layer attacks targeting specific vulnerabilities within online services. Complementing this robust detection capability is a privacy-preserving federated learning module [6, 9, 10], ingeniously designed to address the inherent challenges of data privacy and scalability that often plague traditional AI-based security solutions. By enabling collaborative model training across a distributed network of nodes, each operating on its local traffic data, the federated learning module eliminates the need for centralized data collection, thereby mitigating the risks associated with data breaches and privacy violations [6, 9, 10]. This decentralized learning approach also enhances the scalability of NeuroGuard, allowing it to adapt seamlessly to growing network traffic volumes and evolving attack patterns without compromising performance. Furthermore, a robust blockchain-based security and trust layer [7, 8] underpins the entire NeuroGuard architecture, providing an immutable foundation for secure communication, data integrity, and transparent operation. Blockchain technology is employed to create a tamper-proof audit trail of all traffic management decisions, ensuring accountability and preventing unauthorized modifications to the system's configuration. It facilitates the secure and transparent sharing of threat intelligence information among participating nodes [6], fostering a collaborative defense ecosystem where insights into emerging threats are rapidly disseminated and acted upon. Access control mechanisms, also secured by blockchain, ensure that only authorized and authenticated nodes can participate in the federated learning process and contribute to model updates, thus mitigating the risk of malicious infiltration and data poisoning [7, 8]. Empowered by these advanced technologies, NeuroGuard operates as an Autonomous AI Defense Network (AADN) [2–6], capable of making intelligent, real-time decisions on how to respond to DDoS attacks. The system leverages AI algorithms to analyze the information provided by the traffic analysis engine, the federated learning module, and the blockchain layer, determining the most appropriate mitigation actions based on the specific characteristics of the attack. These actions may include dynamic rate limiting, intelligent traffic filtering, automated traffic redirection to alternative resources, and blacklisting of malicious IP addresses [1, 5]. NeuroGuard is designed to continuously learn and adapt to evolving attack strategies, optimizing the effectiveness of its mitigation actions over time. By offering real-time DDoS detection and mitigation, adaptive threat intelligence sharing, automated response and remediation, secure and transparent operation, and privacy-preserving federated learning, NeuroGuard represents a significant advancement in DDoS defense, providing online services with a robust and resilient shield against the ever-present threat of disruption and compromise.

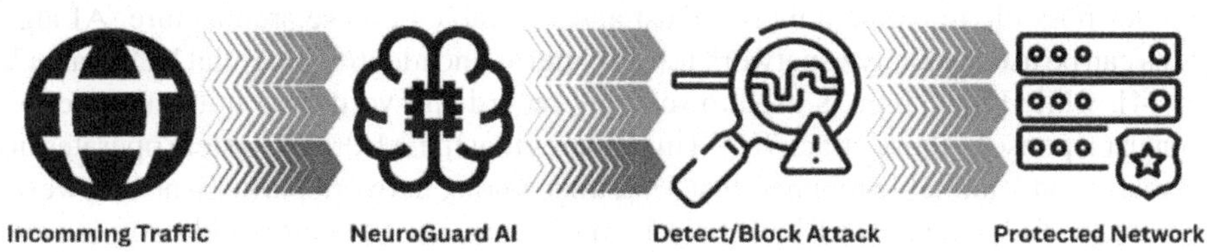

Fig.2. Workflow of NeuroGuard

3.1 Blockchain Traffic Management

The Blockchain Traffic Management represents a paradigm shift in how network traffic, particularly in the context of Distributed Denial-of-Service (DDoS) defense, is governed and secured. By integrating blockchain technology into traffic management systems, it becomes possible to address longstanding challenges related to trust, transparency, and accountability [7, 8]. Blockchain's inherent properties – decentralization, immutability, and transparency – offer a robust foundation for building more secure and resilient networks. Traditionally, traffic management systems rely on centralized authorities and proprietary protocols, creating potential single points of failure and vulnerabilities to manipulation. Blockchain Traffic Management addresses these shortcomings by distributing control across a network of nodes, each maintaining a copy of the traffic management ledger [6]. This distributed architecture eliminates the reliance on a single authority and makes it significantly more difficult for attackers to compromise the system. One of the key applications of blockchain in traffic management is the creation of a tamper-proof audit trail of all traffic management decisions. Every action taken to manage network traffic, such as rate limiting, traffic filtering, or IP address blacklisting, is recorded as a transaction on the blockchain [6]. This ensures that all actions are transparent and auditable, providing a verifiable record of how the network responded to specific events. The immutability of the blockchain guarantees that these records cannot be altered or deleted, providing a high degree of trust in the integrity of the traffic management system. Furthermore, blockchain facilitates the secure and transparent sharing of threat intelligence data among network participants [6]. Threat intelligence, such as indicators of compromise (IOCs), blacklisted IP addresses, or attack signatures, can be securely recorded on the blockchain and shared with authorized nodes. This allows network operators to proactively identify and mitigate potential threats before they can cause significant damage. The use of blockchain ensures that the threat intelligence data is authentic and trustworthy, as each entry is cryptographically signed and verified by multiple nodes in the network. Access control mechanisms, secured by blockchain, play a crucial role in maintaining the integrity and security of the traffic management system [7, 8]. Only authenticated and authorized nodes are permitted to participate in traffic management decisions or contribute to the shared threat intelligence repository. This prevents malicious actors from injecting false or misleading information into the system or from manipulating traffic flows to their advantage. The integration of blockchain with AI-driven systems, such as NeuroGuard, represents a powerful synergy [2–6]. By combining the intelligence of AI algorithms with the trustworthiness of blockchain, it becomes possible to create a more robust and verifiable defense architecture. AI algorithms can be used to analyze network traffic patterns and identify potential DDoS attacks [11–14], while blockchain is used to securely record and verify the mitigation actions taken in response to those attacks [6]. This ensures that the AI-driven system operates in a transparent and auditable manner, fostering trust among network participants. However, realizing the full potential of Blockchain Traffic Management requires addressing several challenges. Scalability, interoperability, and regulatory compliance are all important considerations. Blockchain networks must be able to handle the high volume of transactions associated with network traffic management, and they must be able to interoperate with existing network infrastructure. Furthermore, regulatory frameworks must be developed to address the legal and ethical implications of using blockchain technology in traffic management systems. Despite these challenges, Blockchain Traffic Management holds immense promise for enhancing the security, transparency, and resilience of networks in the face of increasingly sophisticated cyber threats. As given in the Fig. 3

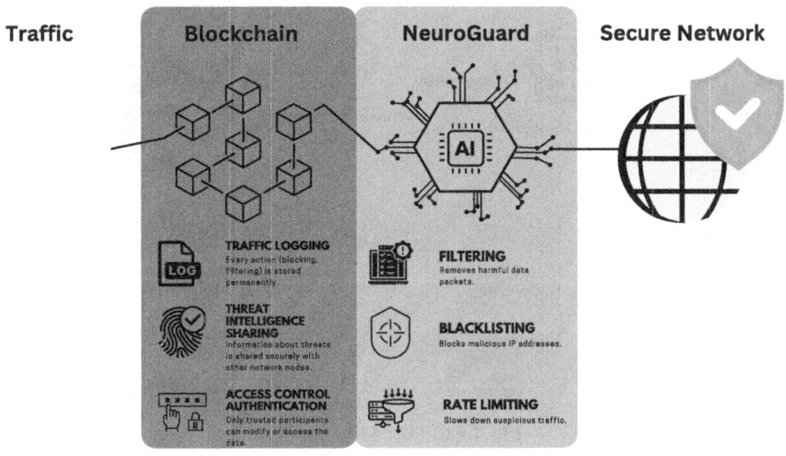

Fig.3. Blockchain Mechanism

3.2 Reporting Mechanism

The reporting process, as graphically outlined, starts with the detection of a "Bad Log," a given event highlighted for holding anomalous or malicious activity identified by [7, 8] This event initiates a chain of processes to alert network staff regarding the perceived security breach. As shown in the picture, on identifying a suspicious entry in system logs, the system goes ahead to "Record Incident." The step entails writing down a comprehensive record, perhaps in a special incident management system, that retains all relevant details such as the nature of suspicious activity, timestamps, source IP and destination IP addresses, and other relevant data [6]. Next, the captured data is then processed to "Generate Statistical Images" which can include visualizations such as graphs, charts, or heatmaps, thus converting raw data into a consumable format highlighting trends and patterns of the incident [2–6]. These incident information and statistical images are then forwarded to a "Mailing SMTP Server." The Simple Mail Transfer Protocol (SMTP) server is used to send the alert notification via an email so that the data will be received by the target recipient, i.e., a security administrator or incident response team. The last step in the reporting process is the delivery of the alert to the "ISP Inbox." The graphical representation depicts the email being delivered to the administrator inbox. On arrival, administrators are able to analyse the generated content and respond appropriately. The picture depicts a streamlined and automated alert process that utilizes logging analysis, statistical imaging, and email communication to quickly notify stakeholders of possible cybersecurity breaches within the network [11–14]. The immediate response serves to secure the data and reduce the impact of the attack. The integration of automated logging processing, visualization reporting, and effective distribution is beneficial in dealing with network incidents and security vulnerabilities without much effect on the system. Represented as in Fig. 4

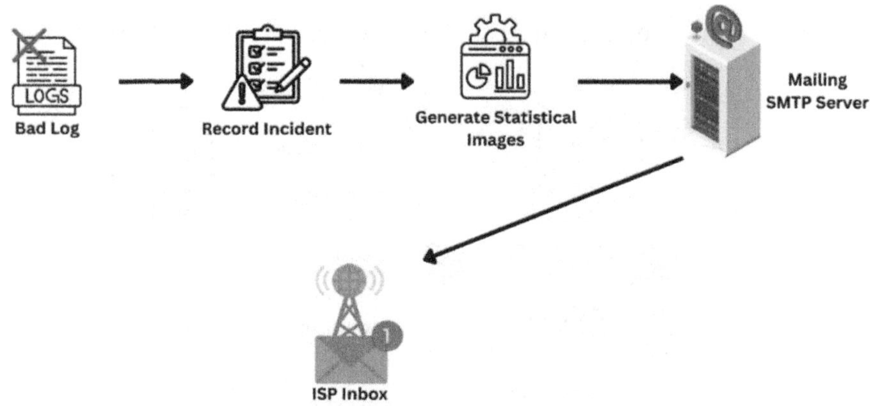

Fig.4. Report Mechanism

3.3 The Adaptive Federated Learning and Response Mechanism.

Federated learning is a critical component in bolstering NeuroGuard's adaptive response and traffic management capabilities by allowing collaborative intelligence gathering and model training on a distributed network of engaged nodes without compromising data privacy, while enhancing scalability [6, 9, 10]. This method circumvents the constraints of conventional, centralized machine learning methods, where the sensitive network traffic information would have to be gathered and centralized, posing a high security and privacy threat. With the use of federated learning, NeuroGuard enables each node to learn from its local network traffic information without ever sharing the raw information itself, creating a safer and privacy-aware setting for DDoS protection [6, 9, 10].The fundamental concept of federated learning in NeuroGuard is to spread the model training process among the network, so each node can contribute to the system's overall intelligence without revealing its sensitive information. Each involved node, be it a network provider, data center, or even a major enterprise, trains a local deep learning model (using CNNs and RNNs as outlined earlier [11–14]) on its local observed network traffic patterns. These local models are subsequently updated from time to time using new arriving traffic to ensure that they stay adaptive and reactive to changing attack tactics. Rather than uploading the raw traffic data to a central server, each node transfers only the model updates – the modifications to the local model made during training – to a central aggregation server [6, 9, 10]. This aggregation server, either controlled by a trusted third party or even decentralized via blockchain technology, aggregates the model updates from all the nodes in the network to produce a global, more generalized model. Different aggregation methods, like federated averaging, can be used to make sure that the global model captures the collective knowledge of the network while reducing the influence of biased or noisy data from any one node. The global model is then shared back to every participating node so that they can enhance their local DDoS detection and mitigation functions. This loop of local training, model update sharing, global aggregation, and model redistribution goes on constantly so that NeuroGuard's defense systems are always updated and adaptive to the changing threat landscape of DDoS. The advantages of employing federated learning in NeuroGuard are numerous. First and foremost, it greatly increases data privacy by removing the requirement of centralized data collection, minimizing the threat of data breaches and privacy infringement [6, 9, 10]. Second, it enhances the scalability of the system by spreading the computational load across many nodes, making it possible for NeuroGuard to manage larger and more sophisticated networks without performance degradation. Third, it encourages a more collective and decentralized way of DDoS defense, allowing network operators to pool their knowledge and resources together to counter the common threat of DDoS attacks.

4 Results and Evaluation

4.1 DDoS Detection Accuracy

The DDoS Detection Accuracy Comparison graph showcases the effectiveness of NeuroGuard against signature-based and traditional machine learning (ML) methods across SYN Flood, HTTP GET Flood, UDP Flood, and DNS Amplification attacks, as measured by the F1-score; consistently, NeuroGuard exhibits superior performance, achieving higher F1-scores for all attack types, indicating its improved accuracy in detecting diverse DDoS attacks, particularly for those aforementioned attacks. As shown in Fig. 5 with the data of Table 1.

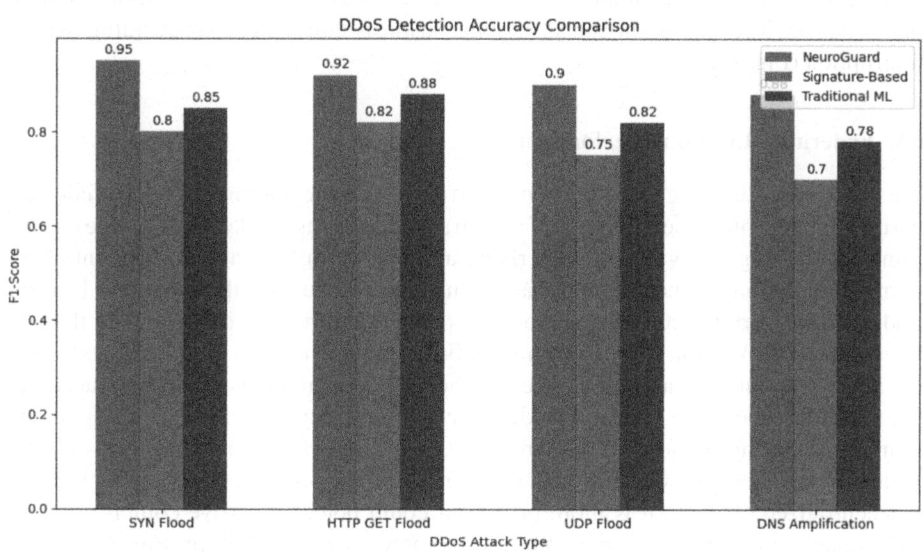

Fig.5. DDoS Detection Accuracy Comparison - Simulated data

Table 1. DDoS Detection Accuracy Comparison (F1-Score)

DDoS Attack Type	NeuroGuard	Signature-Based	Traditional ML
SYN Flood	0.95	0.80	0.85
HTTP GET Flood	0.92	0.82	0.88
UDP Flood	0.88	0.75	0.82
DNS Amplification	0.88	0.70	0.78

4.2 DDoS Mitigation Effectiveness

The "DDoS Attack Mitigation Effectiveness" chart displays the time evolution of a DDoS attack and the efficiency of NeuroGuard in mitigating it. The red line signifies the volume of attack traffic (in Gbps) hitting the target server without NeuroGuard. This line stays at a fairly constant high level, reflecting an ongoing attack. The green line shows the volume of attack traffic with NeuroGuard enabled. This line demonstrates a sharp and dramatic decline over time, indicating NeuroGuard's capability to rapidly cut the volume of malicious traffic to the server.The graph illustrates an important performance characteristic: NeuroGuard actively blocks and filters malicious traffic, keeping it from flooding the target. The exponential decline of the green line demonstrates an adaptive mitigation approach, whereby NeuroGuard learns and refines its defenses to stop more advanced attack patterns. The gap between the red and green lines visually shows how much attack traffic NeuroGuard successfully diverted. By lowering the volume of the attacks to near zero in a short period of time, NeuroGuard is effective in protecting the defended server and guaranteeing service availability throughout the duration of the DDoS attack. It is important for sustaining business continuity and avoiding service interruption (Fig. 6).

4.3 Federated Learning Performance

The "Federated Learning Convergence" chart illustrates the training curve of a federated learning model (blue line) and that of a centralized learning model (orange line) in 100 rounds of training. They both have a rising accuracy with training, but the centralized learning model has higher accuracy and convergence rate than the federated learning model. At the start, the centralized model has better performance improvement than the federated model. With an increase in the number of training rounds, the centralized model can achieve about 99% accuracy, whereas the federated model is about 98% accurate. The difference between the two models' accuracies starts decreasing the higher the number of training rounds. This discrepancy in accuracy between the two models can be due to the discrepancy in where the training is being performed. Federated learning is decentralized. Though it is more private, it could potentially have compromises on performance since the data is not gathered and processed in one place (Fig. 7).

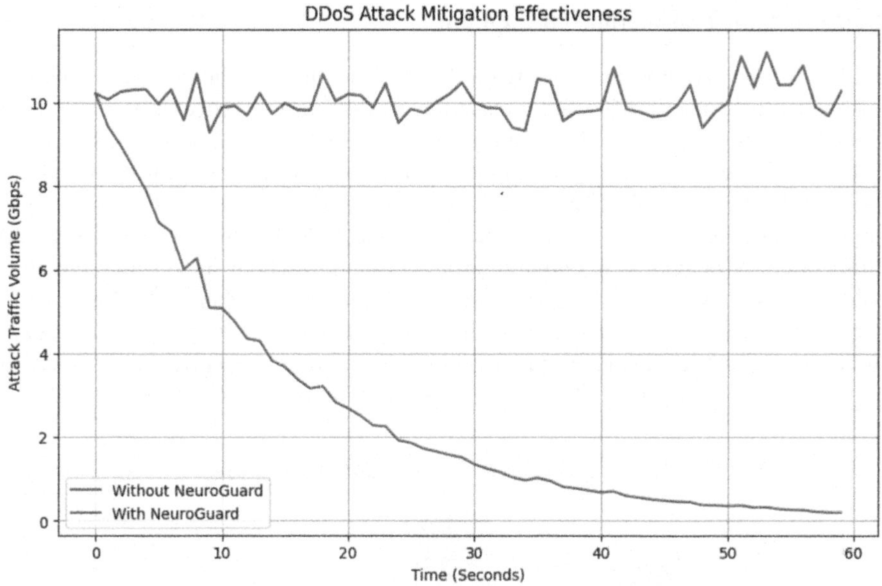

Fig.6. DDoS Mitigation Effectiveness - Simulated data

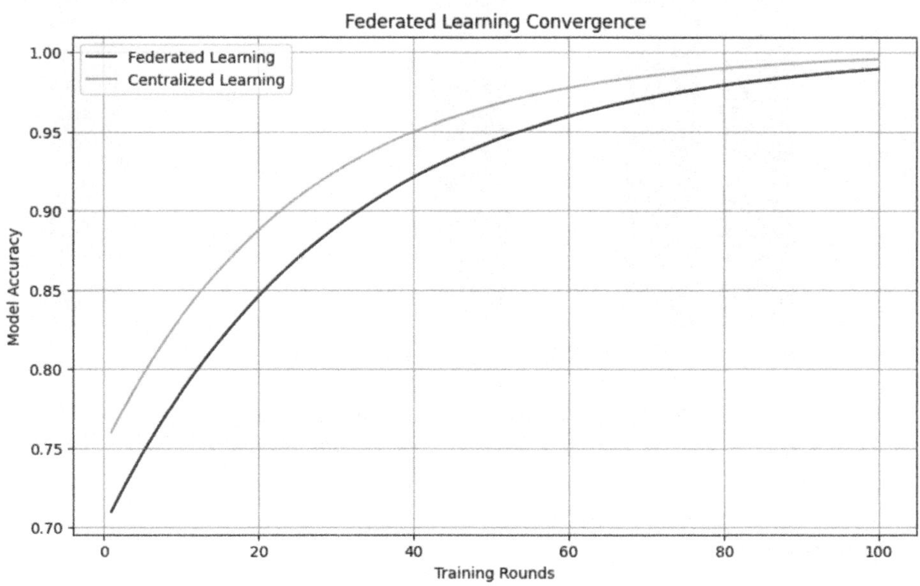

Fig.7. Federated Learning Performance-Simulated Data

4.4 Blockchain Transaction Throughput

The "Blockchain Transaction Throughput" bar chart displays the correlation between blockchain block size (in MB) and transaction processing capability (in terms of Transactions Per Second, or TPS). It is apparent that with the increase in block size from 1 MB to 4 MB, the transaction throughput also increases, hitting a high of around 1300 TPS at 4 MB. When the block size is increased to 8 MB, the throughput reduces slightly to about 1100 TPS. This implies that there is an ideal block size (approximately 4 MB in this example) for achieving maximum transaction throughput since very large blocks would incur processing overhead and might decrease the number of transactions that can be processed per second. The evidence shows a trade-off between block size and transaction throughput. Thus, in a practical implementation, the particular infrastructure would need to be experimented with to achieve optimal transaction throughput (Fig. 8).

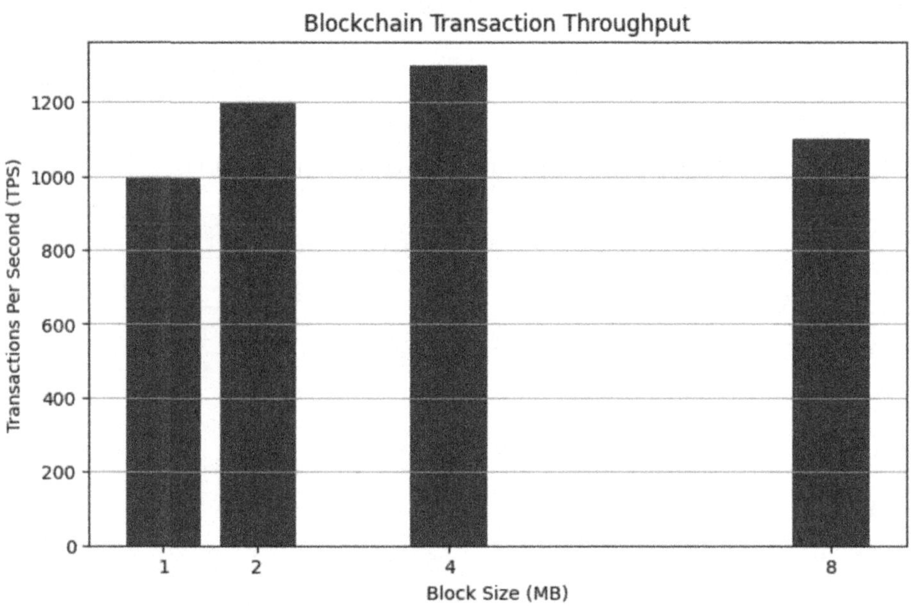

Fig.8. Blockchain Overhead - Simulated Data

5 Conclusion

In In summary, this paper presented NeuroGuard, a revolutionary Autonomous AI Defense Network (AADN) to counter the increasing menace of DDoS attacks. Embracing the limitations of conventional defenses against increasingly advanced and distributed attacks, NeuroGuard synergistically integrates deep learning, federated learning, and blockchain technologies for a stronger, adaptive, and privacy-protecting solution.

NeuroGuard's foundation is a deep learning-driven traffic analysis engine using CNNs and RNNs to provide high-accuracy, real-time identification of malicious traffic. Dynamic in nature, it adjusts to changing attack methods, staying effective against the dynamic DDoS environment. Solving for data privacy and scalability constraints, NeuroGuard has a federated learning module built-in. This allows for collective model training in a distributed network while maintaining each participant's data privacy and still reaching a global intelligence, thus ensuring robustness and scalability. Additionally, blockchain technology adds security, transparency, and trust in the form of a tamper-proof record of traffic management decisions and secure threat intelligence exchange. Integration allows NeuroGuard to dynamically respond to threats as determined through real-time risk evaluation, enforcing smart traffic filtering, rate limiting, and blacklisting to neutralize DDoS attacks while keeping legitimate users' impact at a minimum. This work adds a new AADN architecture combining deep learning, federated learning, and blockchain. Initial findings show the feasibility and efficacy of NeuroGuard in DDoS protection while maintaining data privacy and system integrity. Future research involves performance optimization, investigation of new federated learning methods, and more advanced blockchain security features. NeuroGuard is a step towards a stronger and safer internet, showing how combined technologies can produce more resilient cybersecurity measures. The paper provides a solid foundation for cybersecurity researchers of the future.

References

1. Cao, Y., Gao, Y., Tan, R., Han, Q., Liu, Z.: Understanding internet DDoS mitigation from academic and industrial perspectives. IEEE Access **6**, 66641–66648 (2018)
2. Das, A.K., Bera, B., Saha, S., Kumar, N., You, I., Chao, H.C.: AI-envisioned blockchain-enabled signature-based key management scheme for industrial cyber–physical systems. IEEE Internet Things J. **9**(9), 6374–6388 (2021)
3. Gupta, B.B., Joshi, R.C., Misra, M.: Distributed denial of service prevention techniques. arXiv preprint arXiv:1208.3557 (2012)
4. Haider, S., et al.: A deep CNN ensemble framework for efficient DDoS attack detection in software defined networks. IEEE Access **8**, 53972–53983 (2020).
5. Kim, H., Park, J., Bennis, M., Kim, S.L.: Blockchained on-device federated learning. IEEE Commun. Lett. **24**(6), 1279–1283 (2019)
6. Li, L., Fan, Y., Tse, M., Lin, K.Y.: A review of applications in federated learning. Comput. Ind. Eng. **149**, 106854 (2020)
7. Mittal, M., Kumar, K., Behal, S.: Deep learning approaches for detecting DDoS attacks: a systematic review. Soft Comput. **27**(18), 13039–13075 (2023)
8. Mohamed, N.: DDoS attacks mitigation: a review of AI-based strategies and techniques. In: 2024 15th International Conference on Computing Communication and Networking Technologies (ICCCNT), pp. 1–6. IEEE (2024)
9. Pal, O., Alam, B., Thakur, V., Singh, S.: Key management for blockchain technology. ICT express. **7**(1), 76–80 (2021)
10. Shaaban, A.R., Abd-Elwanis, E., Hussein, M.: DDoS attack detection and classification via Convolutional Neural Network (CNN). In: 2019 Ninth International Conference on Intelligent Computing and Information Systems (ICICIS), pp. 233–238). IEEE (2019)
11. Sumathi, S., Rajesh, R., Lim, S.: Recurrent and deep learning neural network models for DDoS attack detection. J. Sensors **2022**(1), 8530312 (2022)

12. Wani, S., Imthiyas, M., Almohamedh, H., Alhamed, K.M., Almotairi, S., Gulzar, Y.: Distributed denial of service (DDoS) mitigation using blockchain—A comprehensive insight. Symmetry **13**(2), 227 (2021)
13. Yang, K., Sunny, J.J., Wang, L.: Blockchain-based decentralized public key management for named data networking. In: The International Conference on Computer Communications and Networks (ICCCN 2018) (2018)
14. Zhang, B., Zhang, T., Yu, Z.: DDoS detection and prevention based on artificial intelligence techniques. In: 2017 3rd IEEE International Conference on Computer and Communications (ICCC) 2017 Dec 13, pp. 1276–1280. IEEE [14]

Challenges in Information Security Management System

Mariya Evtimova-Gardair(✉) and Frederique Segond

INRIA, Paris, France
{mariya.evtimova-gardair,frederique.segond}@inria.fr

Abstract. The article investigates the security management system challenges. The limitations of the current information security systems investigated are sovereignty, storage and access control, security, privacy, and safeguarding. The statement of improvement of this limitation is investigated. Self-sovereign AI information management system concerning identity is proposed as a solution that ensures the principles for sovereign, secure, reliable, and generic. A model for self- sovereignty AI system is proposed that uses blockchain. The analysis includes an investigation of the various features to determine the effectiveness in coping with the dynamic requirements for identity and its current challenges. It is proposed a result assessment scores and the evaluation of the results. The model is evaluated and it is defined as adherence level the High adherence.

Keywords: AI · Self- sovereign · Identity management · Sovereignty principles

1 Introduction

Using digital identity is an important cyber security aspect of each software system or platform. But it is also a difficult area to provide a secure solution for identity management that can be closely related to the physical identity world. In the literature are described different models [1–4] for identity management but they cannot provide a complete solution to ensure the sovereignty of identity and control over personal and confidential data storage. Identity sovereignty is related to other issues like security, privacy, and safeguarding [5, 6]. A solution is proposed concerning those issues using blockchain technologies and identifying a self-sovereign identity management model [7]. The implementation of blockchain technology contributes to the creation of a new identity management model called self-sovereign identity (SSI) that can solve all of the above issues and provide a user full sovereignty of their identity and storage- control of their corresponding personal and confidential data [8, 9]. The ownership of identity provides access to the private information in a Digital Wallet that is under the user's ownership and control. The Digital Wallet is considered to be a physical wallet that can save all the digital credentials as physical entities [10]. But the difference that can be observed with the physical wallet is that in the digital wallet, the credentials are digitally signed and verifiable which makes them faster. However, the model is peer- and to- peer that not

Published by Springer Nature Switzerland AG 2025
D. Verdejo and E. Mercier-Laurent (Eds.): AI4GS 2024, IFIP AICT 743, pp. 143–152, 2025.
https://doi.org/10.1007/978-3-031-96522-7_11

include another supplier or third- party for connection of the user and the organization. Another model that complements the self-sovereignty model is the self-sovereignty AI model. When applied to AI, this concept ensures that users maintain full control over how the data is used, shared, and processed by AI systems. It is important to mention that there is the predecessor of the self-sovereign identity management model which is the centralized identity management model and the federated identity management model. The centralized identity management model is the oldest IDM (identity management model), where the organization issues credentials to its users to let the users exploit their services. The relationship of trust between the organization and the user is defined by a shared secret that is usually represented by a login password and associated username. The control over the user identity data storage (personal or confidential) is performed by the organization. Also, the user needs to repeat the described process and requires credentials for each organization or system if they want to obtain service access.

The Federated Identity management model is a predecessor to the self-sovereign model. However, this model has a main problem in that the user does not have control over the information (personal or confidential) because it is stored in IDP (Identity provider) and is coming from a third-party provider.

The content of the paper includes section two which defines an overview of the self-sovereign principal definition, section three which defines self-sovereign AI challenges, section four which includes the self-sovereign measurement criteria, and then follows the self-sovereign model description and evaluation methodology and results. In the end, the conclusion is presented that summarizes the main contributions and defines future directions.

2 Self-Sovereign AI Challenges

The self-sovereign principles description is presented overall in Fig. 1 that represent also the main challenges for the self-sovereign artificial intelligence (SSAI). That can be categorized into the following groups: control, consent, portability, security, privacy, transparency, interoperability, ownership, decentralization, and longevity [11, 12].

Other related challenges more particularly for AI that can be considered as a subgroup of those presented in Fig. 1 are:

Technical complexity- SSAI models can be developed and managed using technical expertise and computational resources. However, user-friendly interfaces and accessible tools are crucial for wider adoption, but many are rudimentary.
Explainability and Trust- ensuring transparency about the decision taken from SSAI models and how that can be performed when identifying potential biases and building trust with users remains challenging.
Ethical Considerations-Ethical issues related to data privacy, algorithmic bias, and potential misuse are of particular concern for artificial intelligence especially in autonomous systems.

2.1 Control

User can perform complete control over their digital identity and personal data.

User Control: Users own and manage their own SSAI model, deciding on its training data and learning parameters and even setting ethical guidelines for its behavior. This empowers users to tailor the AI to their needs and ensure it aligns with their values.

2.2 Consent

Users need to provide explicit consent for data usage or sharing.

Regarding collaboration and sharing, users can choose to share their SSAI model with others. This will allow for the formation of collaborative AI ecosystems where models can learn from each other and benefit from collective intelligence.

2.3 Portability

A user can transfer their identity across systems without restriction. This characteristic refers to the user's ability to transition between different systems, platforms, or environments while maintaining access to their data, preferences, and services.

2.4 Security

That characteristic refers to the attributes or features associated with a user that are used to verify their identity, ensure security, and protect data. Data requires secured storage and the user needs to be protected from misuse or breaches.

2.5 Privacy

User data is safe in a private mode and only necessary data is disclosed.

Regarding privacy, the user's data remains under their own control. SSAI models can learn from their data without directly accessing it, protecting the user's privacy and preventing unauthorized use. Blockchain technology further secures their privacy.

2.6 Transparency

Transparency ensures that the process, systems, and policies related to collecting, storing, and utilizing user identity information are clear, accessible, and understandable to users. As a characteristic transparency also emphasizes accountability, user control, and compliance with legal and ethical standards.

Transparency as a characteristic defines the system the way the data is used and by whom.

2.7 Interoperability

Interoperability assures the identification of the works seamlessly across platforms, systems, and services. Furthermore, interoperability supports the ability of the different systems, platforms, and organizations to seamlessly exchange, understand, and use identity-related information in a secure, consistent, and efficient way. That provides support for interaction with the users across various systems without requiring redundant identity verification or data re-entry.

2.8 Ownership

Ownership defines the control, authority, and responsibility a user or entity has over their digital identity, credentials, and associated data within the system. That definition assures that the individual or organization can manage and dictate how their identity information is created, used, shared, and protected.

Characterize users' control over their identity, rather than relying on centralized authorities.

2.9 Decentralization

Decentralization is defined as shifting control and authority over identity information from centralized entities (like governments, corporations, or organizations) to individuals and distributed networks. It implements technologies such as blockchain or distributed ledger to enable secure, transparent, and self-sovereign identity systems [13].

Identity data is not stored or controlled by a single entity.

Unlike traditional AI models controlled by corporations or governments, SSAI models live on decentralized blockchain networks. This removes single points of failure and ensures transparency and accountability in their development and operation.

2.10 Longevity

Longevity defines the ability of the identity management system to remain effective, secure, and relevant over an extended period, despite evolving technologies, organizational needs, and regulatory requirements. Longevity ensures that the system can sustainably support identity management operations without frequent overhauls or obsolescence.

Identity systems are long-lasting, surviving platform changes.

3 Self-Sovereign Measurement Criteria

3.1 Control

- Availability criteria of tools for managing sharing, or revoking access to data
- Percentage of operations requiring user consent
- Use of decentralized identifiers (DIDs) vs. centralized systems

3.2 Consent

- Audit of user consent for identity actions
- Percentage of actions requiring explicit user consent
- Transparency and ease of withdrawing consent

3.3 Portability

- Number of interoperable systems or services
- Percentage of cases where data can be ported without friction
- Ease of data export and re-import across platforms

3.4 Security

- Incidence rate of data breaches or theft
- Strength of encryption and security protocols
- Use of multi-factor authentication (MFA) or cryptographic proofs for identity verification

3.5 Privacy

- Existence of privacy-by-design practices like zero-knowledge proofs.
- Minimal data disclosure in transactions
- Audit reports on data minimization and anonymization
- data and the model itself.

3.6 Transparency

- Platforms providing transparent data usage logs
- Availability and quality of data usage reports
- Clear and accessible privacy policies

3.7 Interoperability

- Number of platforms or services accepting a specific credential
- Adherence to open standards like W3C verifiable credentials, DID, etc.
- Number of partners or ecosystems using the identity framework

3.8 Ownership

- Percentage of identities using self- sovereign mechanisms vs. centralized ones
- Proportion of identity processes controlled by users
- Use of decentralized identity solutions (e.g., blockchain-based)

3.9 Decentralization

- Use of decentralized storage (e.g., blockchain, IPFS)
- Diversity of validators or authorities in the network
- Decentralized governance models (e.g., community or peer governance)

3.10 Longevity

- Existence of long-term viability strategies for identity providers
- Historical success in transferring identity data
- Support for versioning and upgrades without requiring re-establishment of identity

4 Self-Sovereign AI Model Description

Figure 2 is presented a self-sovereign AI (SSAI) model. It is a model that refers to an artificial intelligence framework that prioritizes individual autonomy, privacy, and control over data. It aligns with the principles of self-sovereign identity (SSI), which emphasizes decentralized ownership of personal data and credentials. When applied to AI, this concept ensures that users maintain full control over how their that is used, shared, and processed by AI systems. The proposed model in Fig. 2 is self- sovereign AI model with blockchain that integrates blockchain technology into the architecture of AI systems to create a decentralized, transparent, and privacy-preserving framework. This model ensures that individuals maintain full control over their data and interactions with AI, leveraging blockchain for trust, security, and accountability.

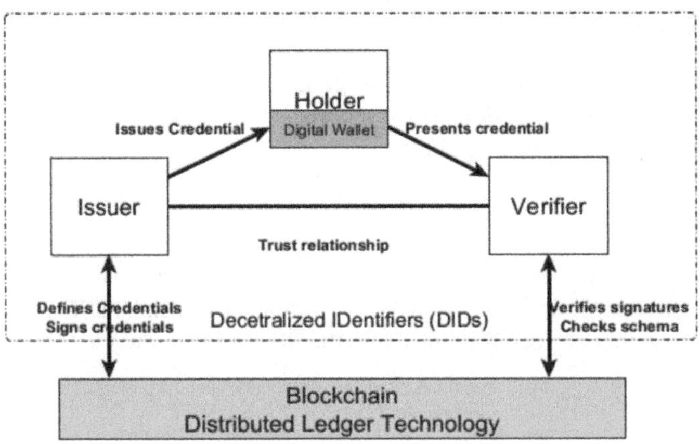

Fig. 2. Self-sovereign AI model description

SSAI considers in its ecosystem three key roles i.e., Issuer, Holder, and Verifier that are shown in Fig. 2. Firstly, an issuer creates and issues credentials to a holder. Then a holder receives credentials from an issuer and can hold the credential until it is required to share that credential with a verifier. The last role is the verifier which can receive and verify credentials that are presented by a holder. This SSAI implementation is based on the Verifiable Credential (VC) and Decentralized IDentifier (DID) standards which are proposed for creating a cryptographically verifiable digital identity that is fully governed by its owner. The use of VC is to present similar information on the web. The DID is a persistent, universally unique identifier and is associated with the private key that owns it. This relationship is completely different from other used identifiers such as mobile number, IP address, and domain name.

5 Evaluation Methodology and Results

5.1 Evaluation Methodology

5.2 Evaluation Results

The represented SSI system model is evaluated based on the 10 principles.

Principle's evaluation based on Levels 1–5(Table 1):

- Control- Level 3

Table 1. Evaluation score

Score range	Adherence Level	Description
1–2	Low adherence	The system shows very minimal adherence to SSI principles. It likely uses centralized structures, lacks user control, and doesn't offer meaningful privacy or portability options. Improvements are necessary
2–3	Partial adherence	The system meets some SSI principles but may lack in critical areas like decentralization or security. There's some level of control for the user, but significant gaps remain in interoperability or privacy
3–4	Moderate adherence	The system demonstrates adherence to most SSI principles. It supports some user control, consent, security, and privacy but could improve in areas like full decentralization or ensuring seamless portability
4–5	High adherence	The system demonstrates adherence to most SSI principles. It supports some user control, consent, security, and privacy but could improve in areas like full decentralization or ensuring seamless portability

Users can manage, share, and revoke access to their identity, but some parts of the process still require third-party approval.

- Consent- Level 5

  Explicit user consent is required for all data-sharing actions. The system is transparent about consent and provides easy options to revoke it.
- Portability- Level 3

  Identity can be moved between a few platforms, but there are limitations with some providers not supporting the standards used.
- Security- Level 4

  Strong encryption is used, and multi-factor authentication is supported, but some minor vulnerabilities have been reported.
- Privacy- Level 3

  Data minimization is in place, but the system doesn't fully implement privacy-enhancing technologies like zero-knowledge proofs.

- Transparency- Level 4
  The system provides clear logs of data usage and transparent reports, but users need more education on how to access this information.
- Interoperability- Level 3
  The system adheres to common standards (e.g., DIDs and verifiable credentials), but it isn't yet fully supported across all major platforms.
- Ownership- Level 5

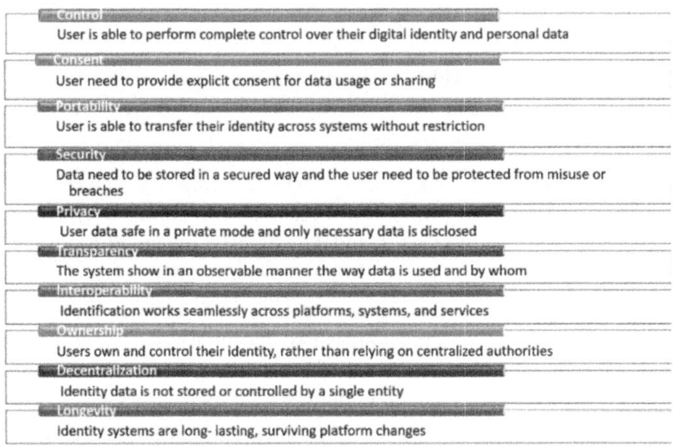

Fig.1. Identification of the main challenges for self-sovereign artificial intelligence model

  Users fully own and control their identity without reliance on third-party identity providers.
- Decentralization- Level 4
  The system uses decentralized storage (blockchain) for identity management, but some components still rely on centralized infrastructure.
- Longevity- Level 4
  The system has a clear longevity plan, including the ability to transfer identity to new systems, but there are some concerns over long-term provider reliability.

After summarization the total score is evaluated through the formula $\frac{\sum_{i=0}^{n} L}{N}$ that define the adherence level as High adherence. (Fig. 3)

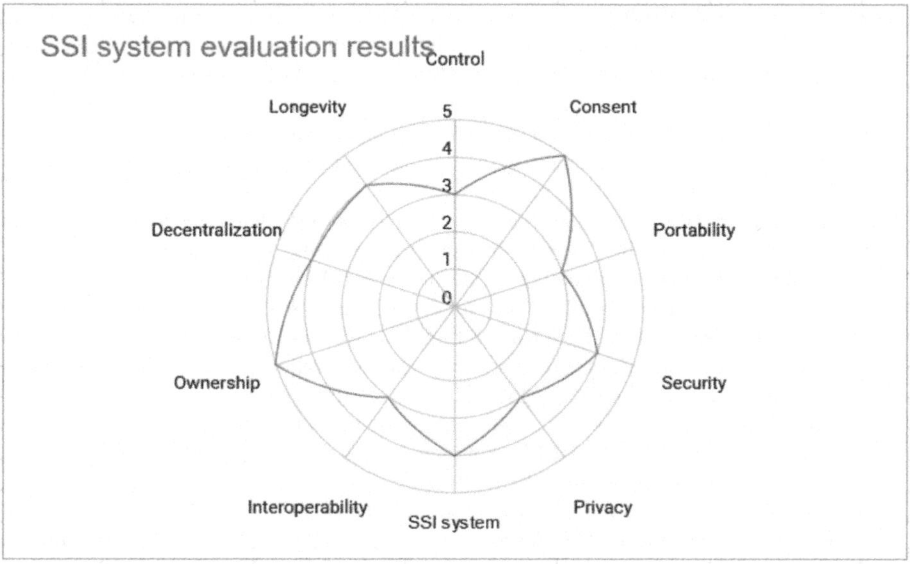

Fig. 3. Evaluation results

6 Conclusion

This paper presents self-sovereign challenges and their characteristics. The investigation leads to the identification of a set of principles with measurable characteristics. A self-sovereign model is introduced, and its evaluation is discussed concerning the proposed self-sovereign principles [14–16]. An evaluation model is also proposed, which is used to assess the self-sovereign model and characterize it as having either moderate adherence or high adherence to these principles.

References

1. Pöhn, D., Hommel, W.: An overview of limitations and approaches in identity management. In: Proceedings of the 15th International Conference on Availability, Reliability and Security, pp. 1–10 (2016)
2. Vrielynck, P.J., Van hamme, T., Ghostin, R., Lagaisse, B., Preuveneers, D., Joosen, W.: A self-sovereign identity approach to decentralized access control with transitive delegations. In: Proceedings of the 29th ACM Symposium on Access Control Models and Technologies, pp. 139–147 (2024)
3. Gavidia-Calderon, C., Kordoni, A., Bennaceur, A., Levine, M., Nuseibeh, B.: The IDEA of us: an identity-aware architecture for autonomous systems. ACM Tran. Softw. Eng. Methodol. **33**(6), 1–38 (2024). https://doi.org/10.1145/3654439
4. Wang, H., et al.: MIS: a multi-identifier management and resolution system in the metaverse. ACM Trans. Multimed. Comput. Commun. App. **20**(7), 1–25 (2024)
5. Tan, K.L., Chi, C.-H., Lam, K.-Y.: Survey on digital sovereignty and identity: from digitization to digitalization. ACM Comput. Surv. **56**(3), pp.1–36 (2023)

6. Aleksandrova, S.V., Vasiliev, V.A., Aleksandrov, M.N.: Problems of implementing information security management systems. In: 2020 International Conference Quality Management, Transport and Information Security, Information Technologies (IT&QM&IS), pp. 78–81. IEEE (2020)
7. Kaneriya, J., Patel, H.: A comparative survey on blockchain based self sovereign identity system. In 2020 3rd International Conference on Intelligent Sustainable Systems (ICISS), pp. 1150–1155. IEEE (2020)
8. Naik, N., Jenkins, P.: Governing principles of self-sovereign identity applied to blockchain enabled privacy preserving identity management systems. In: 2020 IEEE International Symposium on Systems Engineering (ISSE), pp. 1–6. IEEE (2020)
9. Lohmöller, J., et al.: The unresolved need for dependable guarantees on security, sovereignty, and trust in data ecosystems. Data Knowl. Eng. **151**, 102301 (2024)
10. Naik, N., Jenkins, P.: Is self-sovereign identity really sovereign? In: 2022 IEEE International Symposium on Systems Engineering (ISSE), pp. 1–7. IEEE (2022)
11. Grüner, A., Mühle, A., Meinel, C.: An integration architecture to enable service providers for self-sovereign identity. In: 2019 IEEE 18th International Symposium on Network Computing and Applications (NCA), pp. 1–5. IEEE (2019)
12. Dong, C., Jiang, F., Li, X., Yao, A., Li, G., Liu, X.: A blockchain-aided self-sovereign identity framework for edge-based UAV delivery system. In: 2021 IEEE/ACM 21st International Symposium on Cluster, Cloud and Internet Computing (CCGrid), pp. 622–624. IEEE (2021)
13. Dixit, A., Smith-Creasey, M., Rajarajan, M.: A decentralized IIoT identity framework based on self-sovereign identity using blockchain. In: 2022 IEEE 47th Conference on Local Computer Networks (LCN), pp. 335–338. IEEE (2022)
14. Klare, M., Verlande, L., Greiner, M., Lechner, U.: How blockchain and artificial intelligence influence digital sovereignty. In: Papadaki, M., Rupino, P., da Cunha, M., Themistocleous, K.C. (eds.) Information Systems: 19th European, Mediterranean, and Middle Eastern Conference, EMCIS 2022, Virtual Event, December 21–22, 2022, Proceedings, pp. 3–16. Springer Nature Switzerland, Cham (2023). https://doi.org/10.1007/978-3-031-30694-5_1
15. Roberts, H.: Digital sovereignty and artificial intelligence: a normative approach. Ethics Inf. Technol. **26**(4), 1–10 (2024)
16. Usman, H., Nawaz, B., Naseer, S.: The future of state sovereignty in the age of artificial intelligence. J. Law Soc. Stud. **5**, 142–152 (2023)

LLM Based Data Annotation and Augmentation for NER and Relationship Extraction Models Enhancement

Skander Soltani(✉) and Elias Limouni

OPPSCIENCE, 14 Avenue Trudaine, 75009 Paris, France
ssoltani@oppscience.com

Abstract. The foundation of effective analysis and decision-making in Cyber Threat Intelligence (CTI) relies on a robust knowledge basis of concepts (threat actors, tools, malwares,...) and relationships between them (targets, located at,...) enabling analysts to identify, analyze, and mitigate potential threats. STIX (Structured Threat Information Expression) is a serialized structured format that aims to facilitate the exchange of cyber threat intelligence (CTI) data between organizations by interoperability between cybersecurity tools. To enable STIX objects generation from unstructured documents containing emerging objects (threats, actors,...), it is required to automate extracting concepts and the relationships between. These extractions can be tackled as supervised machine learning (ML) tasks. Supervised ML models training requires the availability of a high-quality annotated corpus with enough concepts and relationships. Manual annotation by experts is costly due to the semantic ambiguity between certain concepts and relationships and their scarcity in the documents.

In this paper we present a method based on large language models (LLM) to automate the creation of the annotated corpus. The LLMs twice. First, they are used to automatically annotate a corpus from attack using a couple of prompts fitted to extract STIX concepts and relationships. As some concepts or relationships underrepresented, the corpus is completed by a second synthetic one obtained by asking LLMs to generate new documents inspired by existing one and containing concepts and relation provided in the prompt. Our evaluation of extraction models shows the effectiveness of this approach as the quality metrics are satisfactory.

Keywords: Named entity recognition · relation extraction · corpus annotation · large language model

1 Introduction

Cyber threat intelligence (CTI) aims to gather and share information concerning the occurrence and the assessment of threats description including their nature, their actors... CTI becomes a crucial part of companies' cyber security strategy as it allows them to be more proactive in their approach and determine which threats represent the greatest risks and the more recent ones. One important backbone of CTI is the capacity to automatically build a reliable knowledge base.

Published by Springer Nature Switzerland AG 2025
D. Verdejo and E. Mercier-Laurent (Eds.): AI4GS 2024, IFIP AICT 743, pp. 153–160, 2025.
https://doi.org/10.1007/978-3-031-96522-7_12

One possible option to model CTI data is to use Structured Threat Information Expression (STIX) [5, 9, 14]. STIX is a language and serialization format used to exchange cyber threat intelligence. STIX is open source and free. With STIX, all aspects of suspicion, compromise and attribution can be rep-resented clearly with concepts (malware, attack pattern, campaign, infrastructure…) and relationships (malware authored-by threat-actor, attack-pattern tar-gets location …).

Filling and enriching STIX objects related to any identified threat can be painful as the information should be extracted from unstructured data. In this paper, we propose to automate this task by handling it as a two-stage supervised machine learning: the first one deals with extraction of concepts while the second focuses on the extraction of relationships between them (see [13, 15–18] for similar approaches). Supervised machine learning trains algorithms on labelled data, i.e. data that is already correctly labelled. Labeling a significant amount of data is costly as it requires a certain level of expertise (particularly because of the ambiguity of some concepts).

To tackle the corpus annotation challenge, we automate the process by delegating it to a large language model (LLM). The annotation is handled as a two-step process: the first one for concepts while the second focuses on the relationships between the concepts. Of course, the quality of annotation is an important issue which can be resolved thanks to the process of designing and refining the prompts (prompt engineering). The last key issue is the scarcity of some concepts and relationships which can impact negatively on the models' quality. This issue is solved by data augmentation. As previously, an LLM is used to generate texts with a custom prompt that contains the concepts and relationships to be included in and some examples to guide the generation by LLM (few-shot learning).

After the corpus annotation, training the models for concepts and relationship extraction becomes possible. The used models are based on transformers. The architecture of the models is straightforward: it combines transformers to compute token (word or subword) embedding vectors followed by a specific classification layer. The models can easily be deployed locally, for example as a webservice. There are at least a few advantages to training dedicated models and then use them in production instead of large language models:

- Data privacy: models are deployed locally so there is no need to request external APIs and thus carrying data on the net
- The possibility of continuous improvement of the models with newly annotated data
- The inference time, which is much faster for these models than for LLMs especially when using GPUs.

The models we experimented with in the framework of this paper are in-house ones based on multilingual BERT transformers. See Sect. 3 for more details on their basics and performance.

2 Labelled Data Collection

Collecting labelled data for training models is a crucial milestone as it is the most prominent driver of the trained models' performance. With this in perspective and in the absence of available annotated data, we elaborated a two-stage strategy supported by LLMs.

Our work fits the concepts and relationships specified in a framework under the name of Structured Threat Information Expression (STIX). STIX is a powerful and essential standard that helps the cybersecurity community communicate, collaborate, and ultimately, defend against cyber threats more effectively. Its standardized and structured format, machine-readability, and comprehensive scope make it a cornerstone for modern threat intelligence practices [7]. It is supported by various commercial and open-source tools in the cybersecurity industry and is often used in conjunction with TAXII (Trusted Automated Exchange of Indicator Information) for secure transmission of STIX data.

The key components of the format are:

- STIX Domain Objects (SDOs): like threat Actor, vulnerability, attack pattern, campaign, …
- STIX Cyber-observable Objects (SCOs): file, network traffic, user account, Software, …
- STIX Relationship Objects (SROs): relationship that connects two SDOs or SCOs.

We have made full use of the unannotated data available on the internet. Among the sources we used:

- MITRE ATT&CK GitHub contains a large amount of textual data. Each text contains a sample of the targeted concepts and relations. These texts are gathered from different sources,
- The threatpost website [10] proclaims itself as the first stop for fast-breaking security news, conversations and analysis from around the world. The site has not been updated since 2022 but its content remains valuable for training ML models task,
- Some materials from: f-secure.com [11], Computer Emergency Response Team (in French) [12].

2.1 LLM Based Annotation

Thanks to the emergence of large language models since the release of ChatGPT, datasets annotation can be automated with a high level of quality. This avoids costly and slow annotation campaigns that require a high level of expertise at the cost of rapid engineering and the cost of API requests, which is ultimately much lower than the total cost of manual annotation. The goal of prompt engineering is to craft specific, clear, concise, and well-structured queries to maximize the quality of the LLM response. In our case the prompt should contain the instructions on the response text format that enables the extraction of the concepts and relationships after a parsing step. As stated before, our approach has two steps:

- The first stage focuses on the extraction of concepts contained in the provided text. The prompt in this case will list the targeted concepts with a concise explanation of each as we are dealing with very specialized ones. The prompt requests the extraction of the concepts contained in the provided text and then organize the response as a JSON like string that will make it easier to extract them. See prompt in appendix.
- The second stage focuses on the extraction relationships. In this case we provide the same text with the list of extracted concepts. Again, the prompt requests the extraction of the relationships and then to format the response as a JSON like string. See prompt in appendix.

The observation of the quality of extractions shows the effectiveness of our method as the error rate has been estimated on a random sample to be less than 5% which is an impressive score given the task's complexity. For both annotation steps, we used GroqCloud API to request LLMs [1]. We have restricted ourselves to a selection of concepts and relations to keep the prompts concise.

However, we noticed a lack of some important concepts in the annotated texts ("Infrastructure" and "vulnerability" in particular) and relationships ("compromised" and "delivers" in particular), which lead to a poor quality. This led us to complete the annotated dataset with a step of augmentation which also involves an LLM.

2.2 LLM Based Augmentation

As mentioned above, we employed an LLM to complete the annotated dataset to compensate for the lack of quantity of concepts (Infrastructure and vulnerability) and relationships (compromised and delivers in particular). For this purpose, we listed:

- some values of the concepts as well as those involved in the relationships targeted by the augmentation
- some examples of parts of texts already available containing the targeted concepts and relationships.

These values are then included in the prompt that asks the LLM to generate a text with examples of concepts and relationshipswhich is like one of the texts' parts.

A validation step is necessary to check that the generated texts contain all the concepts and relationships specified in the prompt. When a text is validated, we extract the concepts and relationships in and then use it in training or evaluating the models. Again, we used GroqCloud API to request LLMs [1].

3 Training and Evaluating Models

Now that we have built a good-quality dataset containing sufficient volumes of data, we can consider training models for the annotated concepts and relationships specified in STIX objects. As stated before, we have opted for an approach using two distinct models: one for the concept extraction task and the other one for the relationship extraction one. Both models include the BERT transformer combined with a specific layer for each task. The BERT model generates contextual word representations (embeddings) capturing their semantic meaning in their context [3]. For all the experiments, we used the case insensitive multilingual version [20].

3.1 Concept Extraction Model

Concept extraction is a common task in natural language processing. It is known as named entity extraction (NER). NER involves identifying and categorizing spans of sequences into predefined categories (or tags). Usually, these entities are names of people, organizations, locations, dates, but in our specific case are a subset of concepts specified in the STIX format; see the list of concepts in the result table. We focused only on a subset as the other ones were rare in annotated documents even after the data augmentation step.

The model combines [2, 18, 19]:

- the BERT last layer embeddings,
- a linear layer for embedding adaption,
- a bi-LSTM layer which enhances contextual understanding, feature extraction, dependency handling, and ambiguity resolution
- a linear layer for classifying the sequence tokens

A post-processing step allows creating concepts particularly for the ones with multiple tokens.

Two models were trained: the first uses only the annotated with LLM corpus while the second uses the same data with the generated texts with the data augmentation step. In both cases, the corpus was split into two parts: the first one is used for training the model while the second one is used for its evaluation. Precision, recall and F1-score were used for model evaluation as they are the common metrics for this kind of task.

The quality metrics on the validation part of the datasets are displayed in the following Table 1.

Table 1. Quality metric for concept extraction model before and after data augmentation

	before data augmentation			after data augmentation		
	precision	recall	f1-score	precision	recall	f1-score
ATTACK_PATTERN	0.82	0.44	0.57	0.66	0.56	0.61
CAMPAIGN	0.89	0.61	0.72	0.86	0.65	0.74
DATE	0.87	0.95	0.91	0.89	0.98	0.93
IDENTITY	0.81	0.55	0.65	0.63	0.54	0.58
INFRASTRUCTURE	0.96	0.47	0.64	0.59	0.51	0.55
LANGUAGE	0.75	0.84	0.79	1.00	0.78	0.88
LOCATION	0.55	0.90	0.68	0.90	0.91	0.90
MALWARE	0.00	0.90	0.00	0.79	0.88	0.83
THREAT_ACTOR	0.84	0.84	0.84	0.74	0.82	0.78
TOOL	0.00	0.35	0.00	0.86	0.45	0.59
VULNERABILITY	0.00	0.00	0.00	0.92	0.85	0.88
macro-average	0.59	0.62	0.61	0.82	0.74	0.77
mico-average	0.62	0.74	0.57	0.80	0.78	0.78

We notice that data augmentation improves the quality of almost all types which is confirmed by a significant increase in average metrics.

3.2 Relationship Extraction Model

Relationship extraction is also a common task of natural language processing. The primary goal of Relationship Extraction models is to extract meaningful relationships between entities from text data and classify them into predefined classes. It plays a crucial role in automating information extraction and knowledge graph construction.

We propose here a model based on machine learning. Such models handle entities by pair.

The architecture of the model proposed here is composed of:

- the BERT last layer embeddings,
- locate the couple of entities in a sequence, get the embeddings of the first token of each and then concatenate their embeddings.
- For training samples, samples of each relationship type form a cluster.
- Metric learning is used to construct a custom Mahalanobis distance to separate the clusters
- Then, a prototype is computed for each class in the relationship tagset as the centroid of the samples of this class.

Inference for a pair of entities is achieved as follows:

- Concatenate the embeddings vector of the involved entities
- Identify the nearest prototype to the embedding vector
- Reject the prediction if among the kNN nearest neighbors, a significant number belongs to other relationship classes. This avoids always creating a relationship between concepts.

This kind of method is known as few-shot methods as they require only a few examples to learn robust and powerful models [6–8]. Again, the following Table 2 shows the benefits of data augmentation.

Table 2. Quality metric for relationship extraction models before and after data augmentation

	before data augmentation			after data augmentation		
	precision	recall	f1-score	precision	recall	f1-score
COMPROMISED	1.00	0.20	0.33	0.50	0.44	0.47
DELIVERS	1.00	0.27	0.43	0.70	0.54	0.61
LOCATED-AT	0.71	0.77	0.74	0.93	0.88	0.90
TARGETS	0.75	0.26	0.39	1.00	0.71	0.83
USES	0.69	0.43	0.53	0.86	0.78	0.82
macro-average	0.83	0.39	0.48	0.80	0.67	0.73
mico-average	0.77	0.44	0.52	0.84	0.71	0.76

We notice that the improvements in quality scores are even more significant than for concept extraction.

4 Conclusion

In this paper, we have shown the effectiveness of using LLMs to build low-cost annotated datasets that will be used to learn supervised models for concept and relationship extraction. LLMs have been used to annotate existing documents and to generate synthetic texts containing rare concepts and relations. The creation of a good quality annotated dataset enables training concept and relationship extraction models. The work uses a subset of the STIX objects and relations.

The models trained and evaluated using this dataset show that the data augmentation step improves dramatically the quality of the extractions. These models are much lighter than LLMs and can therefore handle large quantities of data. Furthermore, they are easy to deploy locally, so they preserve the data privacy. Future work will focus on extending the tagset to complete the coverage of all STIX objects and relationships.

References

1. GroqCoud. https://groq.com/. Accessed 12 Sep 2024
2. Xu, L., Li, S., Wang, Y., Xu, L.: Named entity recognition of BERT-BiLSTM-CRF combined with self-attention. In: 18th International Conference, WISA, Proceedings 18, pp. 556–564. Springer International Publishing. Kaifeng, China (2021)
3. Devlin, J., Chang, M.-W., Lee, K., Toutanova, K.: BERT: Pre-training of deep bidirectional transformers for language understanding. In: Proceedings of NAACL-HLT 2019, pp 4171–4186. Association for Computational Linguistics, Minneapolis, Minnesota (2019)
4. Precision and recall. https://en.wikipedia.org/wiki/Precision_and_recall. Accessed 12 Sep 2024
5. ASIS Open, Introduction to STIX. https://oasis-open.github.io/cti-documentation/stix/intro
6. Gao, T., et al.: FewRel 2.0: towards more challenging few-shot relation classification. In: Proceedings of the 2019 Conference on Empirical Methods in Natural Language Processing and the 9th International Joint Conference on Natural Language Processing (EMNLP-IJCNLP), pp. 6250–6255. Hong Kong, China. Association for Computational Linguistics (2019)
7. Liu, J., Qin, X., Ma, X., Ran, W.: FREDA: few-shot relation extraction based on data augmentation. Appl. Sci. **13**(14), 8312 (2023). https://doi.org/10.3390/app13148312
8. Borchert, P., De Weerdt, J., Moen. M.-F.: Efficient information extraction in few-shot relation classification through contrastive representation learning. In: Proceedings of the 2024 Conference of the North American Chapter of the Association for Computational Linguistics: Human Language Technologies, pp. 638–646. Association for Computational Linguistics. Mexico City, Mexico (2024)
9. STIX data format. https://stixproject.github.io/data-model/0
10. https://threatpost.com/
11. http://www.f-secure.com
12. cert.ssi.gouv.fr
13. Marchiori, F., Conti, M., Verde, N.: STIXnet: A Novel and Modular Solution for Extracting All STIX Objects in CTI Reports (2023). https://doi.org/10.48550/arXiv.2303.09999
14. Barnum, S.: Standardizing cyber threat intelligence information with the structured threat information expression (STIX). MITRE Corp. **11**(2012), 1–22 (2012)
15. Wang, X., et al.: Cyber threat intelligence entity extraction based on deep learning and field knowledge engineering, pp. 406–413 (2022). https://doi.org/10.1109/CSCWD54268.2022.9776139
16. Merlano, C.: Enhancing cyber security through artificial intelligence and machine learning: a literature review. J. Cyber Secur. **6**(1), 89–116 (2024). https://doi.org/10.32604/jcs.2024.056164
17. Sarker, I.: Machine learning for intelligent data analysis and automation in cybersecurity: current and future prospects. Ann. Data Sci. **10**, 1–26 (2022). https://doi.org/10.1007/s40745-022-00444-2

18. Shota, F., Kawaguchi, N., Shigemoto, T., Yamauchi, T.: Extracting and analyzing cybersecurity named entity and its relationship with noncontextual IOCs from unstructured text of CTI sources. J. Inf. Process. **31**, 578–590 (2023)
19. Zhou, S., Liu, J., Zhong, X., Zhao, W.: Named entity recognition using BERT with whole world masking in cybersecurity domain. In: 2021 IEEE 6th International Conference on Big Data Analytics (ICBDA), Xiamen, China, 2021, pp. 316–320 (2021)
20. Gasmi, H., Laval, J., Bouras, A.: LSTM Recurrent Neural Networks for Cybersecurity Named Entity Recognition (2024). https://doi.org/10.48550/arXiv.2409.10521

The Definition of Biometric Data in the Context of French Legislative Experimentation and the Implementation of the AI Act

Amélie Turci[1,2](✉)

[1] Université de Rennes, Rennes, France
amelie.turci@univ-rennes.fr
[2] University of Ottawa, Ottawa, Canada

Abstract. Following the publication of EU regulation on artificial intelligence, which came into effect on August 2nd, 2024, the issue of biometric data—as excluded from Article 10 of French legislation of May 19th, 2023, which introduced an experimentation of augmented cameras for the Paris 2024 Olympic Games—arises once again. The definition of biometric data has evolved significantly since the earliest legislations (EU 1995 Directive/46/EC and the 1978 French Law Informatique et libertés), influenced by the opinions of authorities such as WP29, the EDPB, and the CNIL. It has ultimately been enshrined in the GDPR (Article 4, paragraph 14) and the Law Enforcement Directive (Article 3, paragraph 13). The definition therein includes purposes of identification or authentication, which the AI regulation (Article 3, paragraph 34) has moved away from, allowing for the inclusion of categorisation and emotion recognition.

The question then arises regarding the interplay between French legislation and the new European regulation, whose definitional provisions and prohibitions on certain AI systems—such as specific types of categorisation—will be applicable (February 2nd, 2025) before the end of the French experimentation period (March 31st, 2025). Indeed, the purported absence of biometric data in the experimental algorithms has been widely criticized.

Furthermore, there arises a broader question of coherence between the AI regulation and data protection Law (GDPR and the Law Enforcement Directive), with the former needing to be interpreted in light of the latter.

Keywords: Artificial Intelligence · Biometric Data · Olympic Games · AI Act · Data protection

Published by Springer Nature Switzerland AG 2025
D. Verdejo and E. Mercier-Laurent (Eds.): AI4GS 2024, IFIP AICT 743, pp. 161–177, 2025.
https://doi.org/10.1007/978-3-031-96522-7_13

1 Introduction

Beyond its protection by fundamental rights, among which the right to privacy,[1] the processing of biometric data is regulated by data protection law and the AI Act, which will be both the focus here.

There is a broad agreement on the *examples* of biometric data as an ever-ending list.[2] For instance, the WP29's typical examples in 2007 include behavioural characteristics such as a particular way to walk: *"typical examples of [...] biometric data" as "fingerprints, retinal patterns, facial structure, voices, but also hand geometry, vein patterns or even some deeply ingrained skill or other behavioural characteristic (such as handwritten signature, keystrokes,* ***particular way to walk*** *or to speak, etc...)".*[3] Yet many questions are to be raised about the *definition* of "biometrics" and "biometric data", which broadly speaking is the processing of human biological characteristics.[4] The issue we will address here is whether algorithmic systems for recognizing specific behaviours involve biometric data. We will examine the application of the regime under personal data legislation (GDPR[5] and the EU Law Enforcement Directive, hereinafter LED)[6] as well as the upcoming into force legislation on artificial intelligence (AI Act),[7]

---

[1] See CEDH, gr. ch., *S. and Marper v. Royaume-Uni*, 4 December 2008, n° 30562/04 and 30566/04: *"67.* ***The mere storing of data relating to the private life of an individual amounts to an interference within the meaning of Article 8*** *[...]. The subsequent use of the stored information has no bearing on that finding [...]."*

[2] C. CABAL, *Les méthodes scientifiques d'identification des personnes à partir de données biométriques et les techniques de mise en oeuvre*, 12 June 2003, p. 8 (Unofficial translation): *"Today, no character seems to be inherently excluded."*. This may be explained by the fact that *"almost everything, in the anatomy or the behaviour of a person, can be converted into a computer code that allows for identification"* (p.14).

[3] WP29, *Opinion 4/2007 on the concept of personal data*, 20 June 2007, p.8: (emphasis added). The WP29 (Article 29 Working Party) is the predecessor of the EDPB (European Data Protection Board) under the aegis of 1995 Directive/46/EC, i.e. before the GDPR. It is an independent EU body made up of representatives from the EU Member States, the EDPB (European Data Protection Supervisor) and the European Commission.

[4] On the concept of biometric data, see not. M. SZTULMAN, *La biométrie saisie par le droit public: étude sur l'identification et la localisation des personnes physiques*, Bibliothèque de droit public, Issy-les-Moulineaux, LGDJ, 2019.

[5] Regulation (EU) 2016/679 of the European Parliament and of the Council of 27 April 2016 on the protection of natural persons with regard to the processing of personal data and on the free movement of such data, and repealing Directive 95/46/EC (General Data Protection Regulation).

[6] Directive (EU) 2016/680 of the European Parliament and of the Council of 27 April 2016 on the protection of natural persons with regard to the processing of personal data by competent authorities for the purposes of the prevention, investigation, detection or prosecution of criminal offences or the execution of criminal penalties, and on the free movement of such data, and repealing Council Framework Decision 2008/977/JHA.

[7] Regulation (EU) 2024/1689 of the European Parliament and of the Council of 13 June 2024 laying down harmonised rules on artificial intelligence and amending Regulations (EC) No 300/2008, (EU) No 167/2013, (EU) No 168/2013, (EU) 2018/858, (EU) 2018/1139 and (EU)

which interact in an *"ecosystem logic"*.[8] This will helps us understand how French legislation on the experimentation of specific behaviour recognition during the Olympic and Paralympic Games held in France in the summer of 2024 (hereafter the Olympic Games Legislation)[9] fits within the European legislative framework.[10] Indeed, Article 10 of this legislation provides for an experimental processing, from May 20th, 2024, to March 31st, 2025, to detect specified behaviours during certain events through an algorithmic processing of the images transmitted by public space surveillance cameras.[11] The determination of the applicable regime is key because the regime for the category of sensitive data, among which are listed biometric data, provides greater protection for the data subjects (those whose personal data is being processed) than the regime for personal data. Under the GDPR, the processing of sensitive data is generally prohibited (with exceptions),[12] and in the LED, processing is restricted to fewer purposes compared to those permitted for personal data processing.[13]

The concept of biometric data has evolved over time in European digital law and, in consequence, French Law. Originally absent from the first EU legislation on personal data protection, the 1995 Directive,[14] the notion appeared in the 2016 package (GDPR and the Law Enforcement Directive) as personal data that enable or confirm the unique identification of a natural person.

Ultimately the AI Act also includes identification, categorisation, and even emotion recognition within its scope of biometric data.[15] It applies for its provisions on prohibited practices concurrently with the Olympic Games Legislation from February 2nd, 2025

2019/2144 and Directives 2014/90/EU, (EU) 2016/797 and (EU) 2020/1828 (Artificial Intelligence Act). See. not. "Dossier: L'AI Act", *RTD Eur.* 2024 p.533; C. Castets- Renard, "Le règlement européen sur l'intelligence artificielle (AI Act) : quel équilibre entre gestion des risques et protection des droits fondamentaux ?", *Journal de droit européen*, September 2024, vol. 7, n° 311, pp. 318-330.

8 B. Bertrand, "L'AI Act dans l'écosystème normatif européen de la régulation du numérique", *Revue trimestrielle de Droit Européen*, December 2024, n° 4, p. 533 (Unofficial translation).

9 Loi n° 2023-380 du 19 mai 2023 relative aux jeux Olympiques et Paralympiques de 2024 et portant diverses autres dispositions, 20 May 2023.

10 On the qualification of artificial intelligence for the algorithm used under this legislation, see below.

11 Regarding simple video surveillance, see Article L. 252-1, Code de la sécurité intérieure; and chapter II, title IV, book II, Code de la sécurité intérieure.

12 Art. 9: the processing of special categories of personal data is prohibited (para 1), unless explicit consent (para 2, a), necessary to protect the vital interests (c), personal data manifestly made public by the data subject (e), and other exceptions.

13 Art. 10: the processing of special categories of personal data is authorized *"where strictly necessary, subject to appropriate safeguards for the rights and freedoms of the data subject, and only"*: *"where authorised by Union or Member State law"* (a), or *"to protect the vital interests of the data subject or of another natural person;"* (b) or *"where such processing relates to data which are manifestly made public by the data subject"* (c).

14 Directive 95/46/EC of the European Parliament and of the Council of 24 October 1995 on the protection of individuals with regard to the processing of personal data and on the free movement of such data.

15 See not. Recitals 14 to 18, and Article 3(34), (35), (39), (40).

until March 31st, 2025.[16] Yet, personal data legislation will apply at all times. Depending on the context, the French implementation of the LED or the GDPR will apply throughout the entire application period of Article 10 of the Olympic Games Legislation. The LED concerns judicial cooperation in criminal matters and police cooperation (as the directive having repealed the 2008 Framework Decision)[17], and processing *"for the purposes of preventing and detecting criminal offenses, investigating and prosecuting such offenses, or executing criminal sanctions, including protection against threats to public security and preventing such threats"*).[18] The GDPR concerns civil and commercial matters.[19] Yet, this does not affect the definitions of personal, sensitive data or biometric data, which remain consistent across both the GDPR and the LED (hereinafter: the European data protection framework).

Outline. The present study proposes to analyse the definition of biometrics through time, before assessing the applicability of EU legislation on the French experimentation. Researchs' based on the analysis of the EU Institutions' documents will draw some reflections upon the use of what might appear as a special kind of biometrics.

2 The Legal Origin of Biometrics: The Gradual Evolution of Biometric Data Definition

2.1 Biometrics Previously to the GDPR: Biometrics Absent from the Law, yet not Ignored by Data Protection Authorities (DPA)

French law considering biometrics despite their absence from the 1995 Directive. Firstly, despite the legislation vacuum, biometric data had been increasingly used, and it were raising concerns. For example, in its 2001 activity report, the Commission Nationale de l'Informatique et des Libertés (the French Data protection authority, hereinafter CNIL) notes that the proliferation of biometric systems could lead to a *"weakening of the anonymous public space"*.[20] These anxieties remain relevant today.

[16] Yet the political will to continue, and even perpetuate, the experimentation was expressed during the finalization of the assessment report of the Government to the Parliament, pursuant to Article 10, XI, Loi n°2023-380 du 19 mai 2023. See COMPAGNON, S., GAIRAUD, M.-A. et HASSE, B., "Sécurité dans les transports : 'Je veux qu'on puisse utiliser l'intelligence artificielle', annonce le ministre", *Le Parisien*, 8 janvier 2025; REYNAUD, F., "Vidéosurveillance algorithmique : le rapport d'évaluation s'interroge sur l'efficacité du dispositif", *Le Monde*, 15 janvier 2025; THIERRY, G., "Vidéosurveillance algorithmique : le comité d'évaluation dresse un bilan mitigé", *La Gazette des Communes*, 16 janvier 2025.

[17] Council Framework Decision 2008/977/JHA of 27 November 2008 on the protection of personal data processed in the framework of police and judicial cooperation in criminal matters.

[18] Recitals 7 and 11.

[19] Except the *"activities which fall outside the scope of Union law, such as activities concerning national security [...] [and] activities in relation to the common foreign and security policy of the Union."* (GDPR, Recital 16) ; and the *"activities concerning national security [...] [and] activities which fall within the scope of Chapter 2 of Title V of the Treaty on European Union (TEU)"* (Directive, Recital 14). These matters are regulated by national law (in France, the Loi Informatique et Libertés of 1978).

[20] CNIL, *22e rapport d'activité, 2001: prévu par l'article 23 de la loi du 6 janvier 1978*, Paris, la Documentation française, 2002, p.171 (Unofficial translation).

In the same report, the CNIL defines *"biometric systems"* as *"applications allowing the automatic identification or eligibility of a person to be granted certain rights or services (notably the access to) based on the recognition of physical characteristics (fingerprints, iris patterns, hand contours, etc.), traces (DNA, blood, odors), or behavioural elements (signature, gait)"*.[21] The CNIL also states that these data are personal data falling under the scope of the Loi Informatique et Libertés[22] (the French Data Protection Act, hereinafter LIL): *"The purpose of these techniques is essentially to recognize a natural person, to identify, authenticate, and locate them"*.[23]

Indeed, the legal vacuum is not total: personal data, both personal and sensitive have been regulated under EU law since the 1995 Directive (transposed into French law in 2004).[24] And even though biometric data only appeared in 2016 for EU law, since 2004 in French law biometric data has been subject to an authorization regime outlined in Article 25 of the LIL: the *"automated processing involving biometric data necessary for identity control"* are included in the list of processing activities that can only be carried out with the authorization of the CNIL. Thus, the concept of identification was already present.

Opinions of the WP29 subsequent to the 1995 Directive: a work in progress towards a definition of biometric data not restricted to identification. Firstly, in 2003,[25] the WP29 defines biometric data as physical, physiological, or behavioural data that allows the *unique identification* of the data subject, but considers only some of these as sensitive. This is close to the definition of the CNIL in 2007, [26]but it draws away from the GDPR, which a decade later, classifies all identifiable biometric data within the special categories of personal data.[27]

However, later in 2007,[28] the WP29 *does not include identification* in the core of its definition; it rather appears as a **possible use.**[29]

---

[21] pp.157-158.

[22] Loi n°78-17 du 6 janvier 1978 relative à l'informatique, aux fichiers et aux libertés, 6 January 1978.

[23] p.166.

[24] Loi n° 2004-801 du 6 août 2004 relative à la protection des personnes physiques à l'égard des traitements de données à caractère personnel et modifiant la loi n° 78-17 du 6 janvier 1978 relative à l'informatique, aux fichiers et aux libertés, JORF n°182 of 7 August 2004.

[25] WP29, *Working document on biometrics*, 1st August 2003.

[26] CNIL, *Communication de la CNIL relative à la mise en œuvre de dispositifs de reconnaissance par empreinte digitale avec stockage dans une base de données*, 28 December 2007, p. 3 (Unofficial translation): the CNIL defines biometric data as *"data produced by the body itself* ***that uniquely identifies or represents*** *that body and no other, in an immutable manner"* (emphasis added). See also p.12 where the CNIL clarifies that *"the Commission always makes its decisions, of course, 'in the current state of technology'"*.

[27] *Some biometric data could be considered as sensitive in the meaning of Article 8 of 1995 Directive/46/EC and in particular, data revealing racial or ethnic origin or data concerning health."* (p.10)

[28] WP29, *Opinion 4/2007 on the concept of personal data,* 20 June 2007.

[29] Biometric data are defined as *"biological properties, physiological characteristics, living traits or repeatable actions where those features and/or actions are both unique to that individual and measurable, even if the patterns used in practice to technically measure them* ***involve a certain***

In 2012, the WP29 builds upon its previous opinions (2003 and 2007) to define biometric data, while evolving on certain points. It now includes psychological data and adds the mention of *"categorisation/segregation"* alongside identification and authentication, which were carried over from the 2003 definition. The document defines these concepts very clearly,[30] and even recognizes that the trend is towards categorisation. It refers to this type of processing as "*soft biometrics,*" as they complete identification but cannot achieve it on their own.[31]

In another opinion of the same year,[32] the WP29 criticizes the draft regulation of the forthcoming European data protection framework for focusing on what the data allow, rather than focusing on *"what types of data are to be considered biometric data"* (the opinion does not explicitly mention the lack of the notion of categorisation).

In this way, these opinions published before the European data protection framework reveal that the definition of biometric data was heading towards including categorisation, alongside identification and authentication.

2.2 Biometrics Subsequent to the Adoption of the European Data Protection Framework: The Wording of the EU Legislation Still Questioned

The introduction of biometric data in the GDPR: a departure from the WP29 opinions. The concept of biometric data appears in the draft regulation of the GDPR of January 25th, 2012, and is then assigned the status of sensitive data.[33]

As a consequence, national law also has to be updated.[34] From May 25th, 2018, the coming into effect of the GDPR, to June 1st, 2019, the formulation of sensitive data in the LIL shifts to "*data revealing racial or ethnic origin [etc.]*", and "*biometric*

---

degree of probability. *"* (p.8, emphasis added). The WP29 also adds that *"As such, they can work as "identifiers". Indeed, because of their unique link to a specific individual, biometric data may be used to identify the individual."* (p.8)

30 WP29, Opinion 3/2012 on developments in biometric technologies, 27 April 2012, p. 6: *"**Biometric categorisation/segregation**: The categorisation/segregation of an individual by a biometric system is typically the process of establishing whether the biometric data of an individual belongs to a group with some predefined characteristic in order to take a specific action. In this case, it is not important to identify or verify the individual but to assign him/her automatically to a certain category. For instance an advertising display may show different adverts depending on the individual that is looking at it based on the age or gender".*

31 *Mention should also be made to the use of the so-called soft biometrics, defined by the use of very common traits not suitable to clearly distinguish or identify an individual but that allow enhancing the performance of other identification systems."* (p.16). On the development of behaviour data as biometric data, see also the acknowledgment of A. Debet *et al.*, *Informatique et libertés: la protection des données à caractère personnel en droit français et européen*, Les intégrales, n° 10, Issy-les-Moulineaux, Lextenso éditions, 2015, p.1100, para. 2882. Comp. with E.J. Kindt, *Privacy and Data Protection Issues of Biometric Applications: A Comparative Legal Analysis*, 12, Law, Governance and Technology Series, Dordrecht, Springer Netherlands, 2013, p.35, whom employs the notion of "soft-biometrics" in a slightly different way.

32 WP29, *Opinion 01/2012 on the data protection reform proposals*, 23 March 2012, p.10.

33 Resolution passed by the European Parliament on March 13, 2024.

34 Loi n° 2018-493 du 20 juin 2018 relative à la protection des données personnelles, JORF n°0141 du 21 juin 2018.

data for the purpose of uniquely identifying a natural person" is added to the list, thus incorporating biometrics into the *"pantheon of sensitive data"*.[35] From June 1st, 2019, with the transposition of the LED, the principle of the prohibition of sensitive data is moved to Article 6, but the wording remains the same.[36]

In the GDPR, Article 4(14) defines biometric data as data *"which allow or confirm"* the identification of a natural person, and Article 9(1) includes biometric data used *"for the purposes"* of identification in the list of sensitive data. The LED employs the same definition for biometric data (Article 3(13)) and sensitive data (Article 10).[37]

Thus there is both identification ("allow") and authentification ("confirm") in the definition, but only the first is considered as sensitive. And there is no mention made of the purpose of "categorisation". The expression of *"resulting from specific technical processing"* also is a key element, originating from the opinion of the Committee on Bioethics,[38] and which shall be interpreted as resulting from a *biometric system* processing (in other words, a biometric template).[39]

Therefore, *"a biometric data is thus necessarily defined by its **purpose** and not only by its **nature**"*.[40] In this regard, one can refer to Recital 51 of the GDPR:[41] the simple photography (or a database of it, for instance in law enforcement uses) is excluded from the protection of the sensitive data regime. Some authors have perhaps argued that these mere photographies shall be protected as sensitive.[42]

It is worth asking whether the concept of personal data englightens the notion of "identification" in biometric data. To qualify data as personal, the data subject might be

---

[35] M. BOURGEOIS et M. MOINE, "La nouvelle loi Informatique et libertés. Une transposition du GDPR ?", *Cahiers de droit de l'entreprise*, February 2019, n° 1, p. 30 (Unofficial translation).

[36] Modified by Ordonnance n°2018-1125 du 12 décembre 2018.

[37] On the different kinds of personal data, see the classification in A. DEBET *et al.*, *Informatique et libertés*, *op. cit.*, pp. 248-258.

[38] Committee on Bioethics, Opinion on the document of the Consultative Committee of the Convention for the Protection of Individuals with regard to Automatic Processing of Personal Data (T-PD) entitled 'Modernisation of Convention 108: new proposals', DH-BIO (2012) 12 final, Restricted, 21.6.2012, p.6 ('Bioethics Committee, DH-BIO (2012) 12 final').

[39] E.J. KINDT, "Having yes, using no? About the new legal regime for biometric data", *Computer Law & Security Review*, juin 2018, vol. 34, n° 3, p. 531. On the notion of template, see also A. DEBET *et al.*, *Informatique et libertés*, *op. cit*, p.1096, para. 2867.

[40] J. CAREL et L. MEYSONNET, "Définitions et enjeux de la protection des données biométriques", *Dalloz IP/IT*, February 2024, n° 2, p. 81 (Unofficial translation). The sentence continues as this: *"this is why a photograph or a video of an individual is not, in itself, considered biometric data"*.

[41] *"[...] The processing of photographs should not systematically be considered to be processing of special categories of personal data as they are covered by the definition of biometric data only when processed through a specific technical means allowing the unique identification or authentication of a natural person. [...]"*.Pure statistical purposes also are excluded from the definition of sensitive data (see the Datakalab affair in France: Délibération n°2020-136 du 17 décembre 2020 portant avis sur un projet de décret relatif au recours à la vidéo intelligente pour mesurer le taux de port de masque dans les transports., 17 December 2020).

[42] For E.J. KINDT, "Having yes, using no?", *op. cit.*, p. 532, data that *allow* identification should *"be considered in itself of a special category"*, rather than mere personal data (see the four categories of biometric data, notably p. 535).

identified by the data, but also identifiable (identification is permitted by data, e.g. on a photo or video[43]), or indirectly identifiable (e.g. the localisation[44]), even if necessary information are detained by a third party,[45] as long as the means of identification are reasonable.[46] The CNIL even decided that a person being "singularised" would be sufficient for the criterion to be met.[47] The criterion of an *identifiable* data will depend, at the end of the day, of the context.[48] Yet the integration of the finality in the definition of sensitive data prevents from reasoning by analogy with personal data. The notion of identification is difficult to understand in this context where it has different meanings. In the end, it relates to the notion of identity, which is itself subject to interpretation.[49]

The evolution of the understanding of biometric data since the European data protection framework entry into force. Several commentators added to the global understanding of biometric data since 2016, and so made propositions on its evolution. The 2021 document from the Défenseur des Droits (the French Defender of Rights)[50] is particularly interesting in this regard. It distinguishes three types of biometric systems: *"authentication systems", "identification systems"* (***"locating a person within a group of individuals,*** *[...] based on, among other things, [...]* ***behaviour (gait recognition), or any other type of biometric data****"*), and *"**assessment** systems"*.[51] The third category encompasses two distinct types: emotion recognition,[52] and **categorisation** (*"placing*

[43] See for example in France: images captured by drones are considered as personal data, even if they would be blurred between reception and transmission (CE, réf., *Association La Quadrature du Net et la Ligue des droits de l'homme*, 18 May 2020, n°440442, 440445; CE, 10e et 9e ch. réunies, 22 December 2020, n° 446155, *Assoiation. La Quadrature du Net*, pt 7, préc. n° 29). See also CEPD 2007 (see above), p.8: *"Images of individuals captured by a video surveillance system can be personal data to the extent that the individuals are recognizable."*

[44] See also EDPB, *Guidelines 01/2020 on processing personal data in the context of connected vehicles and mobility related applications*, Version 2.0, 9 March 2012: technical data (e.g. *"data relating to the driving style"* permit the *"direct or indirect identification"* of the driver (p.3, pp.4-5).

[45] CJUE, 19 October 2016, C-582/14, *Breyer c. Bundesrepublik Deutschland* , pt 44. See also CJUE, 4th ch., 11 December 2014, C-212/13, *František Ryneš c. Úřad pro ochranu osobních údajů*, pt. 22; CJUE, 2nd ch, 14 February 2019, C-345/17, *Sergejs Buivids*, pt 31.

[46] *Ibid*, pt 45 and 46. See also GDPR, Recital 26.

[47] CNIL, *Délibération n°2013-420 de la formation restreinte prononçant une sanction pécuniaire à l'encontre de la société X*, 3 janvier 2024: *"In other words, the accumulation of data that it holds on a single individual allows it to singularise them based on one or more elements that are unique to the person. These data must, as such, be considered identifying rather than anonymous."*

[48] WP29, *Opinion 4/2007 on the concept of personal data, op. cit.*, p. 13: *"Even ancillary information, such as 'the man wearing a black suit' may identify someone out of the passers-by standing at a traffic light."*

[49] See not. A. DEBET et al., Informatique et libertés: la protection des données à caractère personnel en droit français et européen, Les intégrales, n° 10, Issy-les-Moulineaux, Lextenso éditions, 2015, p.243, para. 492: *"data conflate with the individual's identity"*.

[50] DÉFENSEUR DES DROITS, *Technologies biométriques : l'impératif respect des droits fondamentaux*, 20 July 2021 (Unofficial translation).

[51] Emphasis added.

[52] p.5: *"identifying or inferring emotions, personality traits, or intentions"*.

the targeted individuals into specific categories, ***such as*** *sex, age, hair color, eye color, ethnic origin, or sexual or political orientation, in order to take specific measures"*).[53] These specific categories sometimes overlap with data already considered as sensitive in Article 9 GDPR and Article 10 LED (e.g. *"personal data revealing racial or ethnic origin"*).

Even if the Defender of Rights considers that the regime for sensitive data is not, in principle, applicable to biometric assessment (although *"such an interpretation is not yet stabilized"*) it **recommends** that *"these assessment methods should be subject to* ***specific protective measures****, as they involve the same types of data as those used for identification purposes and their use is equally risky"*. The Defender of Rights also notes that identification and categorisation can be combined (as expressed by the EDPB in 2019[54]). Other distinctions of biometric data including categorisation are put forwards by other actors, such as French deputies.[55] In 2022, the Defender of Rights perfects its position, by presenting the same three categories, with the third one being renamed *"evaluation"*. Regarding categorisation, it takes the example of ***"detecting so-called abnormal behaviours*** *to combat theft in supermarkets"*.[56]

The same year, the CNIL classifies categorisation as "augmented cameras" (e.g.*"detect a fight or dangerous behaviours in a crowd"*), and distinguishes it from biometric data processing, for the reason that this type of use does not imply the "unique identification" (defined as ***"the recognition from one camera to another"***) of the data subject, and by consequence does not imply the processing of physical, physiological or behavioural data).[57] Yet with this meaning of unique identification, to consider the French experimentation as restricted outside of biometric data is rather dubious: some uses (such as the failure of a person to comply with the common direction) imply to single out the person of whom the behaviour is analysed.

The evolution of the concept of biometric data appears to be moving towards an extension of its purposes beyond mere identification. This tendency follows the development of the second generation biometrics, such as behavioural data which allow categorisation. This has been undertaken by the AI Act: whilst its first version of April

---

53 p.6.

54 EDPB, Guidelines 3/2019 on processing of personal data through video devices, 9 January 2020, pt. 82, p.19.

55 M.-P. Daubresse, A. de Belenet et J. Durain, *sur la reconnaissance faciale et ses risques au regard de la protection des libertés individuelles*, fait au nom de la commission des lois, 10 May 2022. This parliamentary information report also puts forward an interesting distinction between four levels of image processing systems using AI, specifically distinguishing identification from two other levels: (1) Detection of the presence of an object or person without determining its nature; (2) Recognition of categories; (3) Identification of a person or object based on non-biometric characteristics, without assigning an identity to the person; (4) Recognition of an individual based on biometric characteristics."

56 Défenseur des droits, *Perception du développement des technologies biométriques en France. Entre manque d'information et manque d'encadrement*, 6 October 2022, pp.2-3.

57 CNIL, *Caméras dites 'intelligentes' ou 'augmentées' dans les espaces publics - Position sur les conditions de déploiement*, 19 July 2022, p.5 (Unofficial translation).

21, 2021 (the European Commission proposal)[58] had merely copied the definition of biometric data from the GDPR and the Law Enforcement Directive,[59] it now proposes in a definition of biometrics no longer limited to the unique identification. Perhaps the disappearance of the notion of uniqueness is preferable, as several different definitions have been suggested.[60]

3 The Interplay of the Legislations: The Contrast of Biometrics Definitions Blurs the EU Effort to Protect the Data Subject from the Undue Use of Their Biometric Data

3.1 The GDPR and the AI Act: Two Legislations on Overlapping Subjects that Create Twofold Obligations

The notion of biometrics in the AI Act. The final version of the AI Act provides a definition of biometric data that omits the mention of *"unique identification"* (Article 3(34)) and specifies that the concept should be interpreted *"in light of"* the GDPR and the Law Enforcement Directive (Recital 14)[61]. This means the European data protection framework is not influenced by the AI Act yet the contrary is true. The definition of Article 3(34) states as follow: *"'biometric data' means personal data resulting from specific technical processing relating to the physical, physiological or behavioural characteristics of a natural person, such as facial images or dactyloscopic data;"*. Thus, all purposes (identification, categorisation, and emotion recognition) are included in the definition of biometric data. Subsequently, the AI Act offers a definition of a *"biometric categorisation system"* (Article 3(40)[62] by using the notion of *"assigning"* natural persons to categories (Recital 16). In its examples of biometric data that could serve as categories, the AI Act specifically mentions *"behavioural traits"*.[63]

---

[58] Proposal for a regulation of the European Parliament and of the Council aying down harmonised rules on artificial intelligence (Artificial intelligence Act) and amending certain Union legislative Acts, COM/2021/206 final. See not. B. BERTRAND, "La proposition de régulation générale pour l'intelligence artificielle dans l'Union européenne : l'IA Act", Chronique Droit européen du numérique, October 2022, n° 3, p. 473.

[59] The AI Act was said to be *"in line with"* the GDPR (Recital 7).

[60] See below, and see not. E.J. KINDT, *Privacy and Data Protection Issues of Biometric Applications*, 12, *op. cit*, p.23. who employs the idea of "distinctiveness".

[61] In Recital 14, the AI Act also clarifies that *"Biometric data can allow for the authentication, identification or categorisation of natural persons and for the recognition of emotions of natural persons"*.

[62] Article 3(40): *"'biometric categorisation system' means an AI system for the purpose of assigning natural persons to specific categories on the basis of their biometric data, unless it is ancillary to another commercial service and strictly necessary for objective technical reasons;"*.

[63] *"The notion of 'biometric categorisation' referred to in this Regulation should be defined as assigning natural persons to specific categories on the basis of their biometric data. Such specific categories can relate to aspects such as sex, age, hair colour, eye colour, tattoos, behavioural or personality traits, language, religion, membership of a national minority, sexual or political orientation. [...]"*.

The broadening of the notion of biometric data might have been influenced by the idea of "biometric-based data".[64] Also interestingly, the EDPB, in its joint opinion with the EDPS on the AI Act proposal, has a different approach yet conveying the same idea: regarding remote biometric identification (hereinafter RBI), it calls *"for a general ban on any use of AI for an automated recognition of human features in publicly accessible spaces"* which includes biometrics as well as other *"behaviour signals"*.[65] On one side, this statement acknowledges that not all behavioural data are biometric data. On the other side, it puts forward a large category which allow to encompass all data originating from the human body, even if they might not qualify as proper biometric data. The idea of a *global* protection of these attributes in personal data law is indeed a recurring issue.

The interplay between the GDPR and the AI Act. According to the CNIL, the European data protection framework systematically applies to prohibited AI systems (which all involve the processing of personal data) and is applicable in many cases to high-risk AI systems.[66] Indeed, the AI Act is grounded on personal data protection regarding the use of biometrics by law enforcement (Recital 3), yet, as written above, the *"EU data protection acquis"* is not affected by the new regulation (Article 2(7), Recital 9, and Recital 10). Regarding prohibited practices, it is emphasised by Article 5(8) (*"This Article shall not affect the prohibitions that apply where an AI practice infringes other Union law."*) and Recital 38 (the AI Act applies as 'lex specialis' to Article 10 LED).

The Commission emphasises in its Guidelines on prohibited practices: *"the AI Act does not affect prohibitions that apply where an AI practice falls within other Union law"*,[67] which means that a system not prohibited by the AI Act might be prohibited or unlawful based on other Union law. The Guidelines, among others, gives the example of *"the lack of a legal basis for the processing of personal data required under data*

[64] C. Wendehorst et Y. Duller, *Biometric Recognition and Behavioural Detection. Assessing the ethical aspects of biometric recognition and behavioural detection techniques with a focus on their current and future use in public spaces*, Policy Department for Citizens' Rights and Constitutional Affairs EN Directorate-General for Internal Policies, August 2021. See notably p.67 (*"While it is certaintly essential to stress the requirement of specific technical processing (for, otherwise, almost any everyday activity might potentially be covered), the requirement that the data must allow or confirm the unique identification of a natural person makes the definition* ***far too narrow****. It essentially reflects the dominant concepts during times of 'first generation biometric technologies' and* ***fails to keep pace with technological developments*** *[…]."*) and p.68 (the best possibility to solve this problem, according to the authors, is *"to include a* ***new definition of 'biometrics-based data'****. This definition would largely coincide with the definition of biometric data, but would differ from that definition in that biometrics-based may or may not allow or confirm the identification of a natural person."*)

[65] CEPD, *Joint Opinion 5/2021 on the proposal for a Regulation of the European Parliament and of the Council laying down harmonised rules on artificial intelligence (Artificial Intelligence Act)*, 18 June 2021, pp.2-3 and pp.11-12. See C. Crichton, "Intelligence artificielle : vers la fin du traitement massif des données biométriques ?", *Dalloz IP/IT*, July 2021, n° 7-8, p. 373.

[66] CNIL, "Entrée en vigueur du règlement européen sur l'IA : les premières questions-réponses de la CNIL", 12 July 2024. See contra E.J. Kindt, "18. Biometric data processing: Is the legislator keeping up or just keeping up appearances?", *in* G. González, R. Van Brakel et P. De Hert (eds.), *Research Handbook on Privacy and Data Protection Law: Values, Norms and Global Politics*, s.l., Edward Elgar Publishing, 15 March 2022, p.383.

[67] p.14, para. 43.

protection law".[68] In conclusion, the AI Act is consistent, as well as complementary alongside the GDPR and LED. This underlines *"the structural role of the GDPR"* in *"the european normative work"* in digital law.[69]

3.2 The Interplay Between the French Law and the AI Act: A Wording that Excludes the Category of Prohibited Practices

The notion of biometrics in the French Law: biometric data that goes unspoken? The question addressed here takes for granted the fact that the *"algorithm"* employed for the experimentation is an AI system (what has since been confirmed by the assessment report, which employs the term of AI).[70] Also, it only addresses the issue of biometric data. Yet it must be acknowledged that other challenges might be addressed, such as the relevance of qualifying this kind of videosurveillance as profiling,[71] or the national security exemption included in both the data protection framework and the AI Act (GDPR Article 23(1)(a) and Recital 16; LED Recital 14; AI Act Article 2(2) and Recital 24).

Article 10, IV of the Olympic Games Legislation specifies that no biometric data is processed.[72] Yet, given the definition of biometric data as explained above, and the

[68] Approval of the content of the draft Communication from the Commission - Commission Guidelines on prohibited artificial intelligence practices established by Regulation (EU) 2024/1689 (AI Act), 4 February 2025, para. 43, p.14. Please note these Guidelines, adopted pursuant to Article 96(1)(b) are not binding for the moment, as they have not been adopted formally yet, and might be examined or modified by the Commission.

[69] B. BERTRAND, "L'AI Act dans l'écosystème normatif européen de la régulation du numérique", *op. cit.* See also C. WENDEHORST et Y. DULLER, *Biometric Recognition and Behavioural Detection. Assessing the ethical aspects of biometric recognition and behavioural detection techniques with a focus on their current and future use in public spaces, op. cit*, p.64: *"As ar as AI systems require the processing of data as training, validation and testing data or, even more importantly, as input and output data, Union and Member State data protection law must apply to the extent that there is no more specific rule under the AIA Proposal that derogates general data protection law."*

[70] C. VIGOUROUX *et al.*, *Expérimentation de traitements algorithmiques d'images légalement collectées au moyen de systèmes de vidéoprotection*, Rapport du comité d'évaluation, January 2025, pp. 98-99.

[71] See not. Article 4(4) and Article 22 GDPR; Article 3(4) and Article 11 LED.

[72] *"The processing activities mentioned in paragraph I of this article do not use any biometric identification system, do not process any biometric data, and do not implement any facial recognition techniques."* (Unofficial translation). This statement is confirmed and emphasised by the assesment report (C. VIGOUROUX *et al.*, *Expérimentation de traitements algorithmiques d'images légalement collectées au moyen de systèmes de vidéoprotection, op. cit.*). See also CONSEIL D'ÉTAT, *Avis relatif aux jeux Olympiques et Paralympiques de 2024 et portant diverses autres dispositions*, 15 December 2022, pt. 24. For an assesment report on the experimentation by Parliament, see A. CANAYER et M.-P. LA GONTRIE (DE), *Gagner la médaille d'or de la sécurisation des jeux Olympiques et Paralympiques de 2024*, 10 April 2024; F. DUMONT et M.-P. DE LA GONTRIE, *sur le bilan de la mise en oeuvre de la loi du 19 mai 2023 relative aux jeux Olympiques et Paralympiques de 2024 (vidéoprotection intelligente et sécurité privée)*, 19 February 2025.

purposes,[73] several authors share the analysis that it rather seems these systems *have to* use biometric data. According to one author, biometric data might be collected by the system, as it *"is subject to an algorithmic computer vision processing that isolates behaviours deemed suspicious"*,[74] which *"may also result in the unique identification of a person [...] even if the identity of that person remains unknown."*[75]

Indeed, this processing was already discussed by the EDPB in 2020 when it defines *"the system [which] is using physical characteristics to detect specific individuals coming back in the range of the camera [...] and tracking them"* as *"a biometric identification method because it is aimed at recognition through the use of specific technical processing."*[76] Even though the EDPB precises that categorisation (*"distinguish one category of people from another", pt. 80, p. 19*) does not fall under the sensitive data regime (Article 9 GDPR), the categorisation accompanied by identification would do so. For example, it would be the case where *"a controller wishes to detect a data subject re-entering the area or entering another area (for example in order to project continued customized advertisement)"* (p.19, para. 82).

[73] Décret n°2023-828 du 28 août 2023 relatif aux modalités de mise en œuvre des traitements algorithmiques sur les images collectées au moyen de systèmes de vidéoprotection et de caméras installées sur des aéronefs, pris en application de l'article 10 de la loi n°2023-380 du 19 mai 2023 relative aux jeux Olympiques et Paralympiques de 2024 et portant diverses autres dispositions, art. 3 (Unofficial translation): *"Predetermined events that an algorithmic processing may aim to detect, as they are likely to present or reveal a risk of terrorism or a serious threat to public safety, include the following: the presence of abandoned objects; the presence or use of weapons, as listed in Article R. 311-2 of the Internal Security Code; non-compliance by a person or vehicle with the designated direction of traffic; crossing or presence of a person or vehicle in a restricted or sensitive area; the presence of a person on the ground following a fall; crowd movement; excessive density of people; and fire outbreaks."*.

[74] S. Etoa, "L'image et le son ? Le déploiement de la surveillance algorithmique dans l'espace public", *Cahiers de la recherche sur les droits fondamentaux*, November 2023, n° 21, pp. 81-87 (Unofficial translation).

[75] p.85.

[76] EDPB, Guidelines 3/2019 on processing of personal data through video devices, 9 January 2020, pt. 82, p.19.

The opinion that some purposes of the French experimentation, such as tracking a person moving upstream through a crowd, are understood as identification is shared by other civil actors,[77] as well as authors.[78]

One of the civil actors also supports the view that the ultimate purpose will be to identify the individual with an abnormal behaviour,[79] as an author has already called attention to.[80] The assesment report recognises that this point is disputed.[81]

The interplay between the French Law and the AI Act. There is a period of nearly two months (from February 2nd, 2025, to March 31st, 2025) during which both Article 10 of the Olympic Games Legislation and some of the AI Act provisions (Chapters I and II) are applicable. These Chapters I and II include the definitions —including the one of biometric data (Article 3)— and the list of the prohibited AI systems (Article 5). This does not affect the provisions on high-risk AI systems, which will only be implemented from August 2nd, 2026 (for Annex III) or August 2nd, 2027 (for the rest).

Two of the prohibited AI systems might apply for a system such as the one experimented by the French legislation: biometric categorisation or identification.

---

77 EDRI *et al.*, "Lettre de la société civile aux députés français sur le projet de loi relatif aux Jeux olympiques et paralympiques 2024", 8 March 2023 (capturing and analyzing individuals' bodies, movements, gestures, and appearance by isolating them from their surroundings constitutes a "unique identification" and, therefore, constitutes biometric data as defined by Article 4(14) of the GDPR) ; CNB, COMMISSION DES LIBERTÉS ET DES DROITS DE LA PERSONNE, *Rapport sur le projet de loi relatif aux jeux Olympiques et Paralympiques de 2024*, 3 February 2023, p. 9; M. ARTIGUELONG *et al.*, "Les atteintes aux droits et libertés pendant la période des Jeux olympiques de Paris 2024", 18 June 2024 ; B. PIÉDALLU *et al.*, "Contribution extérieure de La Quadrature du Net, du Syndicat des avocats de France, du Syndicat de la magistrature, du CREIS-TERMINAL et de la Ligue des droits de l'Homme sur la loi relative aux jeux Olympiques et Paralympiques de 2024 et portant diverses autres dispositions (affaire no 2023-850 DC)", 19 avril 2023; LA QUADRATURE DU NET, *Projet de loi relatif aux Jeux Olympiques et Paralympiques de 2024 : dossier d'analyse de la vidéosurveillance automatisée*, 21 January 2023, p.18 (Unofficial translation): the processing *"allows for the recognition and isolation of a specific person, without necessarily seeking or associating their civil identity"*.

78 C. LEQUESNE and OBSERVATOIRE DE L'ÉTHIQUE PUBLIQUE, *Surveiller les foules. Pour un encadrement des IA « physiognomoniques »*, April 2023, p.52 (Unofficial translation): *"behaviour data* [as used by *"the AI behaviour system necessary for the prevention of crime"* of the French legislation] *consistute biometric data"*

79 LA QUADRATURE DU NET, *Projet de loi relatif aux Jeux Olympiques et Paralympiques de 2024*: *"any use of these systems necessarily aims to enable security agents to take targeted action against the person whose behaviour or body is being analyzed"*.

80 E.J. Kindt, "Having yes, using no?", *op. cit.*, see notably p. 526: *"Another interesting question is whether one could argue that when the controller collects biometric data and stores such in a database (which is considered 'processing'),* knowing *that the storage in a database* permits identification *in the future, this fact of storing in a database could or should be considered processing of biometric data for the* purpose *of uniquely identifying. [...] Any (intended) future use of the data should in our view be taken into account for ascertaining the applicable legal framework."*

81 *Expérimentation de traitements algorithmiques d'images légalement collectées au moyen de systèmes de vidéoprotection, op. cit*, p.96.

Regarding the definition of biometric data in the AI Act, the Commission had confirmed what we have stated above that *"biometric data comprises behavioural characteristics that are based on biometric features"*.[82] So there is less difficulty to consider the data processed by the French algorithm as biometric under the AI Act than the European data protection framework. Yet it is unsure whether it would fall under the definition of biometric categorisation or identification.

Biometric categorisation is defined as an *"AI system for the purpose of assigning natural persons to specific categories on the basis of their biometric data, unless it is ancillary to another commercial service and strictly necessary for objective technical reasons;"* (Article 3(40)). The Commission confirms that within this use, it excludes *"categorisation according to clothes or accessories, such as scarfs or crosses, as well as social media activity"*[83] yet it does include physical characteristics (e.g. facial features and form, skin colour) and behavioural aspects (such as gait).[84] The Commission also specifies that for biometric categorisation to be qualified, the *"natural person must be* ***'individually'*** *categorised"*, which differs from categorising *"a whole group"*. Examples include *"categorising individuals and* ***singling*** *them out based on a specific feature"*,[85] thus "singling out" would be the definition of "individualisation". This criterion, less strict than identification (see below), shall apply to the French experimentation.

Biometric categorisation is then prohibited where it is used to *"deduce or infer"* sensitive data listed such as race and political opinions, except where used *"in the area of law enforcement"* (Article 5(1) (g)). For these two conditions, this prohibited practice cannot apply to the French experimentation.

The qualification as high-risk system (Annex III, Article 1 (b))[86] would also be uncertain, as the categorisation has to be used to infer *"sensitive or protected attributes"*. These attributes are defined by reference to Article 9(1) GDPR (Recital 54): *"Processing of personal data* ***revealing*** *racial or ethnic origin, political opinions, religious or philosophical beliefs, or trade union membership, and the processing of genetic data, biometric data for the purpose of uniquely identifying a natural person, data concerning health or data concerning a natural person's sex life or sexual orientation shall be prohibited."*

According to an author previously mentioned, the term *"revealing"* could be understood as allowing to protect data that can be used for biometric processing in a near future.[87] Plus, the link between the initial processing and the reveal of the sensitive

[82] Commission Guidelines on prohibited artificial intelligence practices established by Regulation, *op. cit.*, para. 277, p. 92.

[83] Commission Guidelines on prohibited artificial intelligence practices established by Regulation, *op. cit.*, para. 277, p. 92.

[84] Commission Guidelines on prohibited artificial intelligence practices established by Regulation, *op. cit.*, para. 278, p. 92.

[85] Commission Guidelines on prohibited artificial intelligence practices established by Regulation, *op. cit.*, para. 282, p.93.

[86] *"AI systems intended to be used for biometric categorisation, according to sensitive or protected attributes or characteristics based on the inference of those attributes or characteristics;"*

[87] E.J. KINDT, "Having yes, using no?", *op. cit.*.

attribute —for instance the system that categorises people going to a certain religious place— might reveal a sensitive attribute —such as, in this example, their religion.

Moreover, authors have argued more broadly on the AI Act that *"the augmented cameras"* (the terminology used by the CNIL to name the AI systems such as the French experimentation one, see above) might be considered as meeting the condition of biometric categorisation.[88]

Regarding biometric identification (RBI), it is defined as *"the automated recognition of physical, physiological, behavioural, or psychological human features for the purpose of establishing the identity of a natural person by comparing biometric data of that individual to biometric data of individuals stored in a database;"* (Article 3(35)) and some of its uses are prohibited under Article 5(1)(h).

The European Commission inconspicuously refers to a standard for the term **'biometric identification'**:[89] The ISO standard defines biometric identification (37.08.02) as the "process of searching against a *biometric enrolment database* (37.03.09) to find and return the *biometric reference identifier(s)* (37.03.19) attributable to a single individual".[90]

Even though the biometric reference identifier does not have to be civil identity, it means the identification is running with a database in which the individual is already present. This is confirmed and exemplified by the European Commission, both for the need of a database,[91] and the link (the prohibited practices start from the recognition of individuals already known by law enforcement and of which a record (of biometric data) has been kept).[92] Eventually, one of the examples given by the Commission Guidelines

---

[88] C. LEQUESNE, "L'encadrement des technologies de surveillance des foules : réflexions sur la démocratie numérique dans l'espace public", in *L'intelligence artificielle face à l'État de droit*, Bruxelles, Bruylant, 2024, at p. 154. See also C. LEQUESNE and OBSERVATOIRE DE L'ÉTHIQUE PUBLIQUE, *Surveiller les foules. Pour un encadrement des IA 'physiognomoniques'*, April 2023: the report gathers facial recognition and "intelligent videosurveillance" into the concept of physiognomonic AI, as they can *"result in discriminatory effects of the same nature"* (p.14, Unofficial translation) The report also emphasises that *"Technological identification can also be relative to categories, and may lead to associations between an individual and certain established or assumed characteristics."* (p.14).

[89] Commission Guidelines on prohibited artificial intelligence practices established by Regulation, *op. cit.*, para. 297, p. 98.

[90] On the evolution of the definition of biometric data in ISO standards, see E.J. KINDT, "18. Biometric data processing: Is the legislator keeping up or just keeping up appearances?", *in* G. GONZÁLEZ, R. VAN BRAKEL et P. DE HERT (eds.), *Research Handbook on Privacy and Data Protection Law: Values, Norms and Global Politics*, s.l., Edward Elgar Publishing, 15 March 2022 p.385. On the notion of the database, already present before the GDPR, see A. DEBET *et al.*, *Informatique et libertés*, *op. cit.*, p. 1096, para. 2867.

[91] Commission Guidelines on prohibited artificial intelligence practices established by Regulation, *op. cit.*, para. 299, p.98: *"For identification performance, the captured biometric data are compared with biometric data already stored in a reference database (such as a repository, e.g. a criminal database containing facial images or templates of suspects)."*. See also para. 309, p.100 (emphasis not added): *"the existence of a reference database is* ***indispensable*** *to perform the comparison for identification purposes"*.

[92] Commission Guidelines on prohibited artificial intelligence practices established by Regulation, *op. cit.*, para. 359, p.113

is a foregone conclusion on the inapplicability of biometric identification to the French experimentation: functionalities of *"object detection and crowd movement"* on *"AI-powered CCTV cameras"* deployed by the police authorities of a busy city are considered as an authorised system, neither prohibited nor high-risk.[93]

4 Conclusion

To conclude, the definition of identification in biometric data does not permit to qualify the French use as a prohibited practice in the AI Act. The classification as categorisation might have been more plausible yet the French use shall not qualify as high-risk system. Assuming that no qualification of biometric data,[94] neither in the EU data protection framework nor in the AI Act can be met, the French experimentation would only qualify as personal data, and a simple AI system. The fundamental rights challenges it poses, notably on anonymity (see the CNIL above) perhaps require a more protective regime. [95]Indeed, the spirit of the AI Act is to prohibit a form of indiscriminate surveillance with many biometric recognition practices falling into Article 5. Yet this kind of surveillance can be achieved, or at least begun, by such categorisation of people in public spaces. Ultimately, this issue leads to a variation of the long-standing question on technology and law: shall technological progress lead regulation, or shall regulation focuses on the fundamental human characteristics to be protected (e.g. physical and behavioural data) regardless of the technical means used?

---

93 Commission Guidelines on prohibited artificial intelligence practices established by Regulation, *op. cit.*, para. 359, p.133: *"The police authorities of a busy city deploy AI-powered CCTV cameras, which can perform live facial recognition technologies. Possibly, different functionalities are being added, such as object detection and crowd movement, on top of facial recognition. They place these cameras at multiple locations, including places of worship, a number of places frequented by the LGBT+ community, doctors' offices, pharmacies, and various restaurants and bars. The installation of biometric-ready cameras as such is not prohibited under the AI Act. Certain uses however, including the unspecified and indiscriminate identification of natural persons, is prohibited."*.

94 See also C. WENDEHORST et Y. DULLER, *Biometric Recognition and Behavioural Detection. Assessing the ethical aspects of biometric recognition and behavioural detection techniques with a focus on their current and future use in public spaces, op. cit.*, pp. 65-66; CCNE, *Questions éthiques soulevées par la situation des personnes ayant des variations du développement sexuel*, 19 September 2019, e.g. p. 16 (Unofficial translation): *"A society that shifts from vigilance to surveillance compromises, under the pretext of a growing demand for collective security, individual freedoms and the right to anonymity and privacy."*.

95 E.J. KINDT, "18. Biometric data processing: Is the legislator keeping up or just keeping up appearances?", *op. cit*, p.398: for any biometric data (including *"biometric data allowing to track and monitor"*) there are high risks for the freedoms of individuals.

Explainability in Fraud Detection: Trustworthy AI and Pattern Detection

Hugues Ali-Mehenni(✉), Steve Bellart, and Ahmad Chamma

Centre de Recherche et Innovation, Talan France, Paris, France
{hugues.ali-mehenni,steve.bellart,ahmad.chamma}@talan.com

Abstract. The use of AI in combating fraud and money laundering is met with considerable skepticism by many specialists. One reason is the inherent difficulty in training an effective AI due to the highly imbalanced nature of datasets, where the vast majority of transactions are legitimate. Additionally, in critical sectors like finance and medicine, where incorrect predictions can have severe consequences, the concept of trustworthy AI is crucial for convincing domain experts to delegate part of their work to AI systems. In this context, explainability tools developed by the scientific community offer new perspectives by unveiling the "black boxes" of AI. These tools provide experts with control mechanisms to evaluate whether AI systems can be trusted. In this work, we first address the challenge of training effective AI in imbalanced settings. We then explore the application of various explainability tools (LIME, SHAP, ANCHORS, PyXAI) on AI models trained for fraud detection. The aim is to identify which of these approaches can help build trust in automated systems with domain experts and whether AI models can learn pre-defined patterned rules or can discover new rules, leading to a better understanding of the decision process. This study highlights the importance of combining effective training techniques with robust explainability tools to enhance the overall trustworthiness of AI in sensitive applications. By examining the different aspects, we aim to contribute to the development of more reliable and transparent AI systems that can effectively assist in fraud detection while retaining the trust of human experts.

Keywords: fraud detection · XAI · tree-based models · interpretability · trustworthy AI

1 Introduction

With the increasing number of transactions and requests generated across various sectors, such as banking and insurance, Machine Learning (ML) has become an essential tool for efficiently distinguishing between legitimate and non-legitimate instances. These distinctions are based on data-driven insights, enabling organizations to better detect and prevent fraudulent activities.

Published by Springer Nature Switzerland AG 2025
D. Verdejo and E. Mercier-Laurent (Eds.): AI4GS 2024, IFIP AICT 743, pp. 178–190, 2025.
https://doi.org/10.1007/978-3-031-96522-7_14

However, a significant challenge persists for AI-based fraud detection systems: the presence of highly-imbalanced datasets. Legitimate transactions vastly outnumber fraudulent ones, making it difficult to accurately detect non-legit instances. To address this issue, various techniques, such as over-sampling methods like SMOTE [7,13], or weight-penalization approaches, are employed to ensure a synthetic or penalized balance between the different classes. These methods help mitigate the bias introduced by imbalanced data and improve the system's ability to correctly identify fraudulent transactions.

Despite the relatively low number of fraud cases detected, the financial impact of these cases on the global economy is significant. In a recent report, the United Nations Office on Drugs and Crime (UNODC)[1] estimates that between 2 and 5% of global GDP is laundered annually, which amounts to between EUR 715 million and 1.87 trillion each year. Such figures highlight the urgency of developing more robust and accurate fraud detection systems to curb the detrimental effects of financial crimes.

While high-capacity models such as tree-based algorithms excel at processing large amounts of data and making predictions, their decision-making process remains opaque due to the complexity of their architecture. This lack of transparency has led to these models being labeled as "Black Boxes". This opacity poses challenges in understanding the reasoning behind certain decisions, particularly in critical applications such as fraud detection.

Explainable AI (XAI) has emerged as a promising subfield within AI, aiming to study the impact of the different variables on the prediction problem via the introduction of local/global perturbations while monitoring the corresponding behavior of the model. XAI techniques allow for the disclosure of feature importances, key rules, and patterns used in identifying the different activities.

2 State of the Art

2.1 Machine Learning and XAI in Fraud Detection

While the use of Machine Learning and Deep Learning models could help identify financial fraud in tasks such as card fraud [19] or money laundering [9], experts need a solid understanding of theeir underlying decision making processes in order to maintain better AI systems. For that purpose, previous studies have already explored the use of XAI for fraud detection and its impact on experts' work. For instance, authors in [11] study instance-level model explanation techniques with feature contribution and local rules extraction to aid a fraud detection team in their work. In [23], the authors use SHAP explanations for fraud cases, and notice that they positively impact the decision-making for fraud alerts. According to [10], XAI for fraud detection has not tackled fraud expert's requirements yet. This would be a crucial step for aligning explanations with experts' rules. The authors thus aim at developing and evaluating principles for user-centric XAI. In this article, we focus on the coherence of the

[1] https://www.europol.europa.eu/crime-areas/economic-crime/money-laundering.

explanations of different explainability tools, which is crucial for trustworth AI. By comparing several XAI tools, our goal is also to contribute to the design of more transparent agents to assist experts in fraud detection.

2.2 Explainable AI

Explainable AI (XAI) is a rapidly evolving field that encompasses a wide range of methods. While there is no universally accepted taxonomy for these approaches, they are frequently classified based on several key dimensions [1,2,10]:

- **Scope** (local or global): Methods can focus on explaining a single "local" instance's prediction or provide explanations for the model's behavior across all instances (global).
- **Agnostic or specific**: Agnostic methods treat the model as a black box, using statistical tools to infer explanations without delving into the model's internal workings. In contrast, specific methods explore the inner structure of the model to make its functioning more comprehensible.
- **Explanation type** (e.g., rules, feature importance): Different methods provide various types of explanations, such as rule-based descriptions or ranking features by their importance to the model's predictions.

In this following, we focus on tree-based-compatible explainability methods, summarized below, as they seem to perform well for the fraud detection datasets [12]. While some explainability tools are model agnostic (LIME, SHAP, etc.), others are more suited to specific models like PyXAI or TreeSHAP (a faster implementation of the SHAP-method suitable for tree-based ML models).

Tree-based models are hierarchical structures for classification or regression that benefit from a certain transparency [1]. Decision trees correspond to a non-parametric supervised learning algorithm based on optimally bisecting the samples space by the mean of a conditioning feature measured by the decrease in a chosen metric (Gini-index, cross-entropy). Despite its wide use, this algorithm suffers from high-variance and a low-performance even after applying pruning techniques. Thus, Breiman [6] introduced in his seminal paper the concept of Random Forests (RF), i.e. the construction of multiple decision trees labelled as weak learners where the decision is based on the ensemble rather than one tree. This structure helps to decrease the variance of the model by using a "bagging technique" where each tree is trained on a subsample of the instances. An alternative to this parallel implementation exists within the "boosting technique" where each tree of the forest is built to correct the errors of the previous tree, thus the decrease also in the bias. XGBoost [8] is an efficient and scalable implementation of Gradient Boosting, with the introduction (among other techniques) of pruning. XGBoost usually outperforms RF on imbalanced data as, if a tree fails on an imbalanced class sample, the next tree will give more weight to that sample.

However, as tree-based ensemble methods such as XGBoost and Random Forests become notoriously complex, XAI methods make a crucial contribution to improving interpretability in a risk-sensitive field such as fraud detection.

LIME stands for Local Interpretable Model-agnostic Explanations [20] and focuses on training multiple local surrogate models to explain individual predictions, i.e. approximating the local behavior of the "black-box" model using known interpretable models. Intuitively, LIME tests what happens to the predictions of the black-box model when variations are introduced into the data. For each instance to be explained, LIME first generates a new dataset of perturbed samples and the corresponding model predictions. Then, it assigns higher weights to samples close to the instance of interest. Finally, it trains a weighted interpretable model that should be a good local approximation of the original model's predictions. More formally, a surrogate model can be expressed as:

$$Explanation(x) = \arg\min_{g \in G} L(f, g, \pi) + \Omega(g)$$

For an instance x, the model g thus tries to minimize a loss L, which measures how close the explanation is to the prediction of the original model f, while keeping the model complexity $\Omega(g)$ low. G denotes the family of all possible explanation models and π the proximity metric.

Anchors [21] is an agnostic method introduced by the same authors which aims at finding decision rules on the features (If-Then rules) that "anchors" a prediction, i.e. variations in other features do not change the prediction. It uses Reinforcement Learning and graph search algorithm to reduce the number of black-box model calls.

SHAP or SHapley Additive exPlanations [16] is a widely used model-agnostic explanation tool in the XAI literature. To explain the prediction of an instance, it assigns each of its features an importance value based on Shapley values [22] derived from game theory. Features are thus considered as actors in a coalition. One of SHAP's main contributions is to define these shapley values as an additive feature attribution method, i.e. a linear model of binary variables, which unifies several explanation methods such as LIME. Mathematically, the explanation of an instance for these methods can be expressed as:

$$g(z') = \phi_0 + \sum_{j=1}^{M} \phi_j z'_j$$

where g is the explanation model, $z' \in \{0,1\}^M$ the simplified input features, M the total number of input features and $\phi_j \in \mathbb{R}$ the feature attribution (i.e. the Shapley values for each feature j in the case of SHAP). Furthermore, by computing the Shapley values, SHAP guarantees a set of theoretical desirable properties, which allows for contrastive explanations.

TreeSHAP [15] is a fast, efficient alternative of SHAP for tree-based models, which accelerates the calculation of local explanations. However it can lead to some counter-intuitive feature attribution [14]. In the following, we denote TreeSHAP by SHAP for simplification.

PyXAI [5] is a python library that provides different types of formal explanations (abductive and contrastive) for tree-based machine learning models (Random Forest, XGBoost). PyXAI offers theoretical guarantees of sufficient conditions (If-Then rules) for the explanation of an instance. In our case, we focused solely on abductive explanations calculated with the PyXAI algorithms for Random Forest [3] and XGBoost [4].

In the following, we discuss the frame of the datasources and the employed models.

3 Methodology

3.1 Datasets

To assess the effectiveness of each explanaibility method on fraud detection, we have chosen 5 open fraud datasets[2], which offer the advantage of reproducibility. These datasets correspond to different domains and vary considerably in terms of number of features and instances.

One characteristic of fraud datasets is that they are usually imbalanced as shown in Fig. 1 (except for the healthcare dataset).

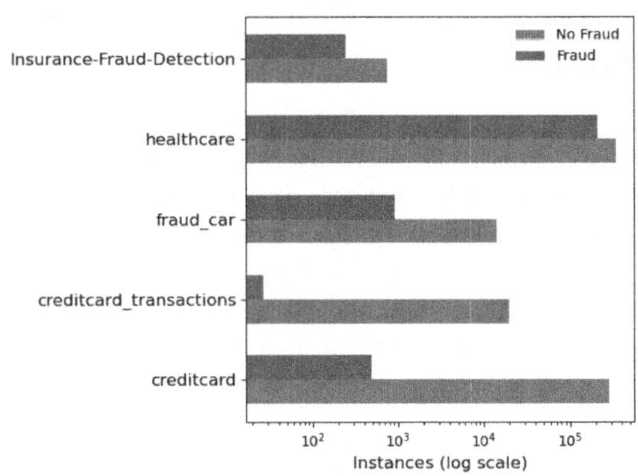

Fig. 1. Proportion of fraud in each of the datasets.

3.2 Classification Models

Two tree-based "black-box" models were chosen for the fraud detection task for each dataset: Random Forest [6] and XGBoost. We used scikit-learn [18] implementation for Random Forest and XGBoost implementation from [8]. Each

[2] https://www.kaggle.com/datasets/.

model was trained separately on 80% of each dataset and fine-tuned with 5-fold cross-validation. Because of the imbalanced nature of the datasets, each model was also trained with and without oversampling, performed with SMOTE. SMOTE [7] or Synthetic Minority Oversampling Technique and is a method for synthesizing new minority samples (fraud samples) by linear interpolation between neighboring original minority samples (SMOTENC[3] was used to handle both numerical and categorical data).

For the classification metric, the F1-score was selected as it gives a better account of the models performance for imbalanced data.

Table 1. Performance comparison of different machine learning models on various fraud detection datasets. The datasets include Fraud car, Insurance, Creditcard transactions, Creditcard, and Healthcare, each with a varying number of instances (#I) and features (#F). The models evaluated are Random Forest (RF) and XGBoost (XGB), both with and without the SMOTE oversampling technique. Accuracy (Acc) and F1-score (F1) are reported for each model and dataset, with results obtained through 5-fold cross-validation and grid search optimization. The metrics are computed on 20% of each dataset left as a testing set.

Model	Stats	Fraud car	Insurance	Creditcard transactions	Creditcard	Healthcare
-	**#I**	15420	1000	19963	284807	200000
-	**#F**	31	39	26	29	47
RF	**Acc**	0.88	0.83	**0.99**	0.99	0.70
	F1	0.26	0.65	**0.89**	0.82	0.59
RF Smote	**Acc**	0.94	0.83	0.99	0.99	0.68
	F1	0.08	0.67	0.57	0.84	0.58
XGB	**Acc**	**0.87**	**0.86**	0.99	**0.99**	**0.82**
	F1	**0.30**	**0.75**	0.57	**0.86**	**0.76**
XGB Smote	**Acc**	0.82	**0.86**	0.99	0.99	0.79
	F1	0.29	**0.75**	0.83	0.84	0.74

The results of our experiment on training efficient models with imbalanced datasets are presented in Table 1. Although the F1-score was used as the optimization metric during grid search, we observe that the accuracy remains relatively high. Interestingly, a constant model that always predicts "no fraud" could outperform in certain cases due to the dataset's imbalance. By choosing the F1-score as the optimization metric, we encourage the model to focus on detecting fraud cases, even if it increases the likelihood of generating more false positives. Overall, the results are consistent, with XGBoost models performing slightly better in general. It's well known that training effective models on highly

[3] https://imbalanced-learn.org/stable/references/generated/imblearn.over_sampling.html.

imbalanced datasets is challenging, we propose leveraging XAI tools to analyze what these models have learned and explore potential improvements based on the findings.

4 Results

In this section, we present our results in three stages. First, we explore rule-based explanation methods to assess whether these approaches can summarize the model's behavior in a few key arguments. Next, we leverage feature importance techniques to highlight the most influential features without relying on complete rule sets. Finally, we focus on the Insurance Fraud Detection dataset, diving deeper into the content of the explanations to evaluate whether these methods can contribute to the development of more trustworthy AI systems.

4.1 Rule-Based Explanations

We used Anchor and PyXAI to generate rule-based local explanations. This means that, for a given instance x, these approaches compute a rule r such that x satisfies the rule r, and any other instance following this rule should be classified by the model in the same way as x. Generally, a smaller rule r is considered a better explanation, as it is easier for humans to understand and can be generalized to a broader range of instances.

The key difference between Anchor and PyXAI lies in their approach. Anchor is a model-agnostic method that uses a statistical approach to compute rules (it can be viewed as an extension of LIME). In contrast, PyXAI is a model-specific method designed for tree ensemble models, such as RandomForest and XGBoost. It opens the "black box" by leveraging the conditions learned by the forest to produce formal rules, highlighting which features are truly important or irrelevant for the model's prediction. Consequently, while an instance x' that follows a rule r generated by Anchor may not always be classified identically to the original instance x, this is impossible with a rule generated by PyXAI, as its rules guarantee consistent classification.

To summarize our results, we present boxplots in Fig. 2, illustrating the distribution of explanation lengths across two datasets: Insurance-Fraud-Detection and Creditcard (the trends are consistent across all datasets). One key observation is that explanations for XGBoost models (both with and without SMOTE) are consistently shorter than those for Random Forest models across all four subgroups. This suggests that, from an explanation and interpretability perspective, XGBoost models may be more advantageous, as they appear to generate simpler explanations using rule-extraction XAI techniques. This could be due to XGBoost learning shallower trees compared to Random Forests.

Additionally, we observe a notable difference in the explanation lengths for instances classified as "fraud" by the model, with no significant distinction between true positives (actual frauds detected) and false positives (non-fraud instances misclassified as fraud). Specifically, the rules extracted for positively

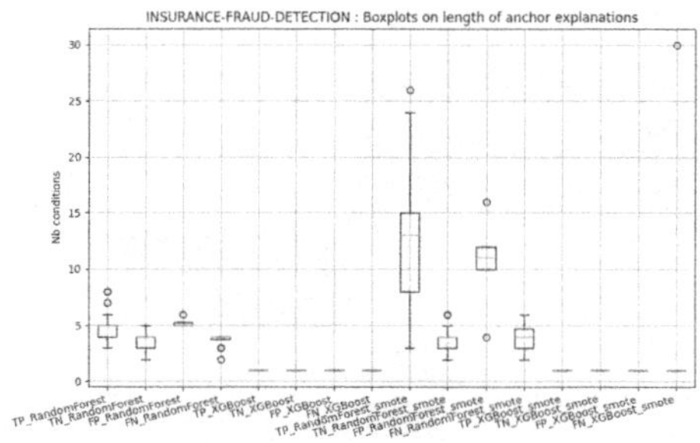

(a) Insurance-Fraud-Detection / Anchor

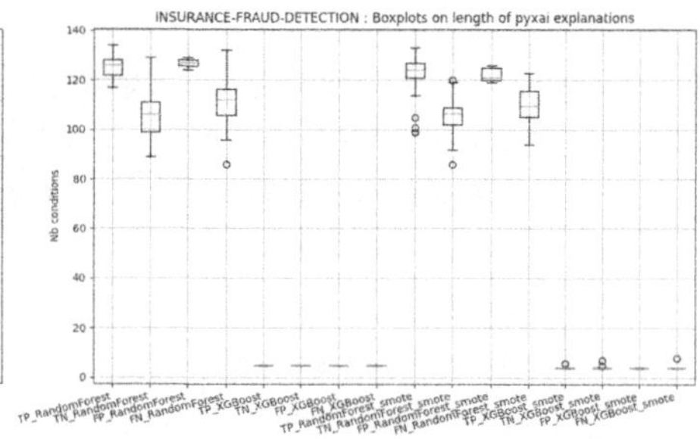

(b) Insurance-Fraud-Detection / PyXAI

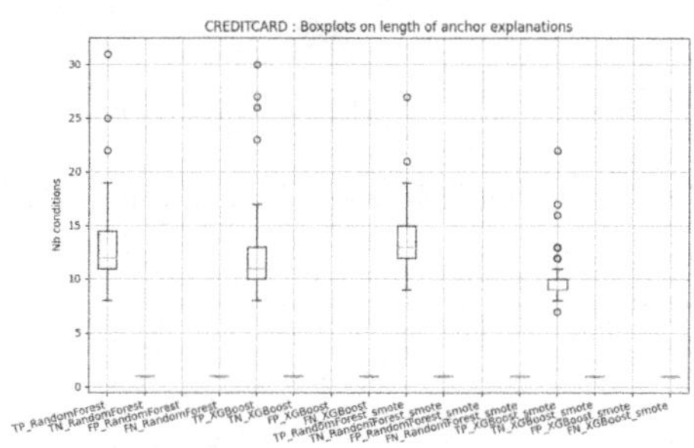

(c) Creditcard / Anchor

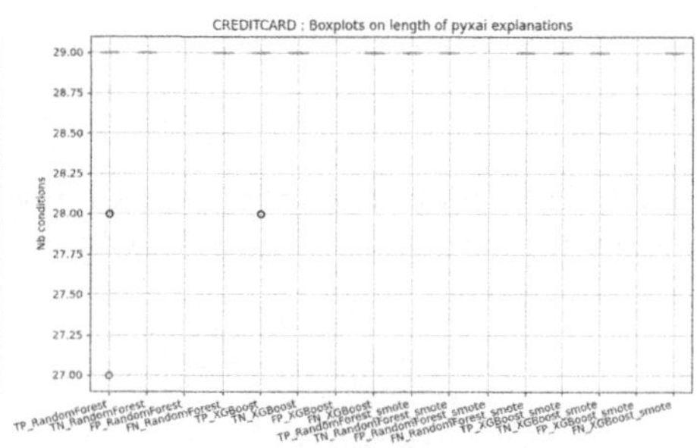

(d) Creditcard / PyXAI

Fig. 2. Boxplots of explanation lengths for each model. For each model, the lengths are grouped by whether the explanation corresponds to a True Positive (TP), True Negative (TN), False Positive (FP), or False Negative (FN) instance.

classified instances are generally longer than those for negatively classified ones. In other words, it seems more challenging to derive simple rules to detect fraud, whereas it is relatively easier to generate straightforward rules for identifying non-fraudulent transactions, revealing clearer patterns for safe transactions.

Finally, we observe a notable difference between the explanations generated by Anchor and those produced by PyXAI. While Anchor's explanations tend to be significantly shorter, they lack formal guarantees, unlike PyXAI. Focusing on the Creditcard dataset, the fact that PyXAI retains all relevant features in its explanation rules, while Anchor can eliminate up to half of them, suggests a need for caution when using Anchor, or more broadly, model-agnostic approaches. These methods are known to have certain limitations [17].

4.2 Feature Importance

While the previous methods introduce different sizes for the judgement rules, i.e. the number of conditions utilized to decide on the legitimacy of a given instance, SHAP and LIME use a pre-defined number of features presenting the ones with the most impact on the prediction (ordered in decreasing order of importance).

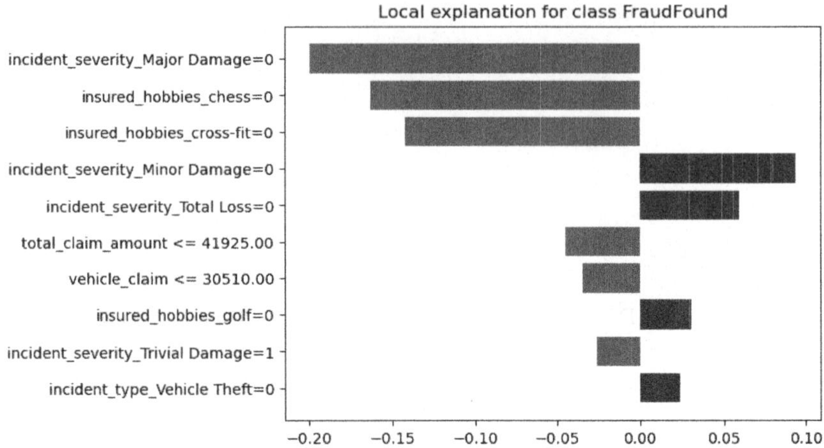

Fig. 3. This figure shows the assigned weights per variable by the LIME method for a random instance in the insurance dataset.

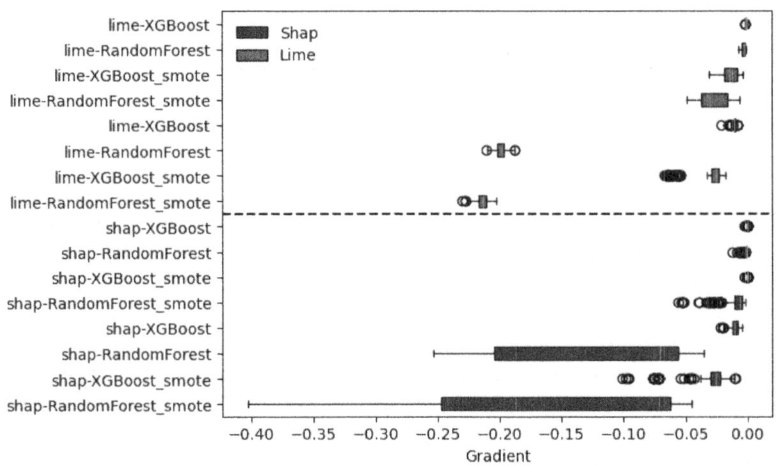

Fig. 4. This figure shows the pattern of the gradient decrease within both SHAP and LIME explanations under the use of the different methods. The dashed line is a visual separation between both explanation methods.

These weights aim to give us a clear numerical-based measure of the impact per variable on the decision process, also what variables' changes are the most important for the prediction. In Fig 3, we present the given weights of the top 10 variables by the LIME method for a random instance. We notice, according to the explanations, that not having a "Major Damage", "cross-fit or chess as hobbies" are essential in reducing the probability of the instance being detected as fraud.

Despite the clear visualization per instance of the variables with the most impact (for LIME and SHAP), identifying the most significant variables is estimated by the mean of the pattern for the decrease in the weights' values, where a faster decrease highlights the use of less variables. In Fig. 4, we measure the gradient of the decrease in the corresponding weights of the different variables within SHAP and LIME across the different models with or without the use of the over-sampling technique for adjusting the imbalance in the insurance dataset. We can observe that, on average, LIME has a higher gradient for the decrease in the assigned weights, indicating that the model focuses on fewer variables to perform the prediction task. Additionally, compared to XGBoost, Random Forest (RF) encounters a larger decrease in the weights' values, suggesting that XGBoost requires more detailed information to make a concise judgment over the instance.

4.3 Variation Between Explanations for a Specific Fraud Dataset

In this section, we delve deeper into the explanations of the Insurance dataset, a small dataset on which the prediction models performed well.

Features importance explainability tools like LIME and SHAP also enables us to find meaningful features in the data to predict a fraud. By comparing to the top conditions found on average in the explanation rules of Anchor and PyXAI, we can then examine whether the different explanation models focus on the same criteria. Figure 5 compares the frequency of the conditions found across the 4 explainability tools on a common "blackbox" model: XGBoost (without SMOTE). Here XGBoost was chosen as it performed the best on this dataset (cf Table 1).

Although the conditions vary from one explainability model to another, we can observe some recurring features. For instance, the "incident_month" feature is common to PyXAI, LIME and SHAP and is even a very frequent feature for the latter two. Furthermore, for Lime and PyXAI, the conditions relating to this feature are similar and concern small values (1 or 2), which corresponds to January or February. In other words, the fact that the incident took place at the beginning of the year could be a determining factor in predicting insurance fraud for this dataset. We can notice that the wordcloud for Anchor only contains one feature about the "policy state", which is only common to the SHAP model. This points out one of the drawbacks of Anchor, which may encourage short explanation rules (unlike a more formal approach like PyXAI).

The wordclouds for the Random Forest model share even more similar features. By way of illustration, we present two of them, one for the Lime model and the other for the PyXAI model in Fig. 6. This indicates a certain consistency between the different explanation models for a same "black box" model. However, for the same explainability tool, we can observe quite different conditions depending on the 2 "black box" models used. This suggests that these 2 models find different decision criteria for predicting insurance fraud. Consequently, it would benefit experts to work with different prediction models, as they may highlight different domain rules.

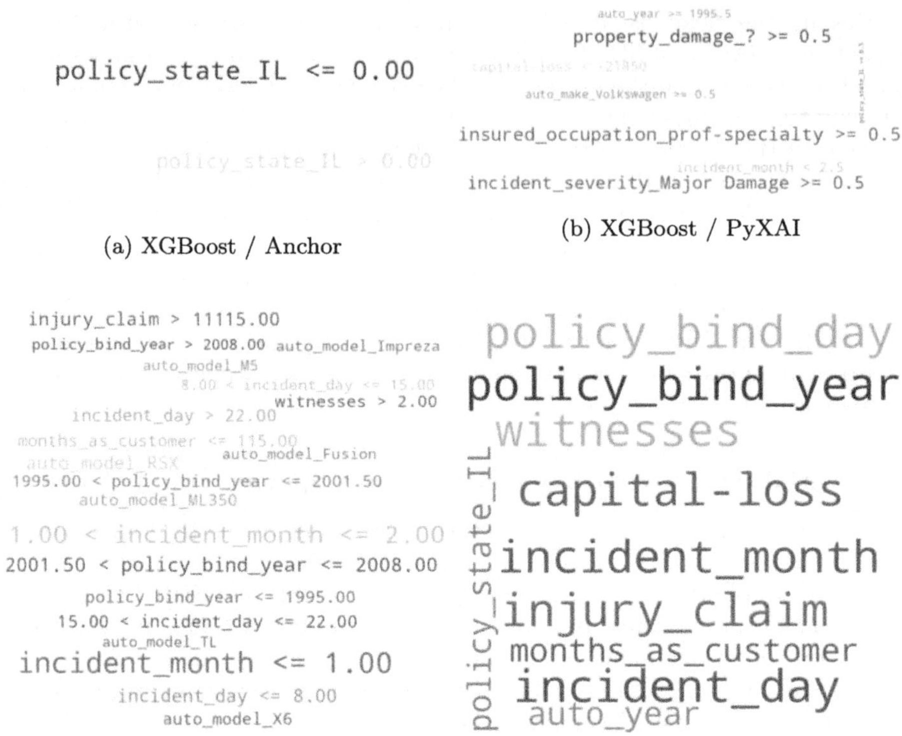

(a) XGBoost / Anchor

(b) XGBoost / PyXAI

(c) XGBoost / LIME

(d) XGBoost / SHAP

Fig. 5. Wordclouds showing the frequency of the conditioning rules found for the XGBoost model across all explanation models for the Insurance dataset.

(a) Random Forest / Lime

(b) Random Forest / PyXAI

Fig. 6. Wordclouds showing the frequency of the conditioning rules found for the Random Forest model with the Lime and PyXAI explanation models for the Insurance dataset.

5 Discussion

Knowing the critical effect of the fraudulent transactions or requests within the different sectors, it is essential to power the experts with the right efficient and robust tools to help in detecting these kind of instances under the challenge of highly-imbalanced datasets, where fraudulent ones represent around 5–6% on average of the different datasources. Therefore, in this work, we aimed to contribute to fulfil this task by evaluating state-of-the-art explainability tools for analyzing high-capacity complex tree-based models.

We conducted our study on open datasets, as fraud often targets sensitive data that can be difficult to acquire. Equipped with rule-based vs feature importance methods for providing local explanations of the different instances, we have found that, on one hand, rule-based methods are essential to determine the conditioning rule under which the legitimacy of the instance is called. This rule can vary in its size, thus highlighting the need for more or less information to detect the fraudulent behaviors. On the other hand, feature importance-based methods helps to perform a feature selection procedure by assigning weights for the different variables based on its contributions to the prediction task. While the different explanation methods can encounter different perspectives of the significance of the variables, we discovered a set of common conditioning variables used across all the models for one given dataset.

While these comparisons enable us to better understand the relevance of each explanation, we could consider - for a more practical approach - building a mixture of models, where each model designs an expert in its own perspective, merging these explainable models into a more robust one. The result is a diverse corpus, which allows for more efficient performance, with a better judgement of the instances. A continuation of our work would be to compare the explanations found with the rules of known experts on more specific domains and in collaboration with companies.

References

1. Arrieta, A.B., et al.: Explainable artificial intelligence (XAI): concepts, taxonomies, opportunities and challenges toward responsible AI. Inf. Fusion **58**, 82–115 (2020)
2. Arya, V., et al.: One explanation does not fit all: A toolkit and taxonomy of AI explainability techniques. arXiv preprint arXiv:1909.03012 (2019)
3. Audemard, G., Bellart, S., Bounia, L., Koriche, F., Lagniez, J-M., Marquis, P.: Trading complexity for sparsity in random forest explanations. In: Proceedings of AAAI 2022, pp. 5461–5469 (2022)
4. Audemard, G., Lagniez, J-M., Marquis, P., Szczepanski, N.: Computing abductive explanations for boosted trees. In: Proceedings of AISTATS, pp. 4699–4711 (2023)
5. Audemard, G., Lagniez, J-M., Marquis, P., Szczepanski, N.: PyXAI: an XAI library for tree-based models. In: Proceedings of IJCAI 2024 (2024)
6. Breiman, L.: Random forests. Mach. Learn. **45**, 5–32 (2001)
7. Chawla, N.V., Bowyer, K.W., Hall, L.O., Kegelmeyer, W.P.: SMOTE: Synthetic Minority Over-sampling Technique. CoRR (2011)

8. Chen, T., Carlos Guestrin, C.: XGBoost: a scalable tree boosting system. In: 22nd SIGKDD Conference on Knowledge Discovery and Data Mining (2016)
9. Chen, Z., Van Khoa, L.D., Teoh, E.N., Nazir, A., Karuppiah, E.K., Lam, K.S.: Machine learning techniques for anti-money laundering (AML) solutions in suspicious transaction detection: a review. Knowl. Inf. Syst. **57**, 245–285 (2018)
10. Cirqueiral, D., Helfert M., Bezbradica M.: Towards Design Principles for User-Centric Explainable AI in Fraud Detection (2021)
11. Collaris, D., Vink, L.M., van Wijk, J.J.: Instance-level explanations for fraud detection: a case study. arXiv preprint arXiv:1806.07129 (2018)
12. Dama, F., Sleiman, R., Bellart, S.: Introduire l'IA dans la lutte contre la fraude : comment choisir et convaincre ?. Ghislain Atemezing, Catherine Roussey. 10 ème Conférence Nationale sur les Applications Pratiques de l'Intelligence Artificielle, Jul 2024, La Rochelle, France. AFIA Association Française pour l'Intelligence Artificielle, Actes de la 10 ème Conférence Nationale sur les Applications Pratiques de l'Intelligence Artificielle (APIA), pp.133-136, Plate-Forme Intelligence Artificielle (PFIA). ffhal-04639488f (2024)
13. Fernández, A., Garcia, S., Herrera, F., Chawla, N.V.: Smote for learning from imbalanced data: progress and challenges, marking the 15-year anniversary. J. Artif. Intell. Res. **61**, 863–905 (2018)
14. Janzing, D., Minorics, L., Blöbaum, P.: Feature relevance quantification in explainable AI: a causal problem. In: International Conference on Artificial Intelligence and Statistics, PMLR (2020)
15. Lundberg, S. M., Erion, G.G., Lee S-I.: Consistent individualized feature attribution for tree ensembles. arXiv preprint arXiv:1802.03888 (2018)
16. Lundberg, S. M., Lee, S-I.: A unified approach to interpreting model predictions. In: Advances in Neural Information Processing Systems (2017)
17. Mirzaei, S., Mao, H., Al-Nima, R., Woo, W.L.: Explainable AI evaluation: a top-down approach for selecting optimal explanations for black box models. Information **15**(1), 4 (2023)
18. Pedregosa, F., et al.: Scikit-learn: machine learning in python. J. Mach. Learn. Res. **12**, 2825–2830 (2011)
19. Patil, S., Nemade, V., Soni, P.: Predictive modelling for credit card fraud detection using data analytics. In: International Conference on Computational Intelligence and Data Science (2018)
20. Ribeiro, M.T., Singh, S., Guestrin, C.: Why should I trust you?: Explaining the predictions of any classifier. In: Proceedings of the 22nd ACM SIGKDD International Conference on Knowledge Discovery and Data Mining. ACM (2016)
21. Ribeiro, M.T., Singh, S., Guestrin, C.: Anchors: high-precision model-agnostic explanations. In: AAAI Conference on Artificial Intelligence (AAAI) (2018)
22. Shapley, L.S.: A value for n-person games. Contrib. Theory Games **2**(28), 307–317 (1953)
23. Weerts, H.J., van Ipenburg, W., Pechenizkiy, M.: A human-grounded evaluation of Shap for alert processing. arXiv preprint arXiv:1907.03324 (2019)

Author Index

A

Ali-Mehenni, Hugues 178
Arumugam, Chamundeswari 91

B

Barik, Kousik 75
Bellart, Steve 178
Billuart, Jérémy 18

C

Camara, Daniel 28
Chabchoub, Yousra 114
Chamma, Ahmad 178
Chockalingam, Sabarathinam 75

E

Evtimova-Gardair, Mariya 143

F

Faizal, J. Mohammed 127
Filardo, Gautier 42

G

Ganesh, N. S. Gowri 127
Gemignani, Romain 18
Govindharaju, Karthi 127
Gumbs, Gauderic 114

H

Heckmann, Thibaut 42

I

Isabelle, Cimino 62

J

Jérôme, Marcenac 62

K

Kandolo, William 100
Karthick, K. J. Dinesh 127
Kvalvik, Petter 75

L

Laurent, Eunika Mercier 1
Limouni, Elias 153

M

Misra, Sanjay 75
Mohanish, K. 127

P

Perrot, Patrick 18, 28, 114

S

Segond, Frederique 143
Soltani, Skander 153
Somasundaram, Manimegalai 91

T

Togbe, Maurras 114
Turci, Amélie 161

V

Verdejo, Dominique 1

Published by Springer Nature Switzerland AG 2025
D. Verdejo and E. Mercier-Laurent (Eds.): AI4GS 2024, IFIP AICT 743, p. 191, 2025.
https://doi.org/10.1007/978-3-031-96522-7

The manufacturer's authorised representative in the EU is Springer Nature Customer Service Centre GmbH, Europaplatz 3, 69115 Heidelberg, Germany. If you have any concerns regarding our products, please contact ProductSafety@springernature.com

Printed and bound by CPI Group (UK) Ltd, Croydon, CR0 4YY
30/09/2026
02225502-0019